IMAGES
of America

The Sons of Italy in Massachusetts

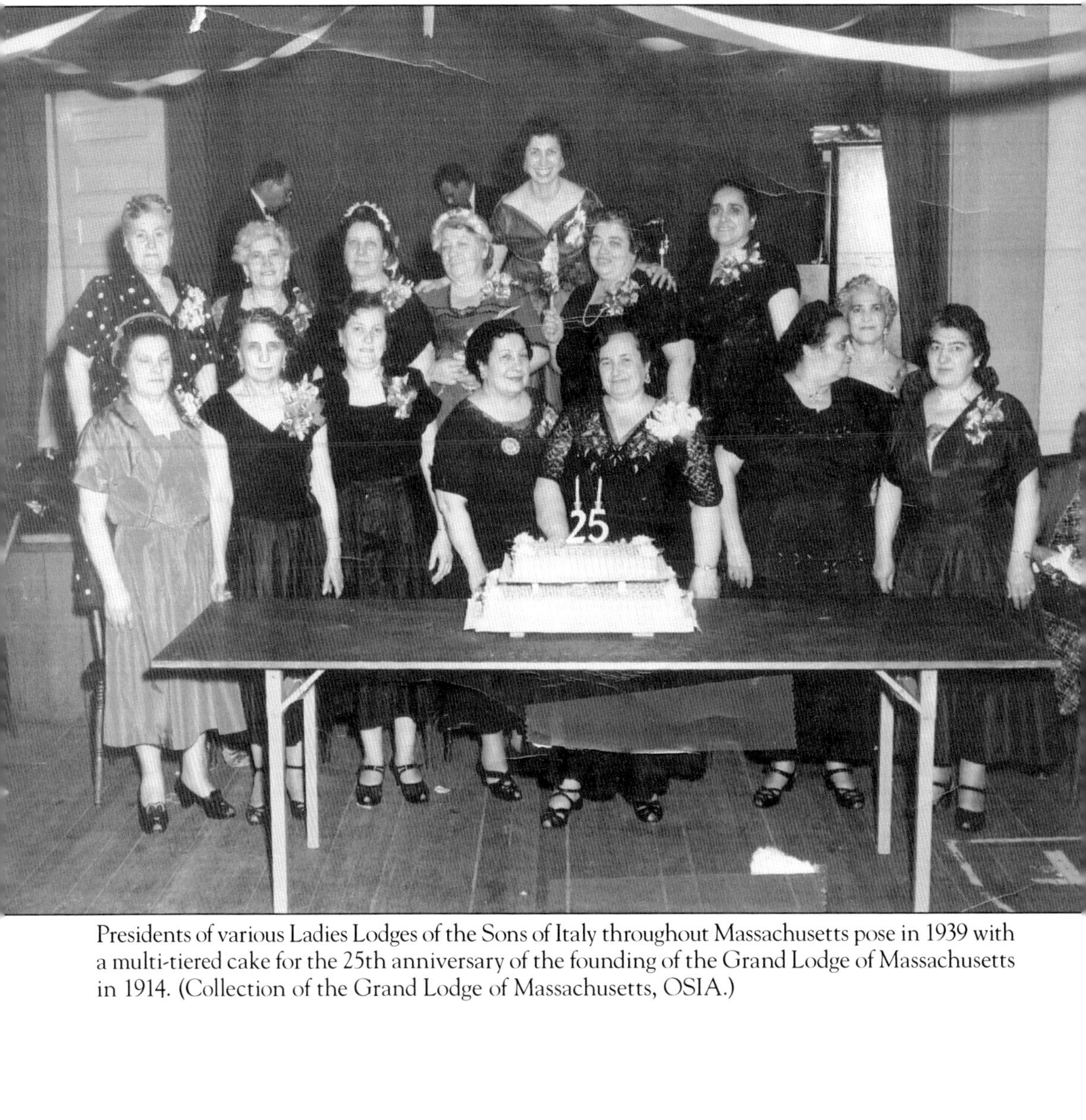

Presidents of various Ladies Lodges of the Sons of Italy throughout Massachusetts pose in 1939 with a multi-tiered cake for the 25th anniversary of the founding of the Grand Lodge of Massachusetts in 1914. (Collection of the Grand Lodge of Massachusetts, OSIA.)

On the Cover: Pictured is a 1956 charity ball of the Sons of Italy in the elegant ballroom of the Copley Plaza Hotel in Boston's Back Bay. Among those in the front are Chairman Modest Mele leading the dance, Lee Mele, Mrs. John Guarino, Hector D'Amato, Elsie Apicella, Frank Libertore, Benjamin Corleto, Paul and Mary D'Agostino, Joseph Silverio, Mary Silverio, Jerry Leone, Sue Ventola, Olindo Ventola, Mr. and Mrs. Joseph Toscano, and Joseph Furnari. (Collection of the Grand Lodge of Massachusetts, OSIA.)

IMAGES of America

THE SONS OF ITALY IN MASSACHUSETTS

Anthony M. Sammarco for the Grand Lodge of Massachusetts,
Order Sons of Italy in America

ARCADIA PUBLISHING

ISBN 978-1-4671-3377-7

Published by Arcadia Publishing
Charleston, South Carolina

Printed in the United States of America

Library of Congress Control Number: 2015931896

For all general information, please contact Arcadia Publishing:
Telephone 843-853-2070
Fax 843-853-0044
E-mail sales@arcadiapublishing.com
For customer service and orders:
Toll-Free 1-888-313-2665

Visit us on the Internet at www.arcadiapublishing.com

This photographic history is dedicated to the members of the Grand Lodge of Massachusetts, Order Sons of Italy in America, past, present, and future.

Lunga può Figli d'Italia in un gruppo popolare e dedicato al futuro benessere di italoamericani in Massachusetts.

Contents

Acknowledgments

I would like to extend my sincere thanks to Carmelita Bello, State President of the Grand Lodge of Massachusetts, Order Sons of Italy in America (OSIA), and Theresa Farina, Chair of the Historical Commission, for their interest and assistance in the researching and writing of this book. Without their assistance in the collection of Lodge photographs over the last year, this book would not have been possible. I would also like to extend my deep appreciation to Dean Saluti and Marjorie Cahn, whose initial interest and assistance spearheaded the writing of this book for the centennial. To Caitrin Cunningham, my ever-patient editor at Arcadia, I express my sincere thanks for all her wise counsel, patience, and assistance.

I would like to thank the following members of the Grand Lodge of Massachusetts State Council: Carmelita Bello, State President; Antonio Sestito, State First Vice President; Ronald Hill, State Second Vice President; James DiStefano, State Immediate Past President; Denise Furnari, State Orator; Marie Jackson, State Recording Secretary; Margaret Olivieri, State Financial Secretary; John Christoforo, State Treasurer; and State Trustees John Argiro, Mary Ann Bello, Stephen Cozzaglio, Charles DeStefano, Larry Giordano, Richard Matlak, Marisa Ranalli, Marissa Sestito, and Rodolfo Viscomi.

The following are Chairmen of Permanent Commissions: Budget and Finance, Arthur Bennett; Charitable and Educational Trust, Angelo Rossi; Charity, Carol Rossi; Commission for Social Justice, Albert DeNapoli, Esq.; Historical, Theresa Farina; Italian Culture, Joan D'Argenis; Judiciary, Philip Privitera, Esq.; Junior Division, Charles DeStefano; Magazine, Pamela Donnaruma; Membership, Ronald Hill; Organization and Education, Antonio Sestito; Public Relations, Michelle DiPlacido; Scholarship, Donna Giuliani; Sports, Steven Cedrone; and State Deputy, Mary Cooper.

Thanks go also to Paul Guida, Executive Director, and Adriana Guida, Executive Assistant, of the Grand Lodge of Massachusetts office.

I would like to thank the following for their assistance and support in the researching and writing of this book: Ruth-Ann Berlandi, Laura Caira, Carmine Cardillo, Cesidio Cedrone, Hutchinson and Pasqualina Cedmarco, Lucy Codella, Jackie Anderson of Colortek of Boston, Stephen A. Cozzaglio, Florence Kane, Richard Leccese, Michael Lombardo, the Sons of Italy Historical Society, Dean J. Saluti, Claire Spagnolo, and Santa Walazek.

I would also like to thank all the Lodges in Massachusetts that shared photographs and information for this centennial book.

All photographs, unless otherwise noted, appear courtesy of the Grand Lodge of Massachusetts, OSIA.

Introduction

The Sons of Italy in Massachusetts was chartered on January 25, 1914, and celebrated its centennial with many events throughout 2014. The Grand Lodge of Massachusetts is the fifth-oldest Grand Lodge in America and is part of the National Order Sons of Italy in America and proud to be part of the oldest, largest, and most geographically represented organization of Americans of Italian heritage in this country. The National Lodge was organized in New York in 1905 by Dr. Vincenzo Sellaro as the Ordine Figli d'Italia in America, and the Grand Lodge of Massachusetts was chartered nine years later in 1914, with Saverio R. Romano of Boston serving as the first President from 1914 to 1919; the original local Lodge was the Ettore Fieramosca #60, which was organized in 1910 in Roxbury, Massachusetts. Today, the Grand Lodge of Massachusetts includes the states of Massachusetts, New Hampshire, and Maine, with thousands of members. The Junior Division was organized in 1931, and over the following five decades, over 100 Junior Lodges were founded throughout the state, considered to be the most successful effort of any Grand Lodge to recruit youth to the Sons of Italy.

The stated purpose of the Order Sons of Italy in America is to "enroll all eligible persons so that we may successfully promote national education, charitable fundraising, secure adequate laws for the benefit of its members, enrich Italian culture and heritage, and to combat discrimination while protecting and upholding the positive image of the people of Italian birth or descent." Since 1928, the Grand Lodge has issued its own monthly publication, *Il Gazzettino*. The publication title was changed in 1931 to the *Sons of Italy Magazine*, with articles in both Italian and English. It changed again in 1966 to its current name, the *Sons of Italy News*. The content has always informed and educated Italian Americans on issues and historical stories that affect members and friends.

Throughout the years, the Grand Lodge of Massachusetts raised funds for many charitable endeavors, among them the Home for Italian Children and the Italian Red Cross, and beginning in the 1950s and for the next three decades, the Grand Lodge assumed a leadership role in raising funds for the Don Orione Home for the Aged and the Madonna Queen Shrine in Boston. During World War II, the Grand Lodge was also active in the war bonds program, purchasing $140,000 worth of bonds. The Grand Lodge was also involved in the Supreme Lodge's successful effort to have the classification of "enemy aliens" removed from Italian immigrants and their descendants. OSIA members in the armed forces were exempt from dues to the Grand Lodge, and the $500 death benefit was paid to the beneficiaries of those who died serving our country. Following the war, members of many Lodges in Massachusetts donated food, clothing, and money to war-torn Italy.

As Grand Venerable Anthony Julian said in 1946 upon his election as President of the Grand Lodge, the basic aim of the Grand Lodge of Massachusetts, Order Sons of Italy in America was to "promote the fundamental conception of Americanism based upon respect for the Constitution, obedience to the laws, devotion to the Government of the Republic, and defense of its institutions."

He went on to state:

> Ours is a successful fraternal organization. Because of its tried principals and its accomplishments in the field of social and charitable activity, it has won the confidence and devotion of its members, and the respect of the community at large. The Order is generally and justly acclaimed as the outstanding representative association of our people in Massachusetts. By our joint efforts we will make it greater and stronger.

The Charitable and Educational Trust of the Grand Lodge of Massachusetts has continued to fund charitable causes. Through the Trust, the Grand Lodge has provided needed medicines and assisted in the construction of an orphanage for the victims of earthquakes in Italy. Today, the Trust provides funding for scholarships awarded to high school seniors named in honor of past Grand Venerables and State Presidents. The Trust also supports the Order's primary charities, which include the Cooley's Anemia Foundation, Alzheimer's Association, Doug Flutie Jr. Foundation for Autism, and the Casa Monte Cassino in Boston's North End. In 1979, members established the Commission for Social Justice of the Grand Lodge of Massachusetts, the anti-defamation arm of the Order.

Today, the Grand Lodge of Massachusetts is made up of over 6,000 members belonging to Lodges in Massachusetts, New Hampshire, and Maine. The State Council is comprised of 18 members, accompanied by the State Past Presidents, a State Chaplain, and 15 Chairmen of Permanent Commissions. The Grand Lodge of Massachusetts office was located for many years in Boston's North End, then in Cambridge, and is presently located at 93 Concord Avenue in Belmont, Massachusetts.

In 2014, Anthony Baratta, National President of the Order Sons of Italy, said, "The Grand Lodge of Massachusetts has . . . been blessed with visionary, active and strong leaders over the years." It has for over a century extolled the preservation and the promotion of Italian heritage and culture and encourages all eligible persons to join a Lodge and assist in the promotion of national education and charitable fundraising, securing adequate laws for the benefit of its members, enriching Italian culture and heritage, and combating discrimination while protecting and upholding the positive image of the people of Italian birth or their Italian American descendants.

One

The Sons of Italy in Massachusetts

Figli d'Italia in Massachusetts

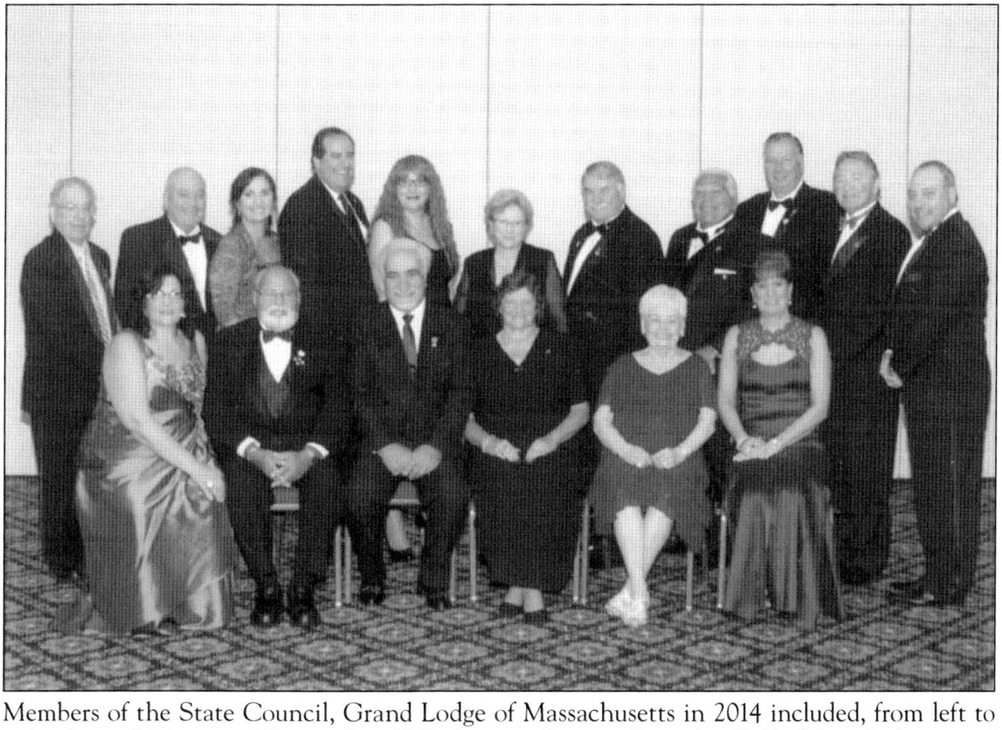

Members of the State Council, Grand Lodge of Massachusetts in 2014 included, from left to right, (seated) Margaret Olivieri, Ron Hill, Antonio Sestito, Carmelita Bello, Marie Jackson, and Denise Furnari; (standing) Stephen Cozzaglio, Charlie DeStefano, Marisa Ranalli, John Arigo, Marissa Sestito, Mary Ann Bello, James DiStefano, John Christoforo, Larry Giordano, Richard Matlak, and Rodolfo Viscomi.

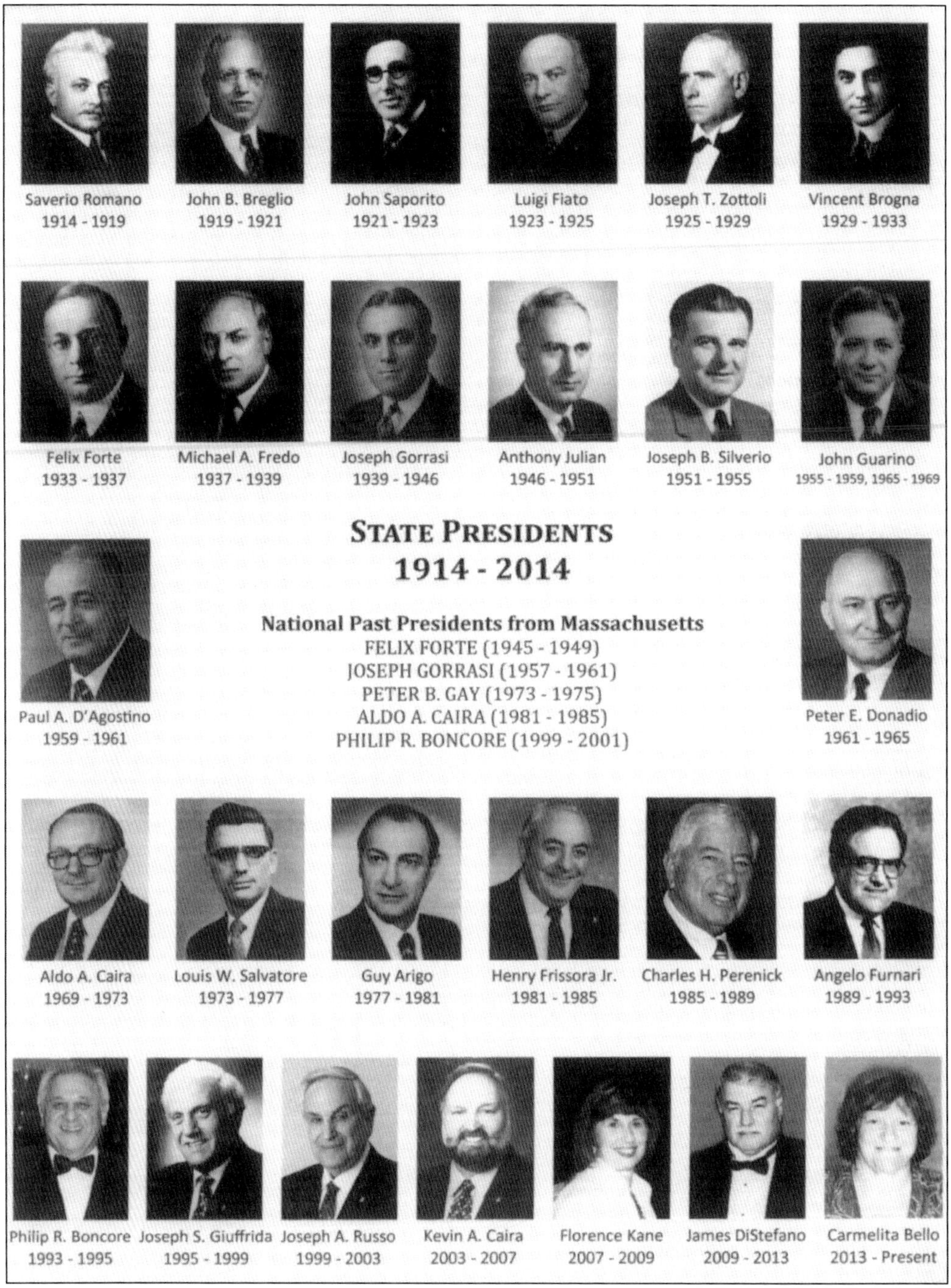

Pictured are all the Venerables and Presidents of the Grand Lodge of Massachusetts from its founding in 1914 to 2014.

Carmelita Bello was elected State President of the Grand Lodge of Massachusetts in 2013. Seen here with her aunt Gladys Bello, who served as a Venerable of the Lodge Princess Maria Gabariella #313 in Worcester, Carmelita is also active in the Worcester Lodge #168.

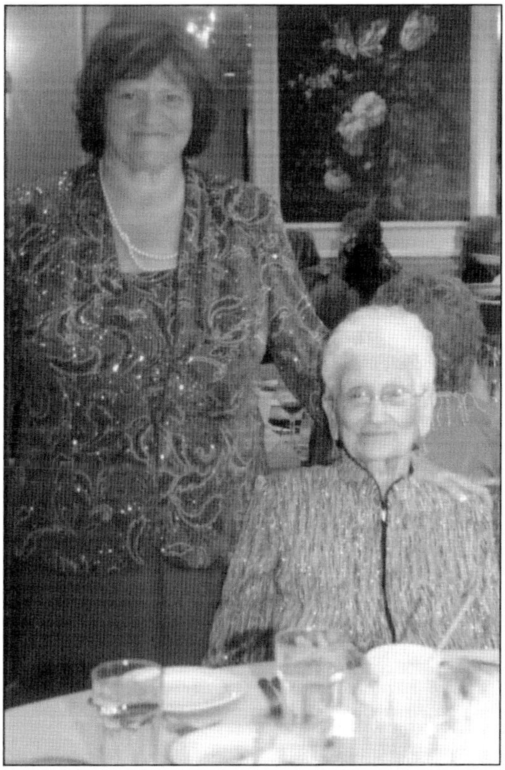

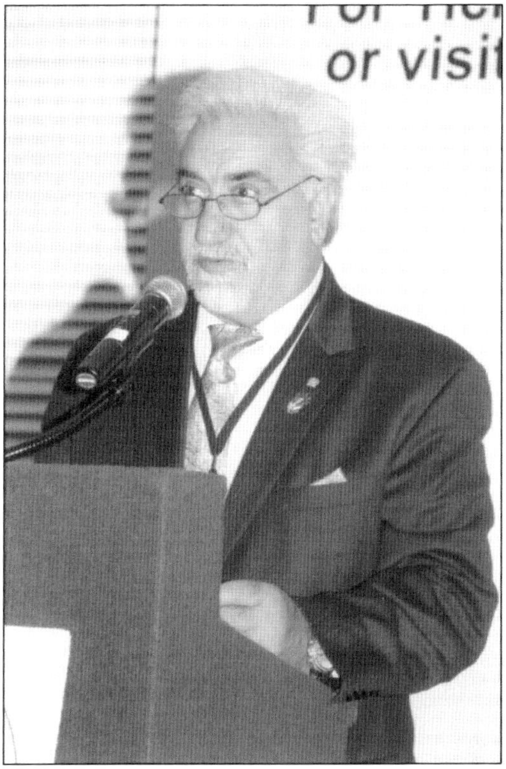

Antonio Sestito, State First Vice President of the Grand Lodge of Massachusetts, is pictured here. He also serves as Chairman of the Organization and Education Commission.

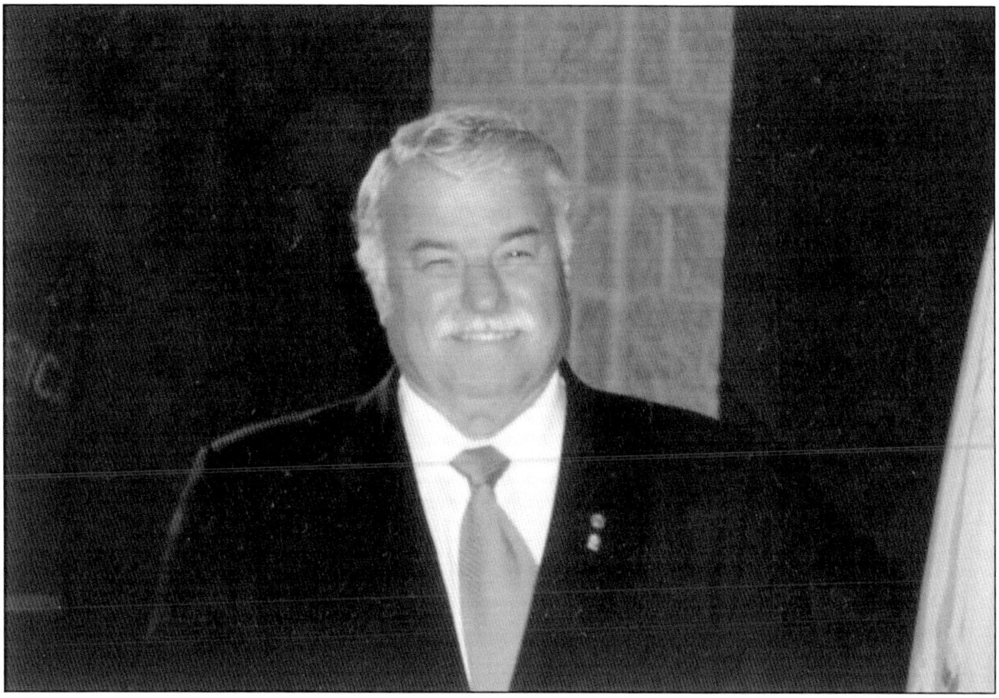

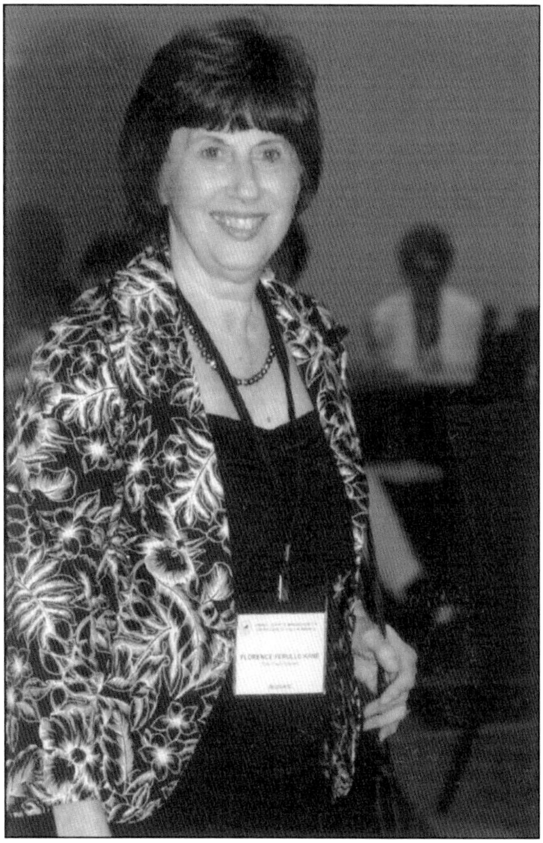

James DiStefano served as President of the Grand Lodge of Massachusetts from 2009 to 2013. He is currently serving as State Immediate Past President on the State Council and as National Recording Secretary of the Sons of Italy.

Florence Ferullo Kane served as President of the Grand Lodge of Massachusetts from 2007 to 2009. She serves as a National Trustee of the Sons of Italy.

Kevin A. Caira served as President of the Grand Lodge of Massachusetts from 2003 to 2007. He is also active in the Angelo Giuseppe Roncalli Lodge #2183, having served as President from 1996 to 1998.

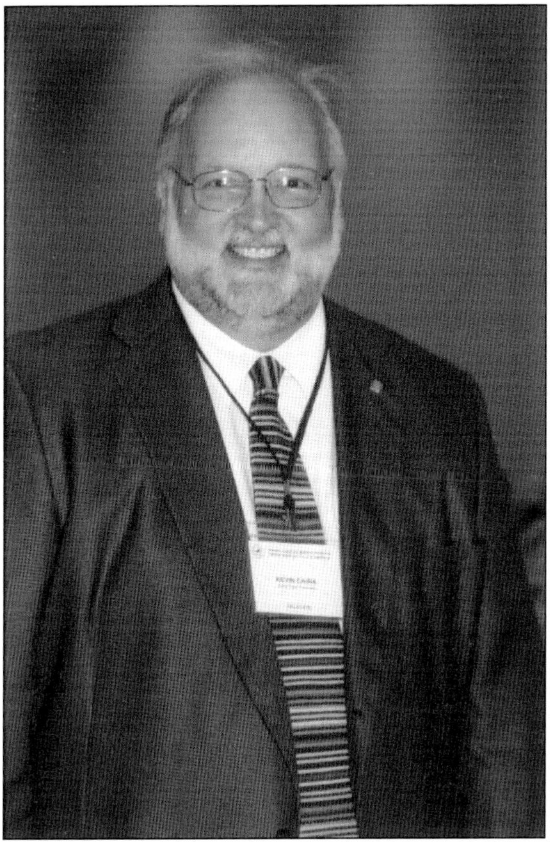

Joseph A. Russo served as President of the Grand Lodge of Massachusetts from 1999 to 2003. He serves as National First Vice President of the Sons of Italy and owns the Joseph Russo Funeral Home in Roslindale. On the left is Dorothy Berlandi of the Braintree Ladies Lodge #1422.

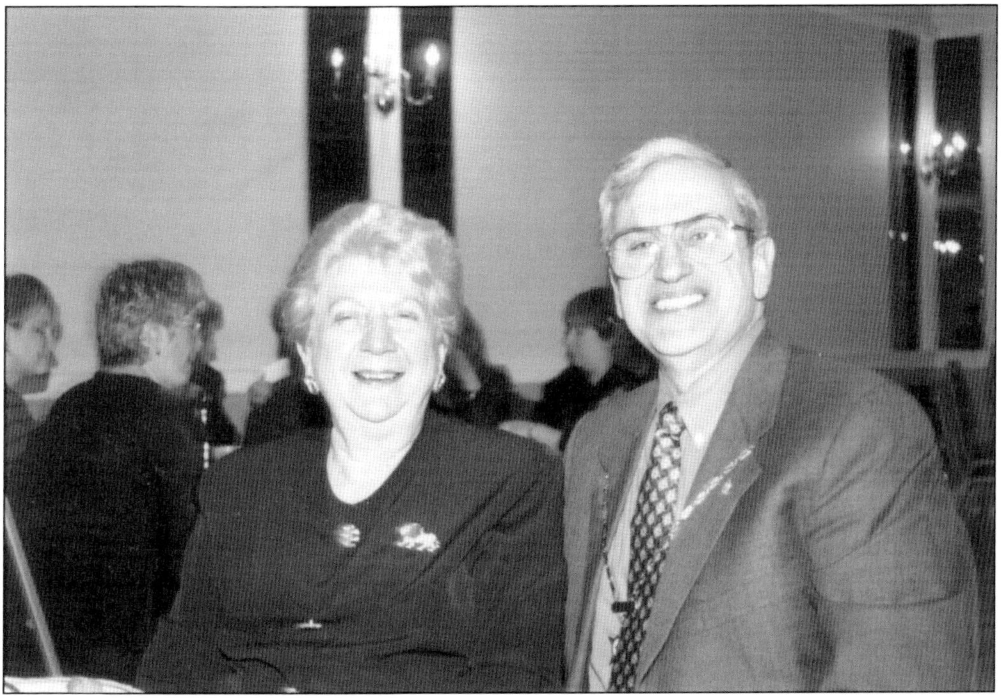

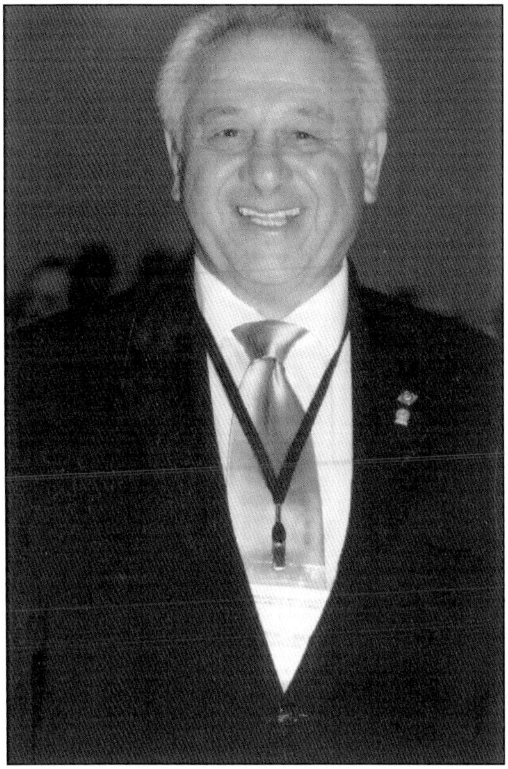

Philip R. Boncore, Esq., served as President of the Grand Lodge of Massachusetts from 1993 to 1995. He also served as President of the Winthrop Mixed Lodge #2057 from 1998 to 1990 and as National President from 1999 to 2001.

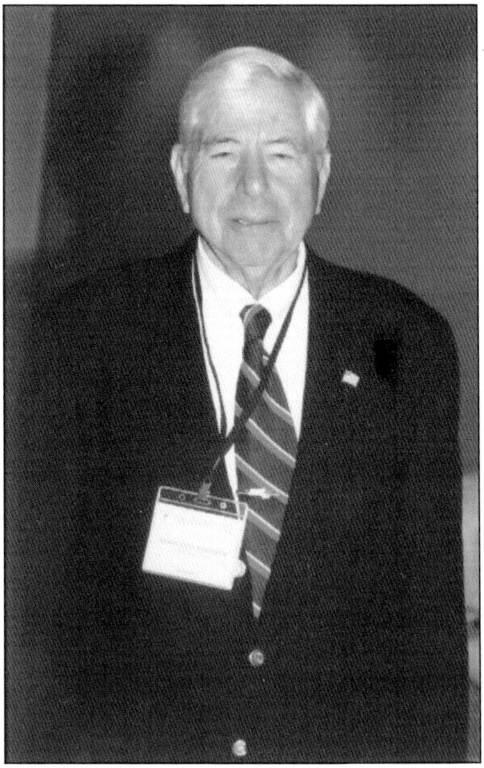

Charles H. Perenick served as President of the Grand Lodge of Massachusetts from 1985 to 1989.

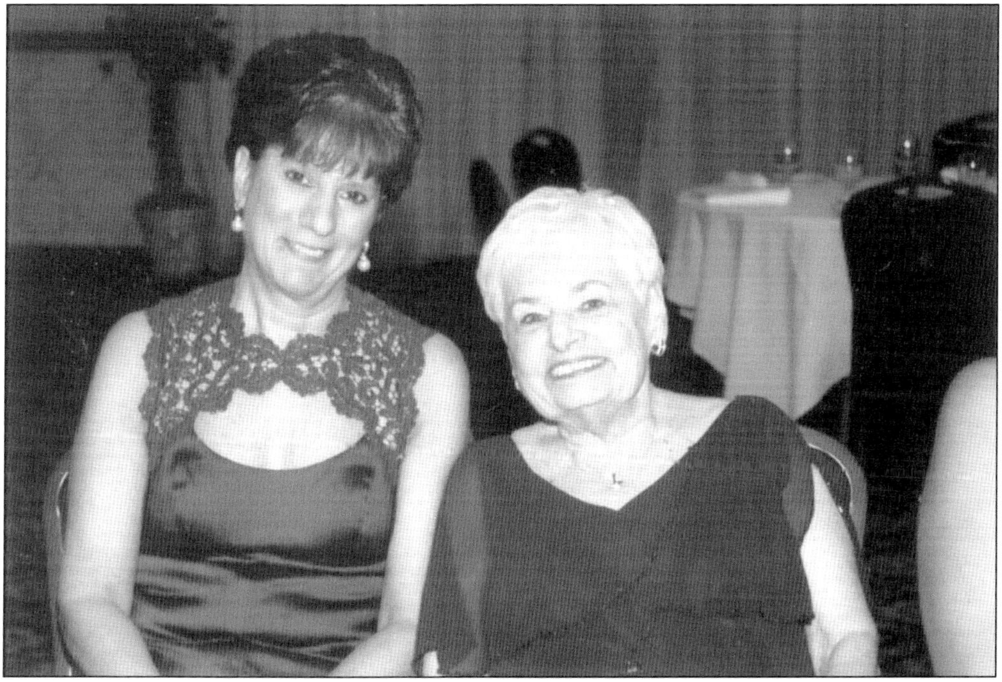

Denise Furnari (left) serves as State Orator, and Marie Jackson (right) serves as State Recording Secretary.

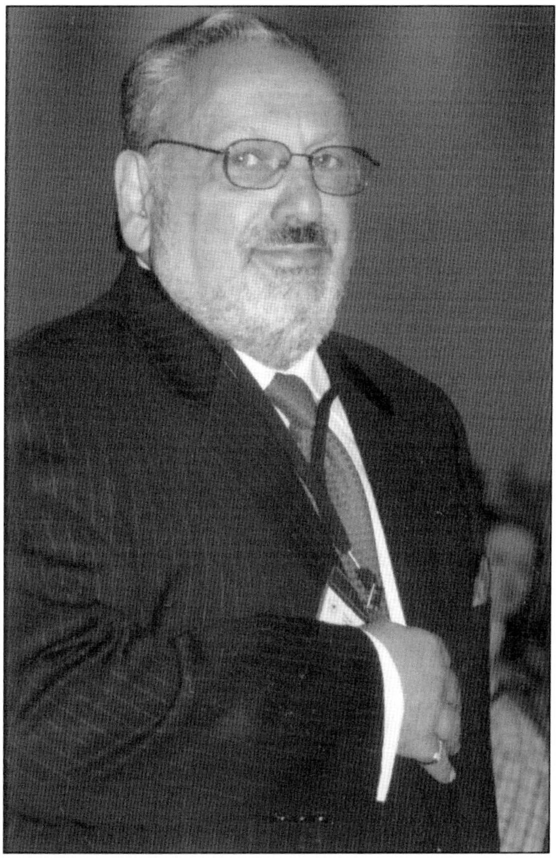

Anthony J. Panaggio Jr. serves as the President of the Benefit Insurance Commission and is the National Historian of the Sons of Italy.

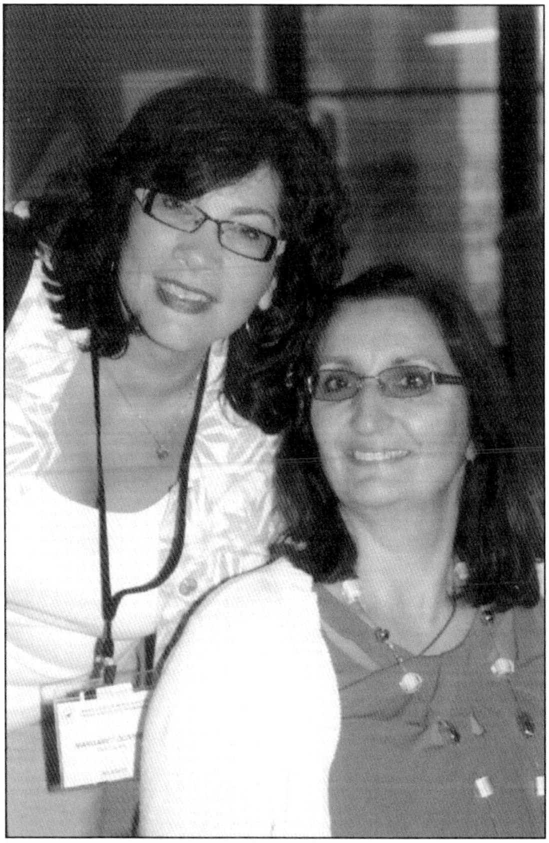

Margaret Olivieri (left) serves as the State Financial Secretary, and Marisa Ranalli (right) serves as a State Trustee of the Sons of Italy in Massachusetts.

Rodolfo Viscomi serves as a State Trustee. He served as a President of the Piave Fiume Lodge #1036 in Watertown. He has been active for over 25 years with the Massachusetts chapter of the Cooley's Anemia Foundation, one of the leading foundations in combating thalassemia and one of the charities supported by the Order Sons of Italy in America.

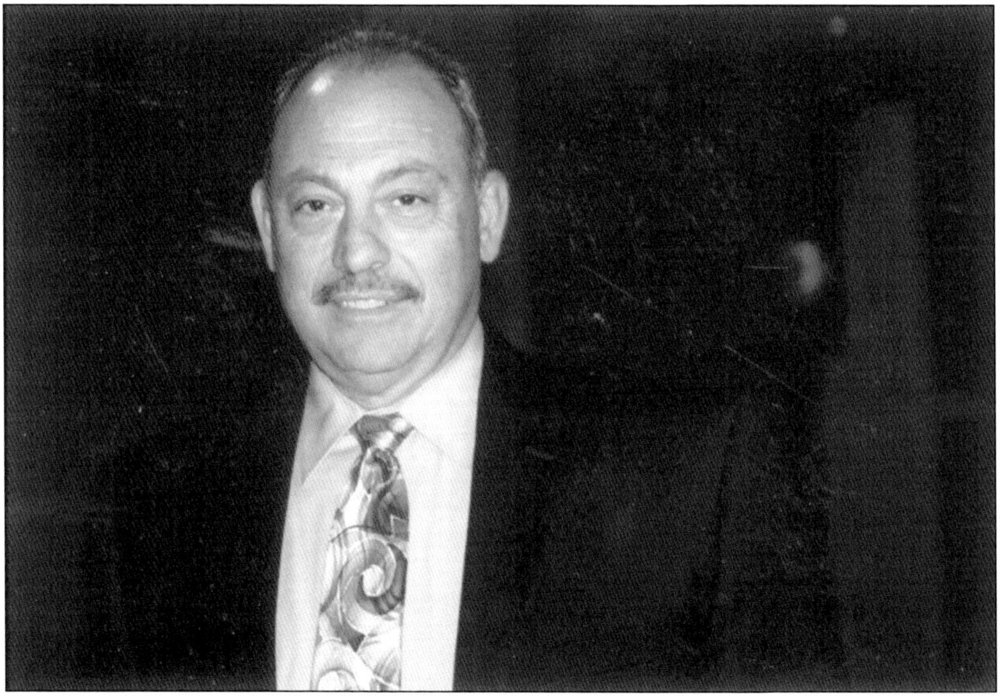

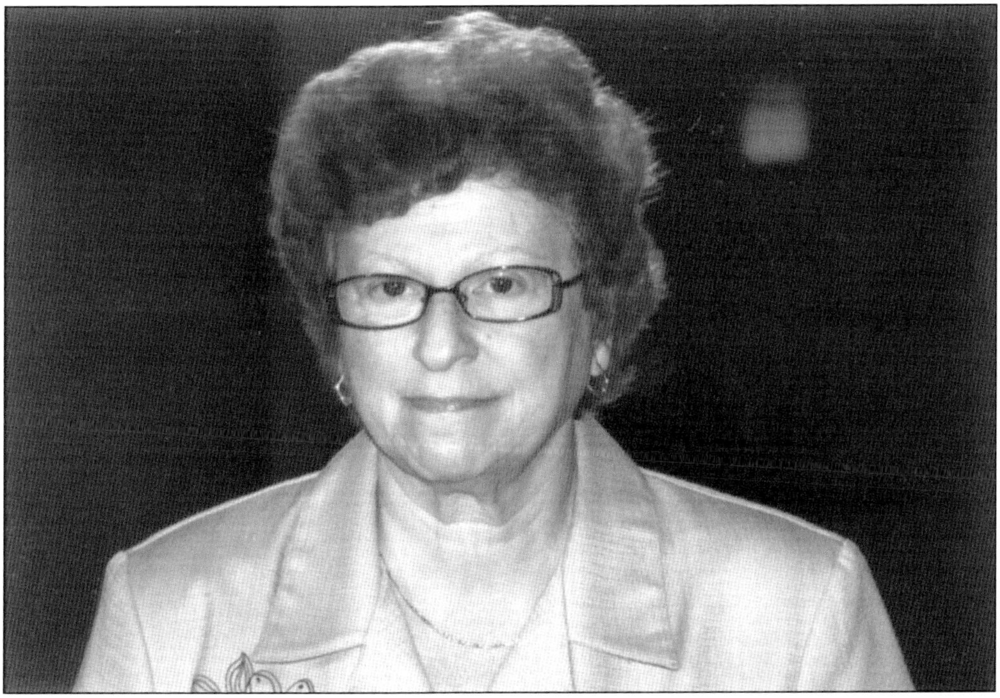

Mary Ann Bello serves as a State Trustee and has also served as President of the Worcester Lodge #168.

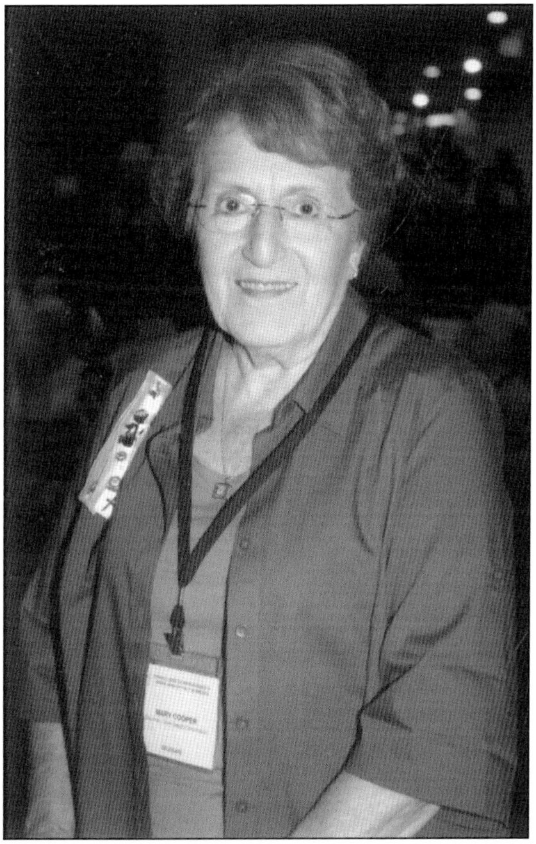

Mary Cooper serves as State Deputy Chairman. She is a Past President of the Cornelia dei Gracchi Lodge #1583 in Watertown.

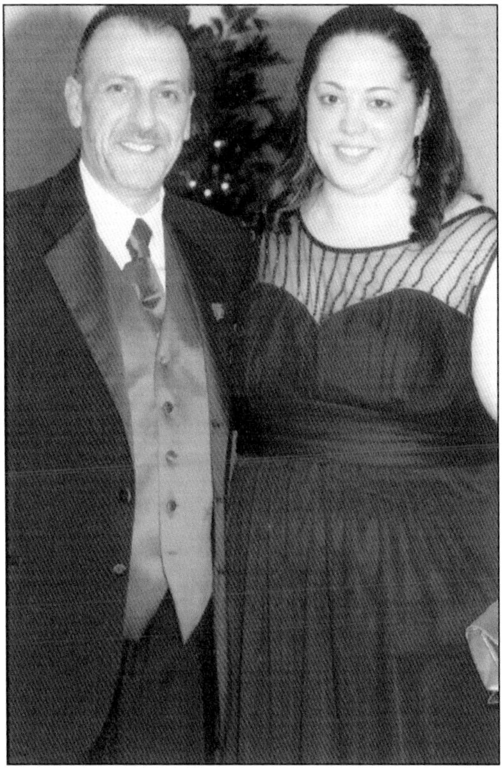

Paul M. Guida is the Executive Director of the Grand Lodge of Massachusetts, and Adriana Guida serves as the Webmaster and Executive Assistant.

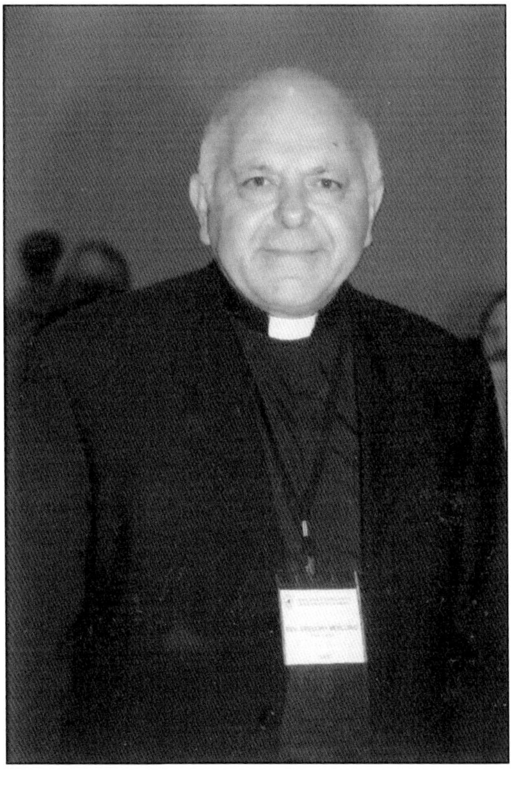

The Rev. Gregory Mercurio serves as the State Chaplain of the Grand Lodge of Massachusetts. He has been pastor at Holy Family Parish in Lynn, Massachusetts; Cardinal Bernard Law knew that Father Gregory's Italian heritage would make him an excellent candidate to serve the Italian church congregation. He is now an administrator at St. Pius V Parish in Lynn.

Two

The Beginnings of the Grand Lodge of Massachusetts

Gli Inizi della Gran Loggia del Massachusetts

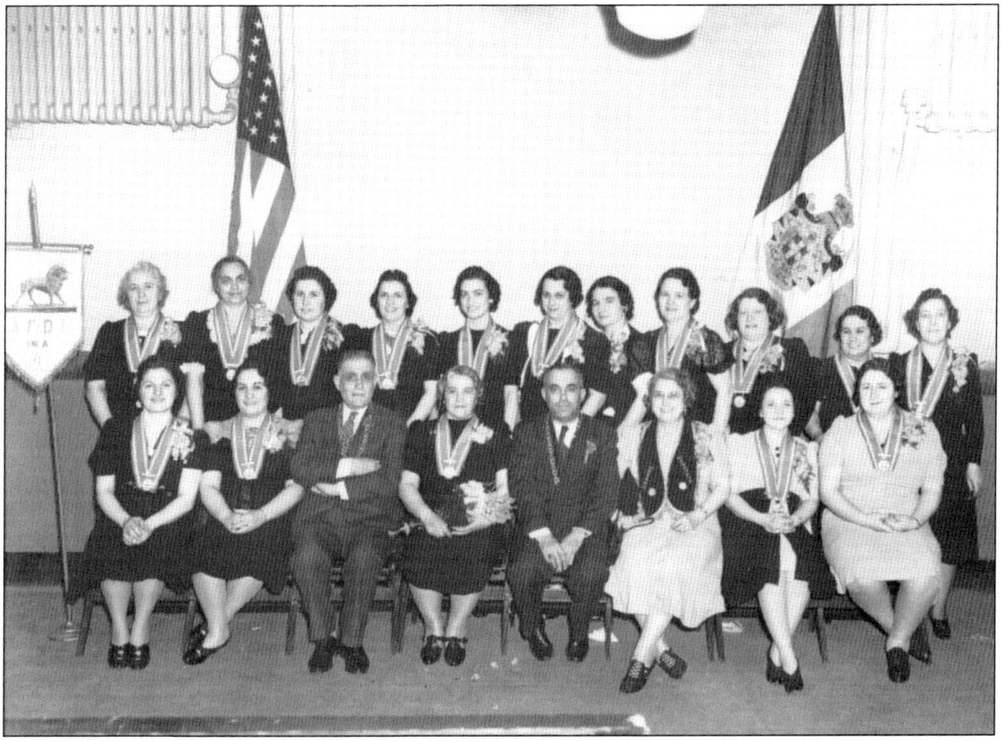

Seen in 1930, members of the Ladies Lodge in Roxbury, Massachusetts, pose for a photograph of their installation, the gentlemen wearing their regalia and the ladies their ribbons with the medallion of the OFDIA, the Ordine Figli d'Italia in America. The Ettore Fieramosca Lodge #60 in Roxbury was organized in 1910 and was an early local Lodge in Massachusetts prior to the founding of the Grand Lodge of Massachusetts in 1914.

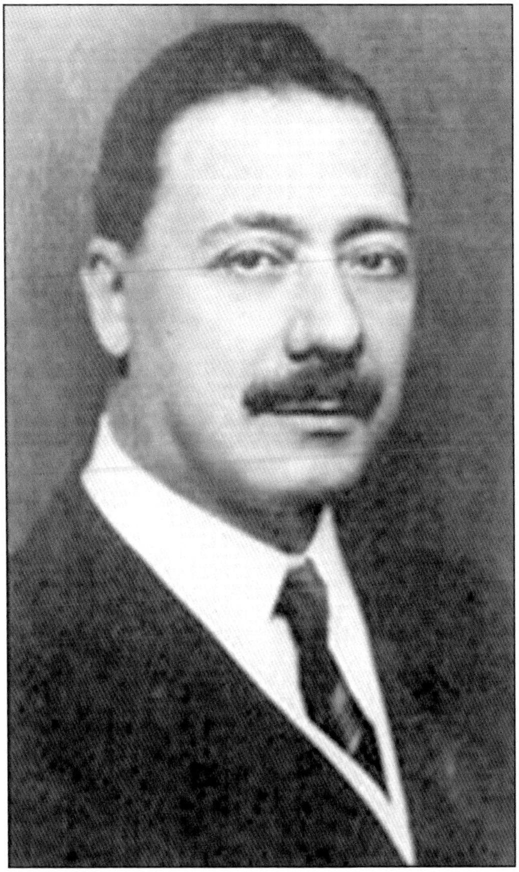

Dr. Vincenzo Sellaro (1868–1932) founded the Ordine Figli d'Italia in America in 1905. Dr. Sellaro wrote the Order's national constitution and outlined the rituals of formal procedures of investiture of officers and other ceremonies. He also founded the first Lodge, the Mario Rapisardi Lodge #1 in New York. In 1922, Dr. Sellaro was knighted by the Italian government for his aid to the Italian American community for establishing OSIA.

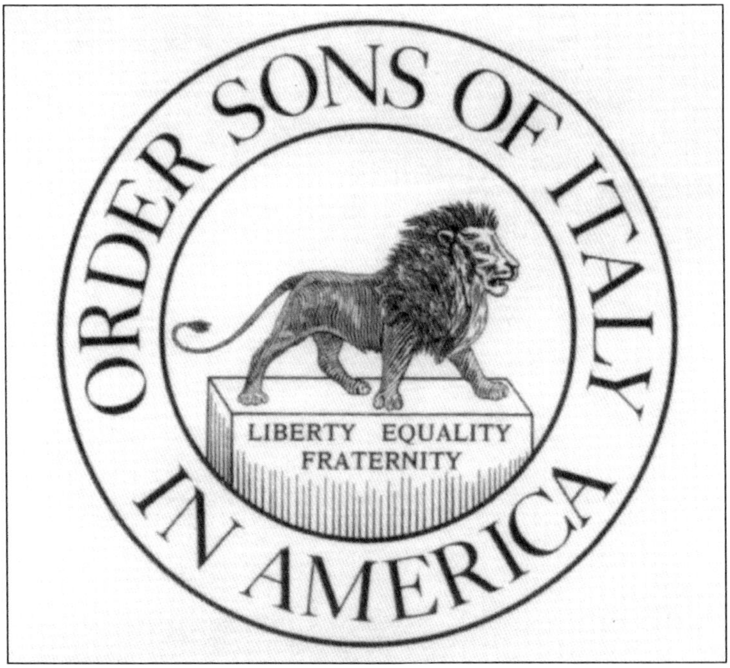

The lion of the Sons of Italy in America has been a proud emblem for over a century for the group that espouses liberty, equality, and fraternity for Italian Americans throughout the United States.

Saverio R. Romano served as the first Grand Venerable of the Grand Lodge of Massachusetts, from its founding in 1914 to 1919. A member of the Republican party, he served as a delegate to the Republican National Convention as an alternate in 1912 and 1924 and as a delegate in 1932 and 1940. He was employed by the City of Boston in the assessing department, and later became an attorney. He lived on Hanover Street in the North End of Boston.

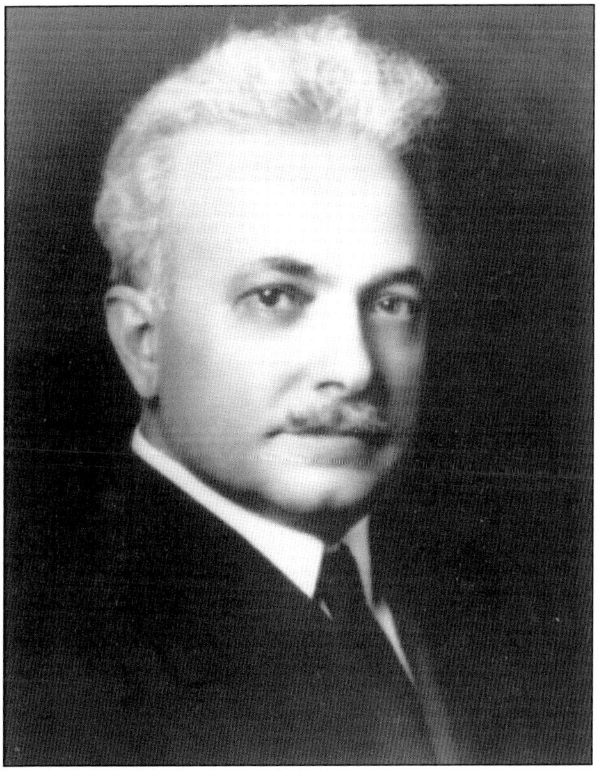

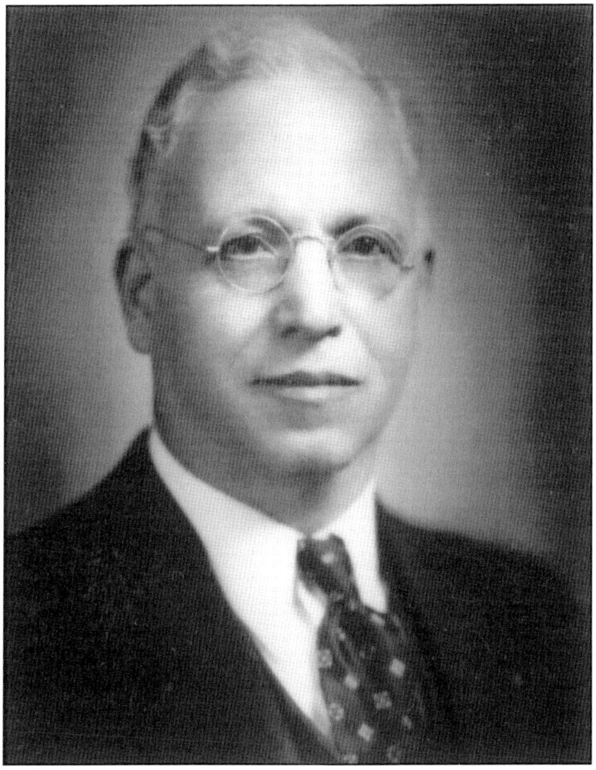

John B. Breglio served as the second Grand Venerable of the Grand Lodge of Massachusetts from 1919 to 1921. He lived in Springfield, Massachusetts.

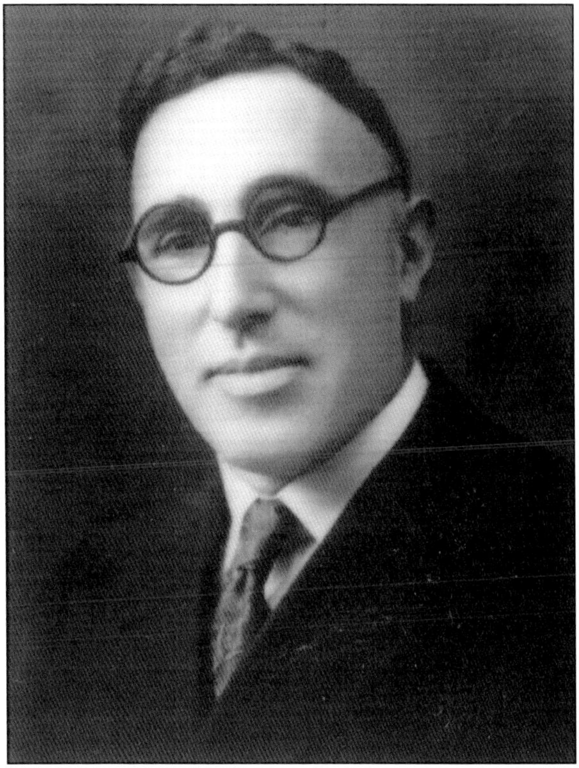

John Saporito served as the third Grand Venerable of the Grand Lodge of Massachusetts from 1921 to 1923.

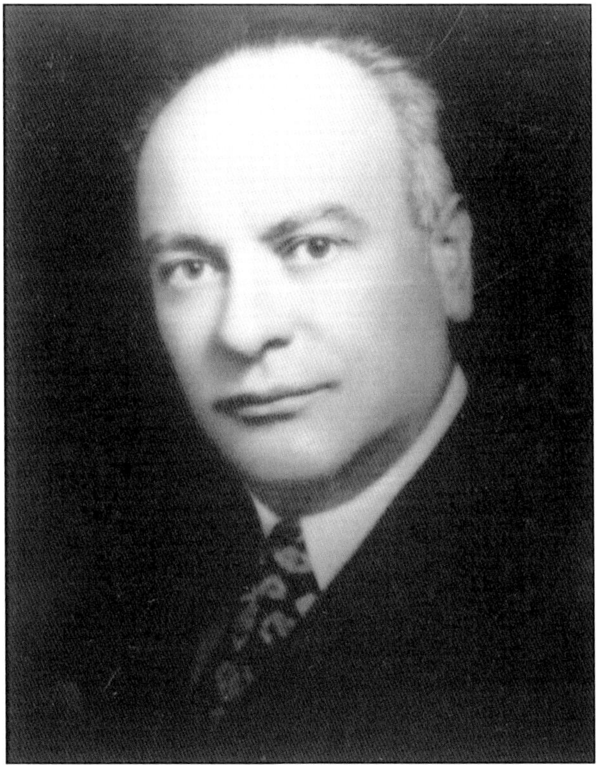

Luigi Fiato served as the fourth Grand Venerable of the Grand Lodge of Massachusetts from 1923 to 1925.

Joseph T. Zottoli served as the fifth Grand Venerable of the Grand Lodge of Massachusetts from 1925 to 1929. A graduate of Boston University Law School in 1903, he was a successful trial attorney on the Suffolk County Bar. His uncle and mentor was Antonio Zottoli, who served as mayor of Salerno, Italy, and was also an attorney.

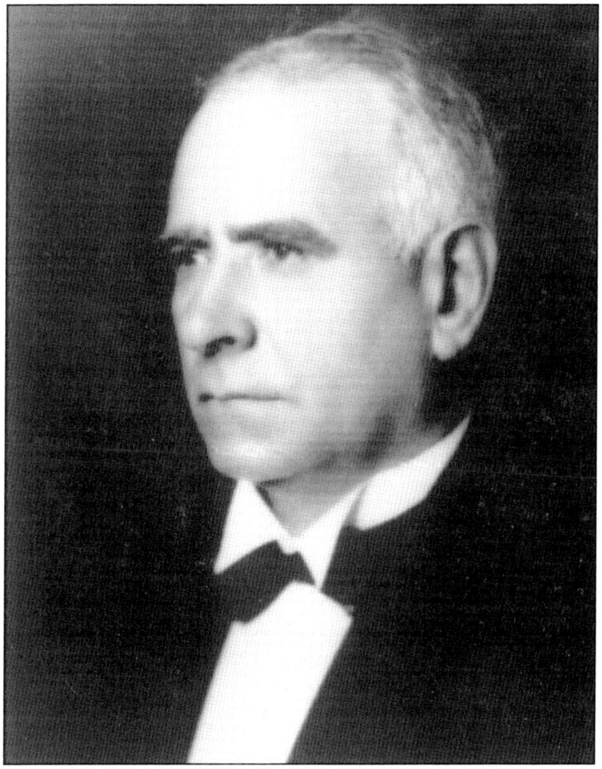

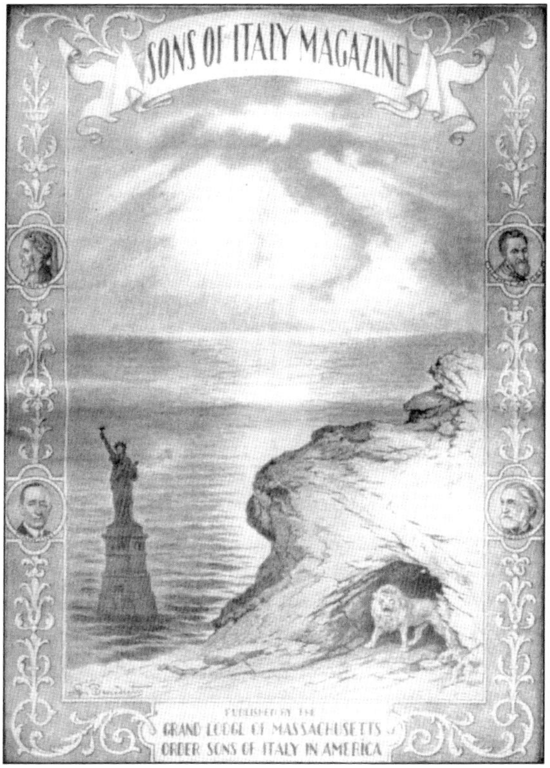

The Sons of Italy Magazine was published monthly by the Grand Lodge of Massachusetts and was initially printed in Italian and, later on, with a few articles in English as well. Here, the July 1934 cover shows the Sons of Italy lion emerging from a cavern with the Statue of Liberty welcoming Italian American immigrants. The lion, representing the champion of the Italian Americans, roars its proud presence.

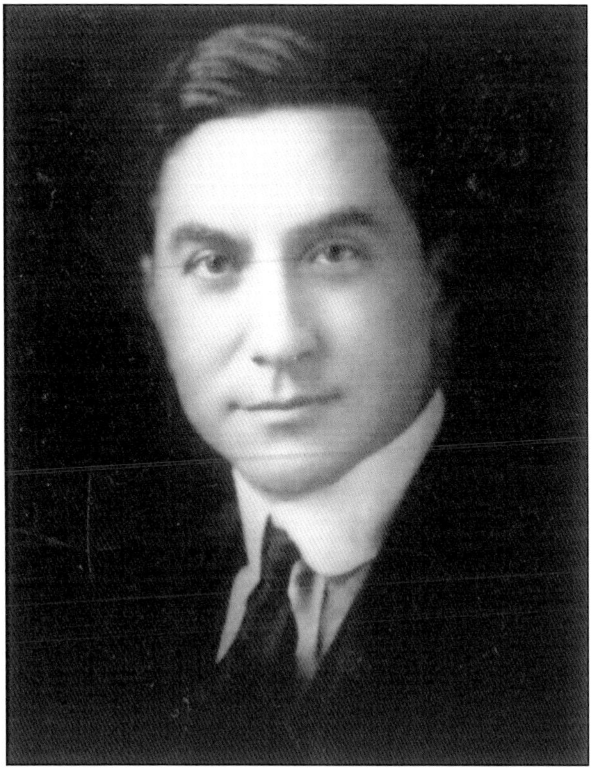

Vincent Brogna served as the sixth Grand Venerable of the Grand Lodge of Massachusetts from 1929 to 1933 and was a well-known judge appointed in 1934 to the Superior Court of Massachusetts. His son Vincent Jr. followed him as a judge; Gov. Foster Furcolo appointed him in 1961. Judge Brogna served as a member of the Massachusetts House of Representatives from 1912 to 1914 and was a delegate and member of the Massachusetts State Democratic Committee.

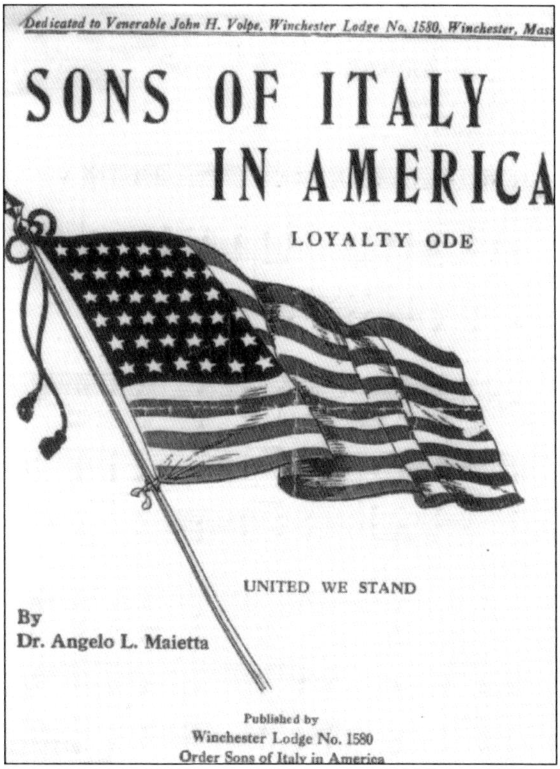

The Loyalty Ode of the Sons of Italy in America was written by Dr. Angelo L. Maietta (1907–1992), a member of the Winchester Men's Lodge #1580. The song was sung at events as members declared "United We Stand" with the flag of the United States proudly depicted. Dr. Maietta served on the staff of Winchester Hospital and as chief of the Carney Hospital's allergy clinic and was also a clinical instructor of medicine at Tufts Medical School.

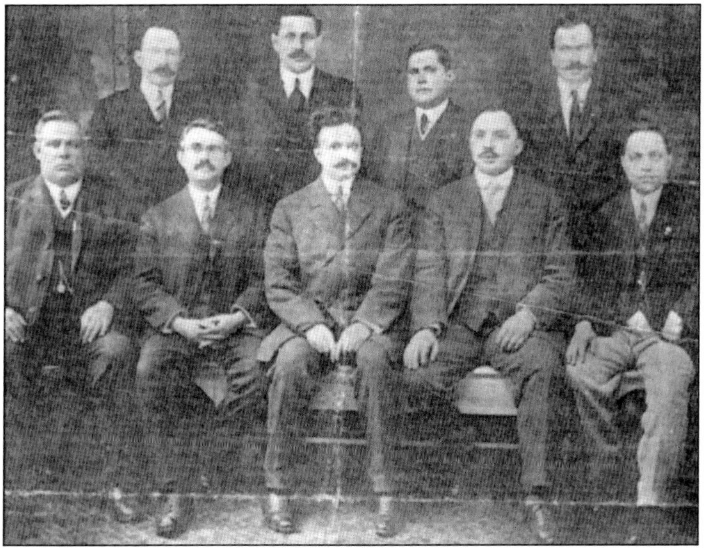

Il Primo Gran Concilio Del Massachusetts posed for a photograph of their installation in January 1939, on the 25th anniversary of the founding of the Grand Lodge of Massachusetts. From left to right are (first row) Giuseppe DeMarco, Gaetano Cuccaro, Saverio R. Romano, Costantino F. Ciampa, and Antonio Tropea; (second row) Enrico Della Donne, Nicola Crispo, Giuseppe Dota, and Salvatore Bello.

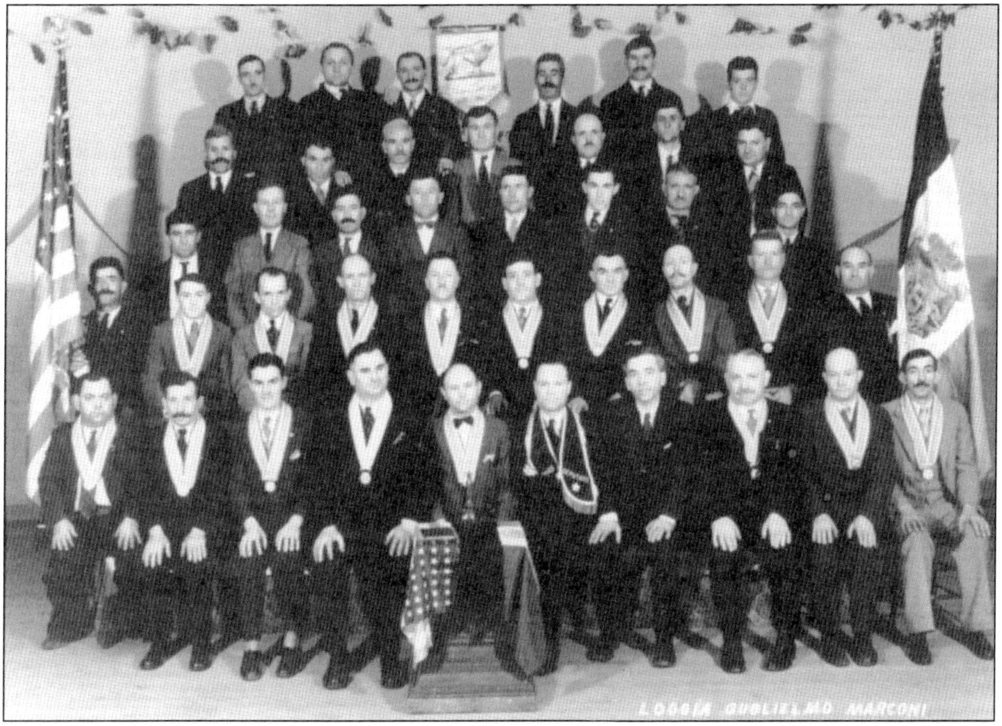

The Guglielmo Marconi Lodge #1620 from Lee, Massachusetts, posed for their installation in 1933. From left to right are (first row) Francesco DelDuca, Charles Termini, Joe Valenti, Louis Cassaniga, Louis DiGrigoli, Enzo Marinaro, Roger Canzano, Piretro Scolforo, Leo Meledio, and Cosimo Sorrentino; (second row) John Passetto, Frank Consolati, Leo Scolforo, Mr. Valenti, Jack Viani, Gus Barbini, Domenic Cavassa, Basilio Baldisserotto, Andrew Bonafin, and Lazarus Buffis; (third row) Peter Fumasoni, Tony Carlino, Peter Coco, Peter Manatti, Gene Sacchiero, Bill Salinetti, Ceasar Serra, and Mr. Bona; (fourth row) A. DiSimoni, Steve DeFrancesco, Mike Tolvo, E. DelBarco, Bondi Salinetti, E. Scapin, and Tony DelDuca; (fifth row) Joseph Longerato, Gene Longo, Joe Galardi, Tony DiSimoni, John Naventi, and Leo Scarafoni.

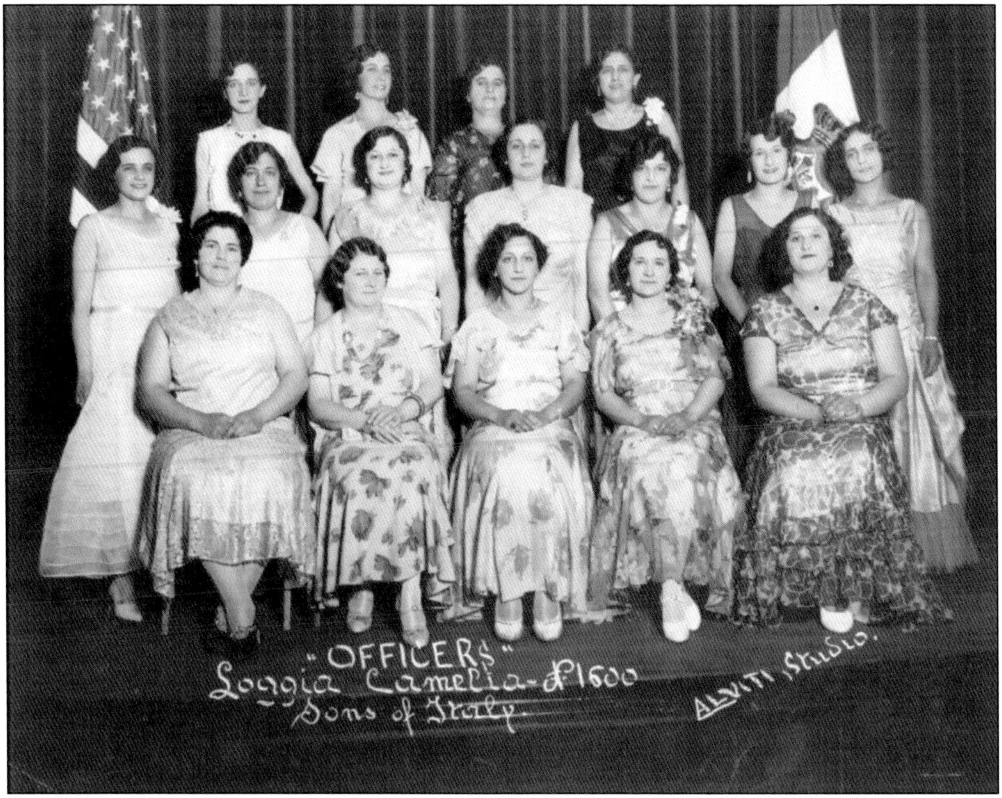

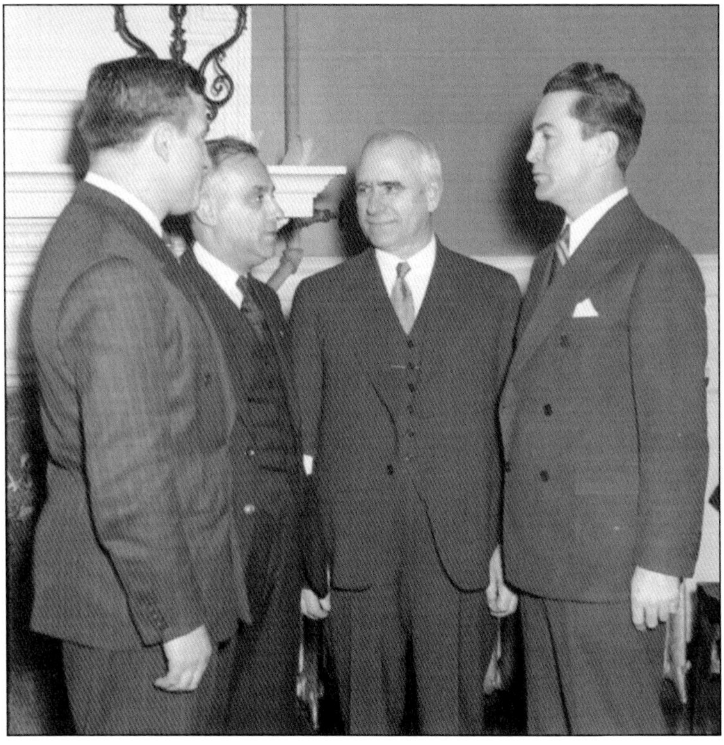

The officers of the Loggia Camelia #1600 in East Boston, Massachusetts, pose for their installation in 1927 with the flags of the United States and Italy flanking the ladies.

Officials of the Grand Lodge of Massachusetts discuss upcoming events in 1939. Joseph T. Zottoli, a former Grand Venerable (1925–1929), is third from the left, and beside him is Pres. Joseph Gorrasi, who served from 1939 to 1946. The two gentlemen on the left are unidentified.

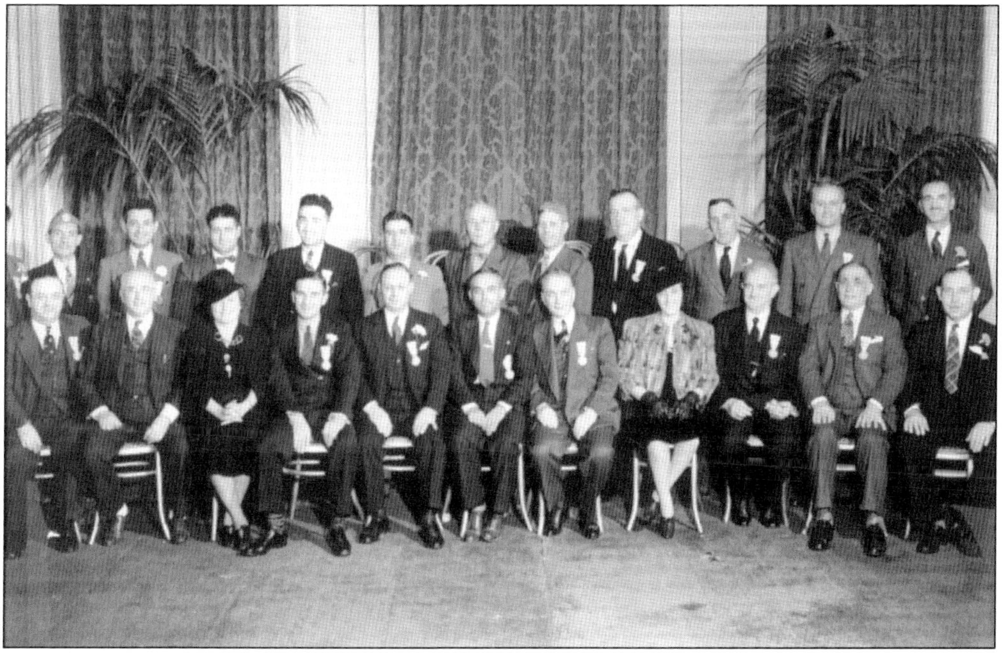

In 1939, the Grand Lodge of Massachusetts traveled to the National Convention in California and posed for a group photograph. Among those in the first row are Brockton attorney Albert Gennaco, Louis Moccia, Judge Felix Forte, Judge Joseph Gorrasi, Edith D'Orazio, Paul D'Agostino, and Anthony Julian.

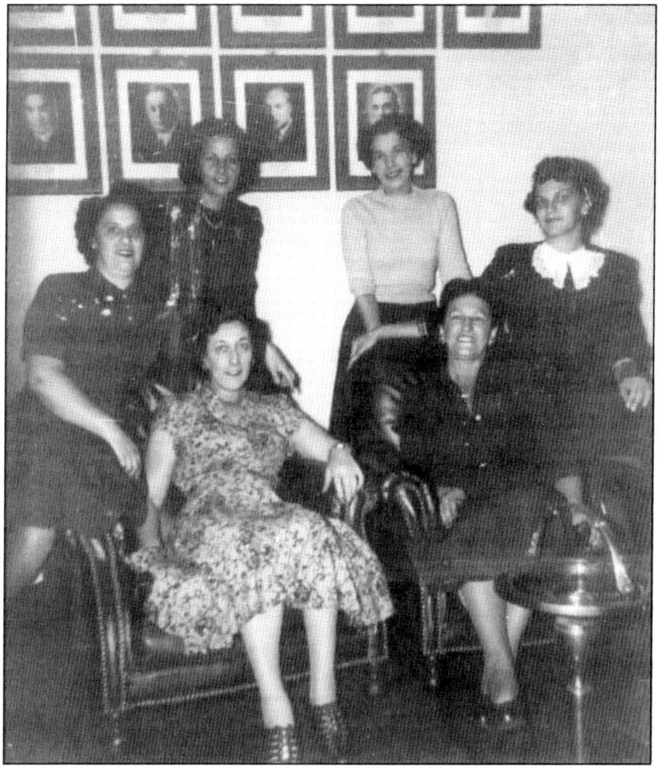

A group of women are seen at the School Street headquarters of the Grand Lodge of Massachusetts in 1940, where it had moved from the North End. On the wall are displayed photographs of the Venerables and Presidents of the Grand Lodge of Massachusetts since its founding in 1914. Today, the headquarters of the Grand Lodge of Massachusetts is at 93 Concord Avenue in Belmont, Massachusetts.

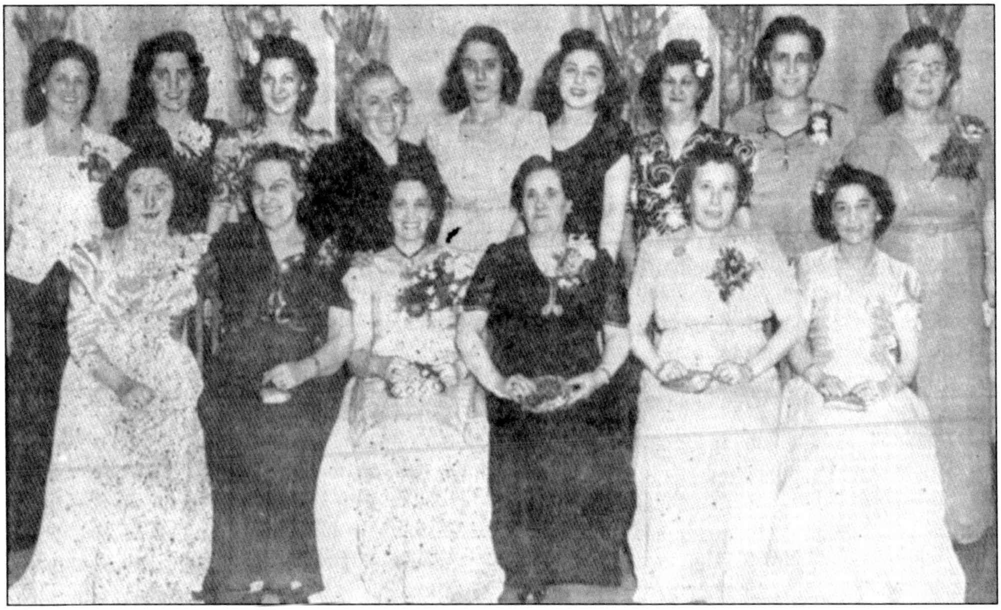

Officers of the Columbia Lodge #1438 in Pittsfield, Massachusetts, in 1946 are, from left to right, (first row) Anita Gloria, Mrs. Joseph Guercio, Chairwoman Mrs. N. Iorio, Mrs. Cesare Vergati, Mrs. George Librizzi, and Delphine Froio; (second row) Clara Tini, Julia Altobelli, Florence Adornetto, Mrs. Joseph Paoli, Rose Cataldo, Benita Bruni, Mrs. Jack Fazio, Connie Quadrozzi, and Mrs. Dan Canzano.

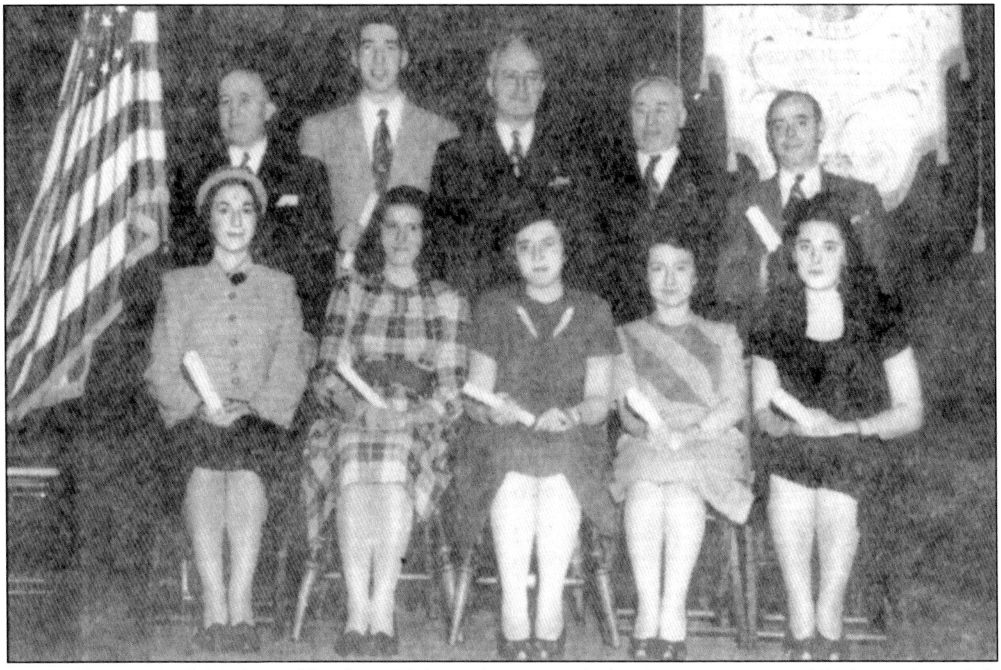

Junior Division of the Grand Lodge of Massachusetts scholarship winners in 1946 are, from left to right, (first row) Marianne Piazza, C. Liusetti, Mary Minerva, Gilda Lalli, and Lola Castelluzzi; (second row) President of Junior Division Joseph Colameta, Frank Lionette, Grand Venerable Anthony Julian, Michael Fredo, and Eugenio Mazzone.

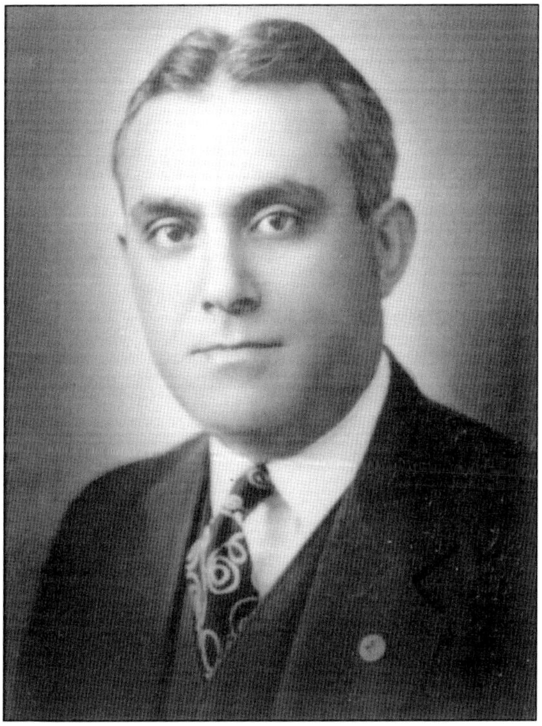

Joseph Gorrasi served as Grand Venerable of the Grand Lodge of Massachusetts from 1939 to 1946. Judge Gorrasi served as a special justice of the Municipal Court of Boston. He was a resident of Woburn, Massachusetts, where he served as Woburn city solicitor from 1964 to 1968; the Joseph Gorrasi Lodge #1406 was named in his honor.

Members of the Winchester Men's Lodge #1580 Degree Team in 1941 are, from left to right, (first row) Alfred DeMinico, Gaspare Muraco, Carmen Frongillo, Dr. Angelo Maieta, John Volpe, Gabriel Vespucci, and Anthony Ficociello; (second row) Alfred Tofuri, Anthony Vespucci, Salvatore Casalinuovo, Philip Muraco, Carmen DeMinico, Peter Fiore, Antonio Jacobellis, and Frank Procopio; (third row) Domenic Provinzano, Andrew Diapella, Francis Muraco, Frank Frongillo, Louis Giacalone, Giacomo Pantaleo, and Lawrence Penta.

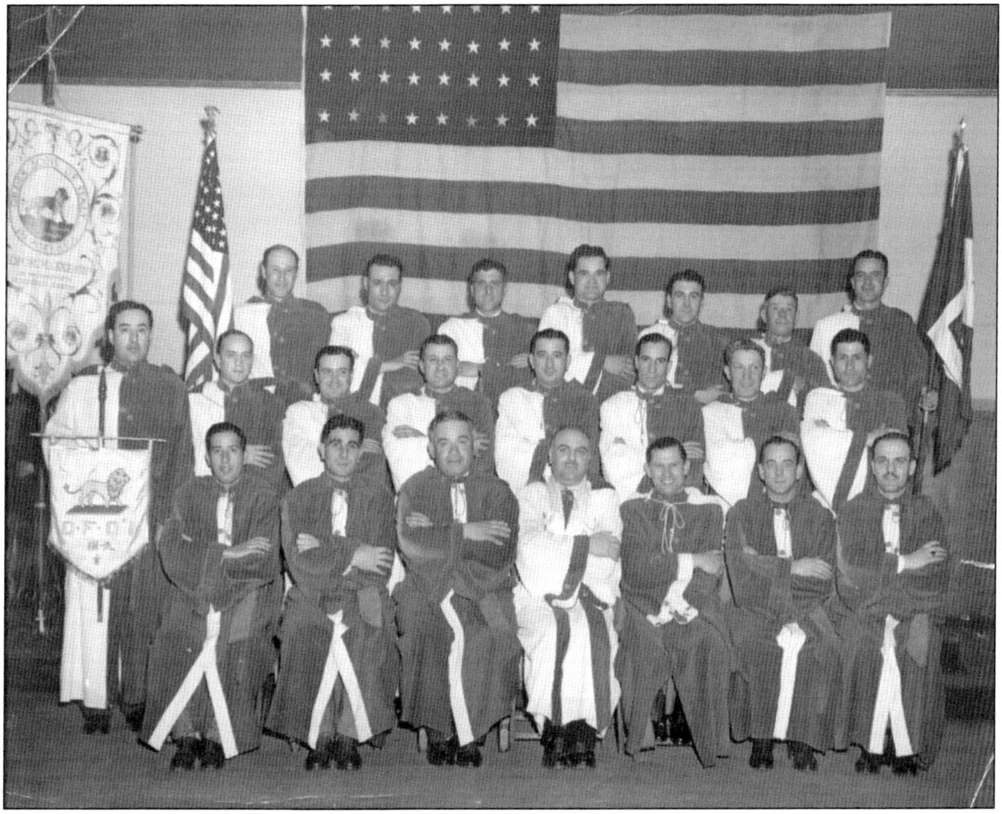

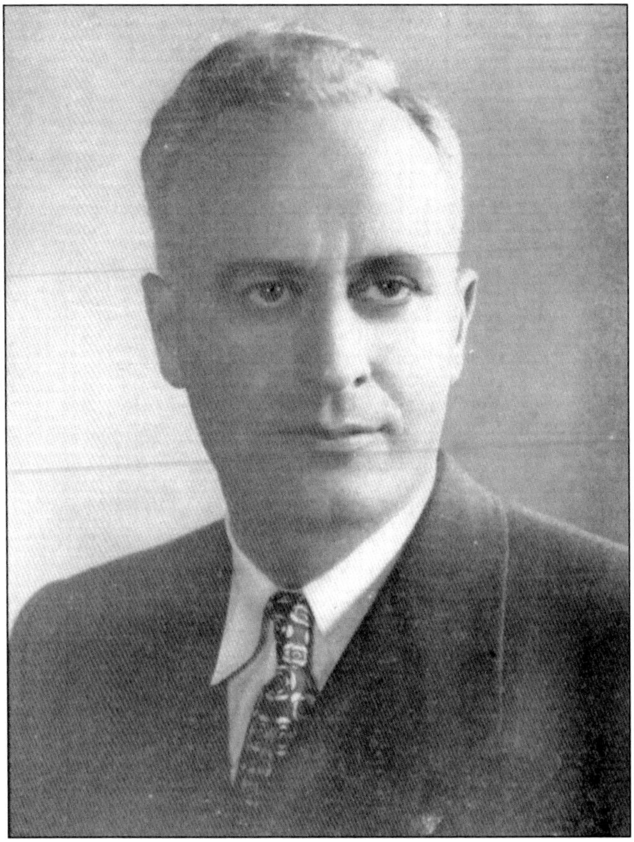

Anthony Julian served as Grand Venerable of the Grand Lodge of Massachusetts from 1946 to 1951. He graduated from Boston College and from Harvard Law School. He was a faculty member at Boston College from 1934 to 1937, and later served in the Massachusetts state legislature from 1937 to 1938. In 1959, Pres. Dwight D. Eisenhower nominated him to a seat on the US District Court for the District of Massachusetts. He was later appointed chief judge in 1971 and remained in that capacity until his death in 1984.

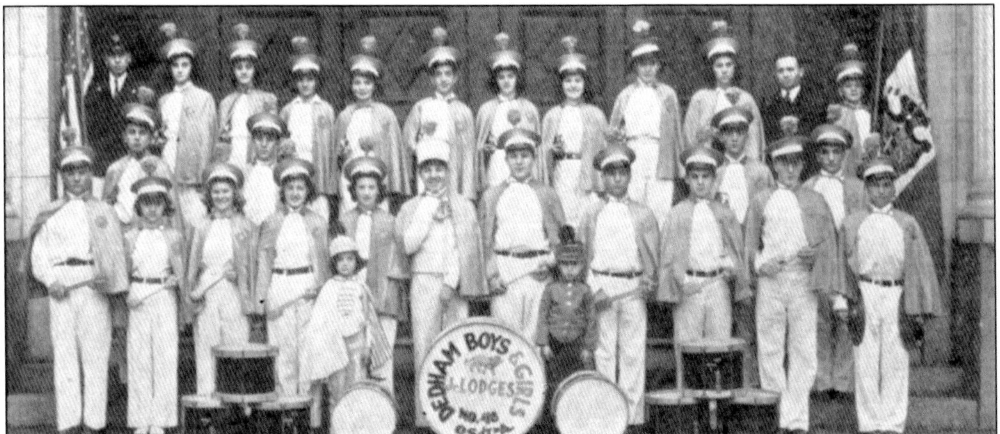

The Dedham Boys and Girls Bugle and Drum Corps of the Sons of Italy, seen in 1939, had 29 members and participated in parades throughout Massachusetts. In the foreground are the corps mascots Florence Angelo and Anthony Cieri. Members are, from left to right, (first row) Nicholas Campagna, Angie Odoardi, Lucy Campagna, Yola Odoardi, Anna Iadonisi, Martin Mastendrea, Roger Capone, John Zonfrelli, Pete Obelli, Frank Sinibaldi, and Paul Zonfrelli; (second row) Elio Mattozzi, Daniel D'Attilio, Evo Petozzi, and Anthony Carpino; (third row) Mr. Gutman, Irene Rinaldi, Carmela Piccone, Eva Angelo, Mary Angelo, Domenic Angelo, Olga Cenzalli, Rose Scampoli, Pauline Angelo, Catherine Araby, Louis Cieri, and Domenic Iadonisi.

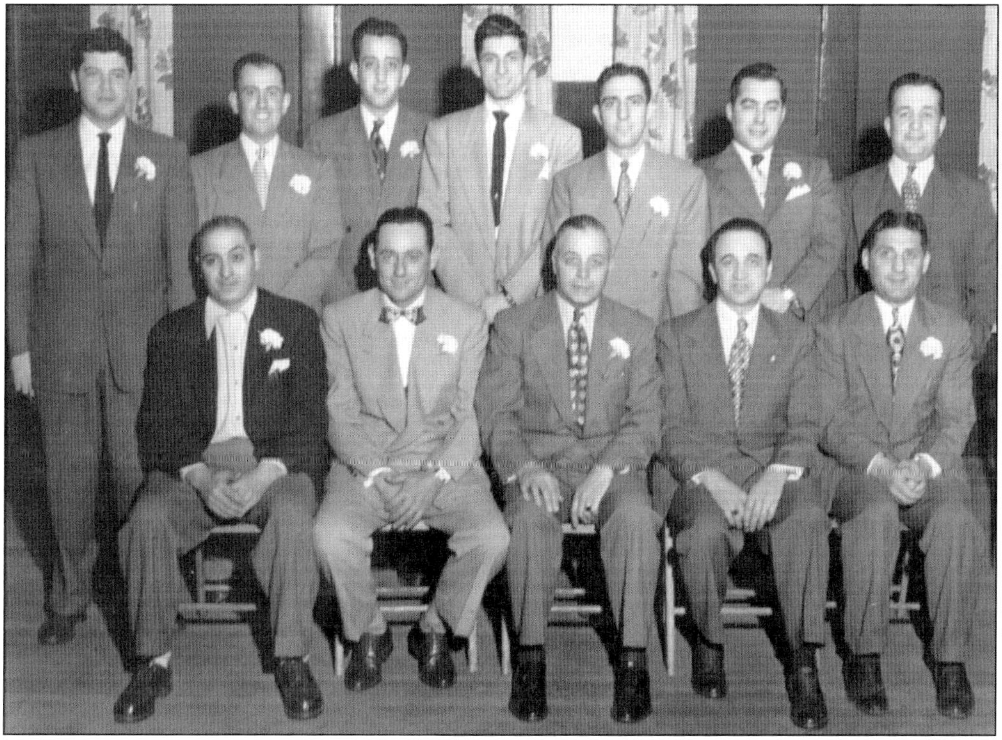

Officers of the Piave Fiume Lodge #1036 in Watertown, Massachusetts, in 1940 include Stranierio D'Antonio, Vincent Failla, Vincent Massa, Frank DiAndrea, John Mannino, Robert Nuovo, Anthony Pane, John Mantenuto, Ray Mussa, Phil Pane, and John Mannino Jr.

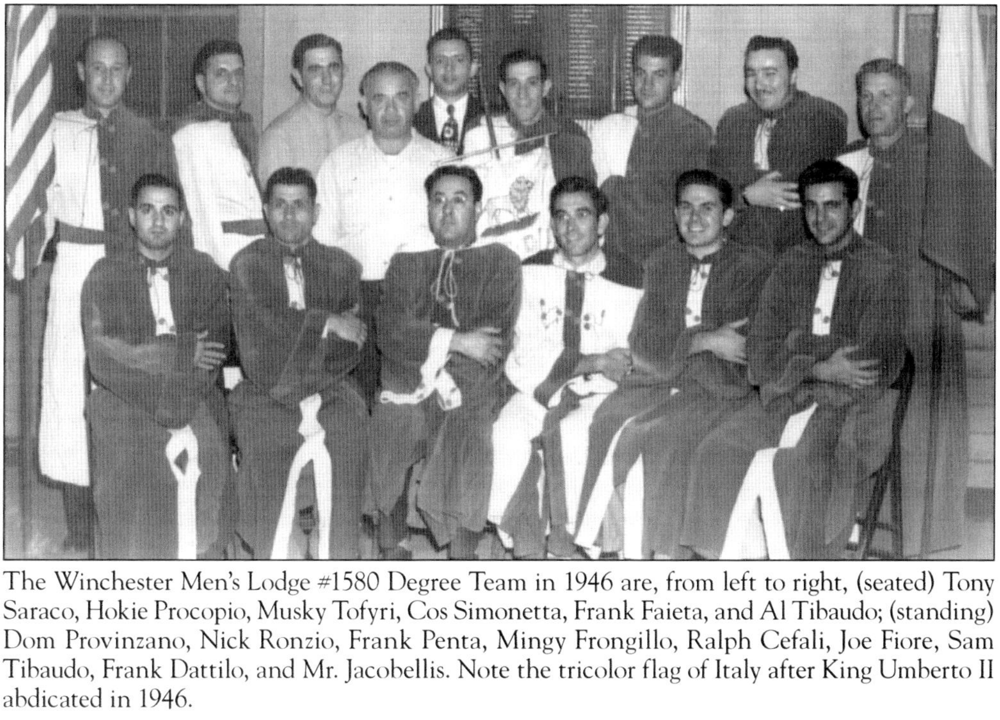

The Winchester Men's Lodge #1580 Degree Team in 1946 are, from left to right, (seated) Tony Saraco, Hokie Procopio, Musky Tofyri, Cos Simonetta, Frank Faieta, and Al Tibaudo; (standing) Dom Provinzano, Nick Ronzio, Frank Penta, Mingy Frongillo, Ralph Cefali, Joe Fiore, Sam Tibaudo, Frank Dattilo, and Mr. Jacobellis. Note the tricolor flag of Italy after King Umberto II abdicated in 1946.

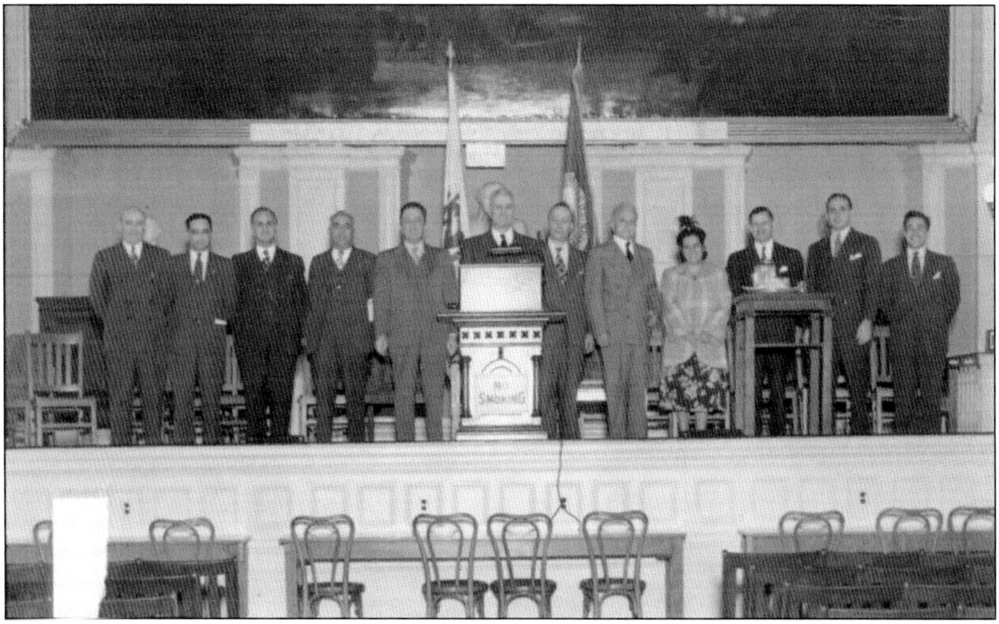

The State Convention of the Grand Lodge of Massachusetts in 1948 was held at the historic Faneuil Hall in Boston, Massachusetts. Among those posing on the stage are Judge Joseph Gorrasi, Nazzareno Toscano, Grand Lodge of Massachusetts Grand Venerable Anthony Julian, Judge Saverio R. Romano, Sophie Gorrasi, Gov. John A. Volpe, and Roy Papalia, Esq.

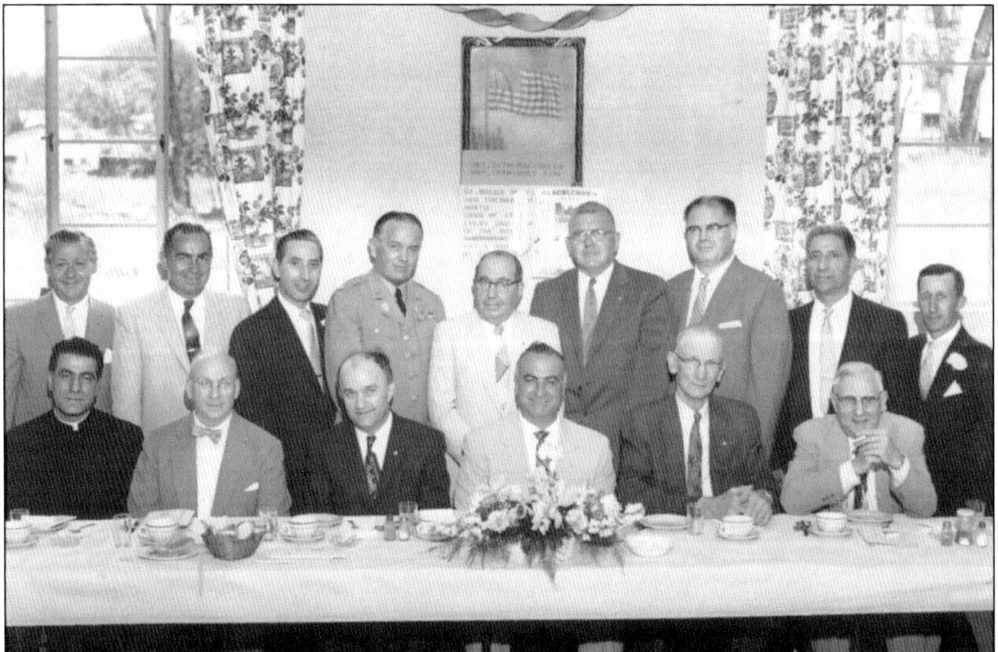

The Worcester Lodge #168 Columbus Day Dinner in 1946 included, from left to right, (seated) Fr. Joseph Valente, Mario DiTroia, Jerry Leone, Jerry Torte, Senator Olson, and Representative Amoroso; (standing) M. Palladino, S. Melchiori, O. Zullo, Lt. Col. Walter Gleason, Ignazio Colombo, Chief L. Brown, Dr. R. Romano, A. Zullo, and D. Sauro.

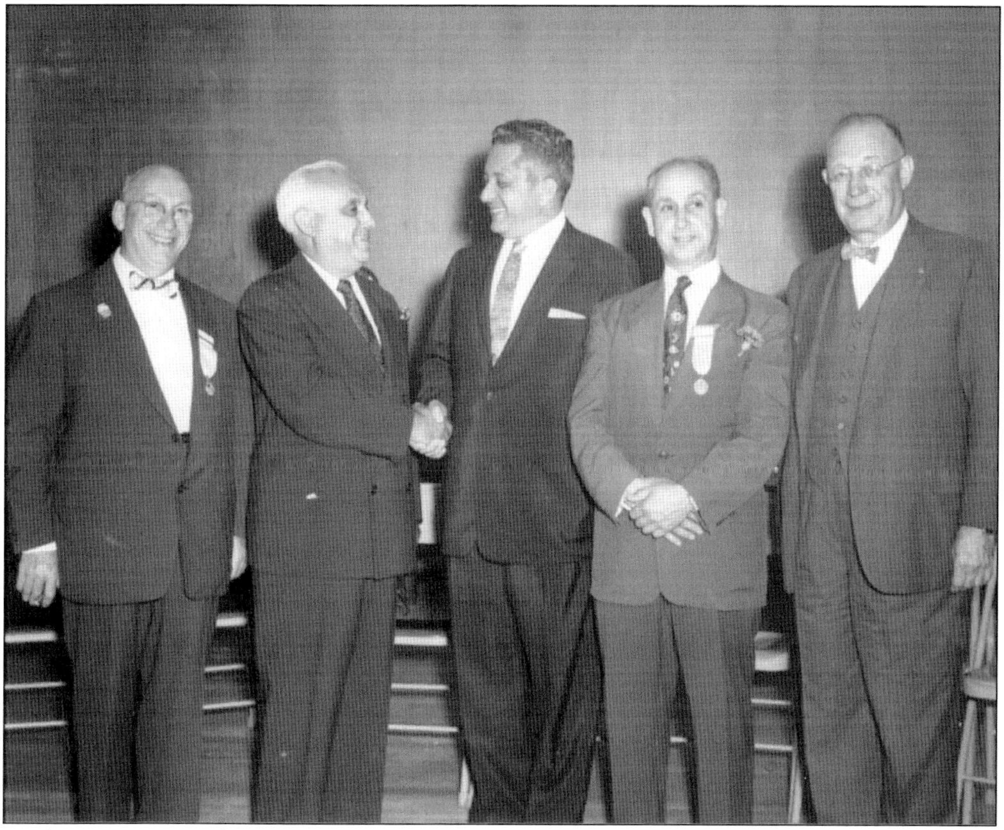

At the 1955 National Convention in San Francisco are Mario DiTroia; Joseph Gorrasi, former State President (1939–1946); John Guarino, then current President (1955–1959 and 1965–1969); Frank Liberatore; and Judge Felix Forte, former President (1933–1937).

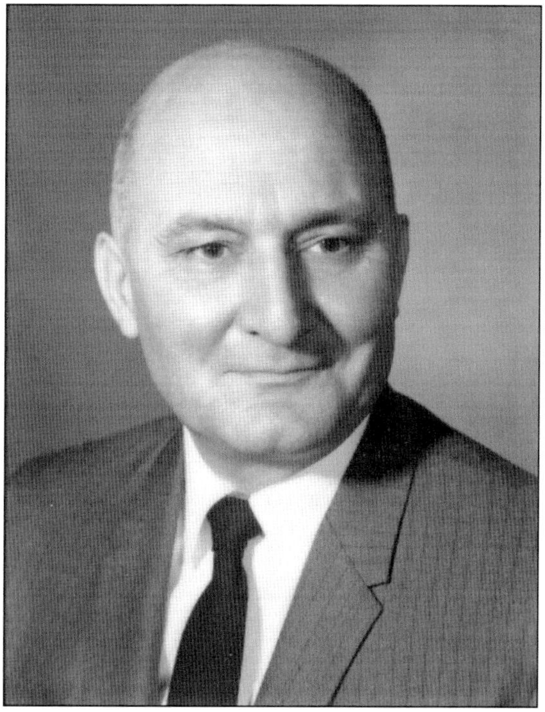

Peter E. Donadio served as Grand Venerable of the Grand Lodge of Massachusetts from 1961 to 1965. A graduate of Boston University, he worked for the Internal Revenue Service. He served the Grand Lodge of Massachusetts as Grand Trustee (1955–1959), First Assistant Grand Venerable (1959–1961), Grand Venerable (1961–1965), and as Third Assistant Supreme Venerable (1969–1975).

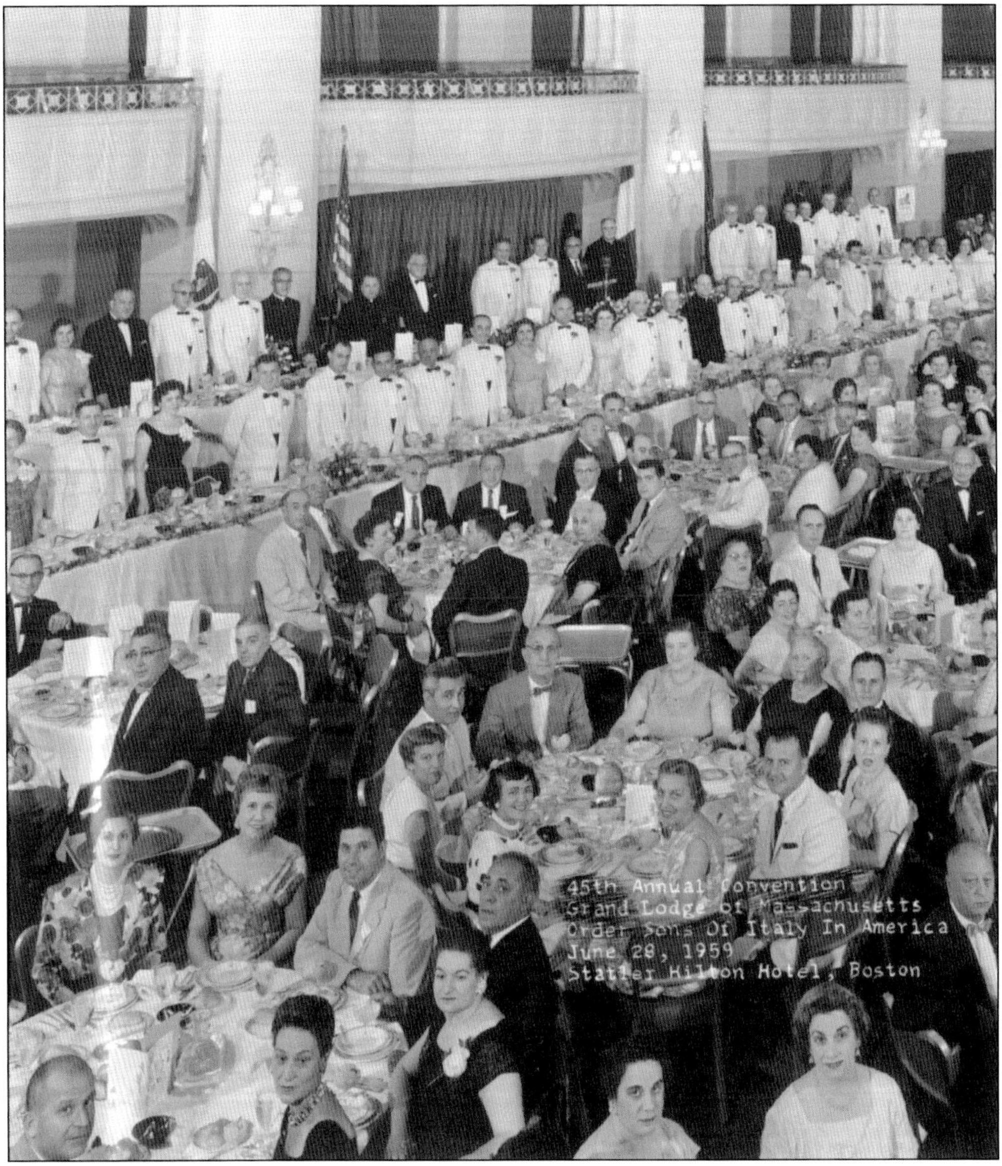

The 45th annual State Convention of the Grand Lodge of Massachusetts was held in 1959 at the Statler Hilton Hotel (now known as the Park Plaza Hotel) in Boston. Built in 1927 by noted hotelier Ellsworth Milton Statler, the hotel was often called a "City within a City," with shops, lounges, reception rooms, and a magnificent ballroom. This is a detail of a much larger group photograph that shows members and friends who attended the convention and dinner.

The Council of Italian American Organizations met in 1952 for a dinner meeting. Seen on the right is John A. Volpe, a member of the Winchester Men's Lodge #1580 and a well-respected politician who would serve as governor of Massachusetts from 1961 to 1963 and from 1965 to 1969, as the US secretary of transportation from 1969 to 1973, and as the US ambassador to Italy from 1973 to 1977.

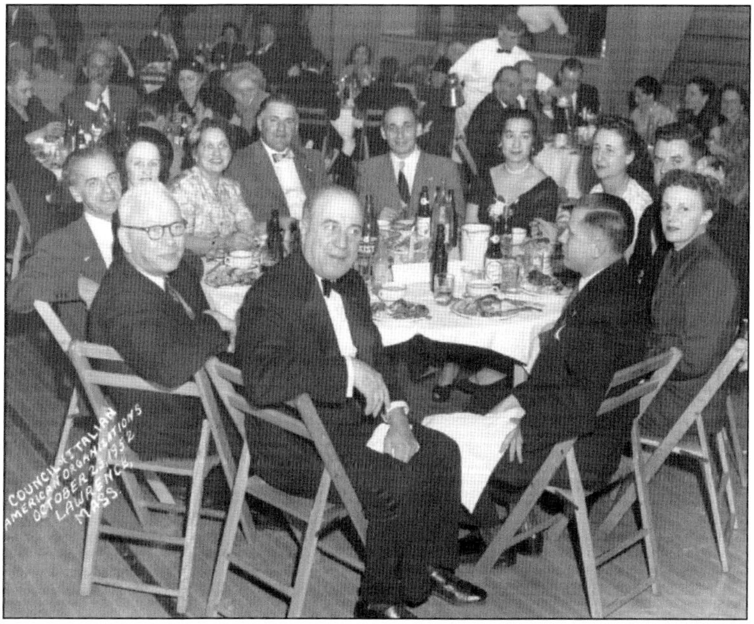

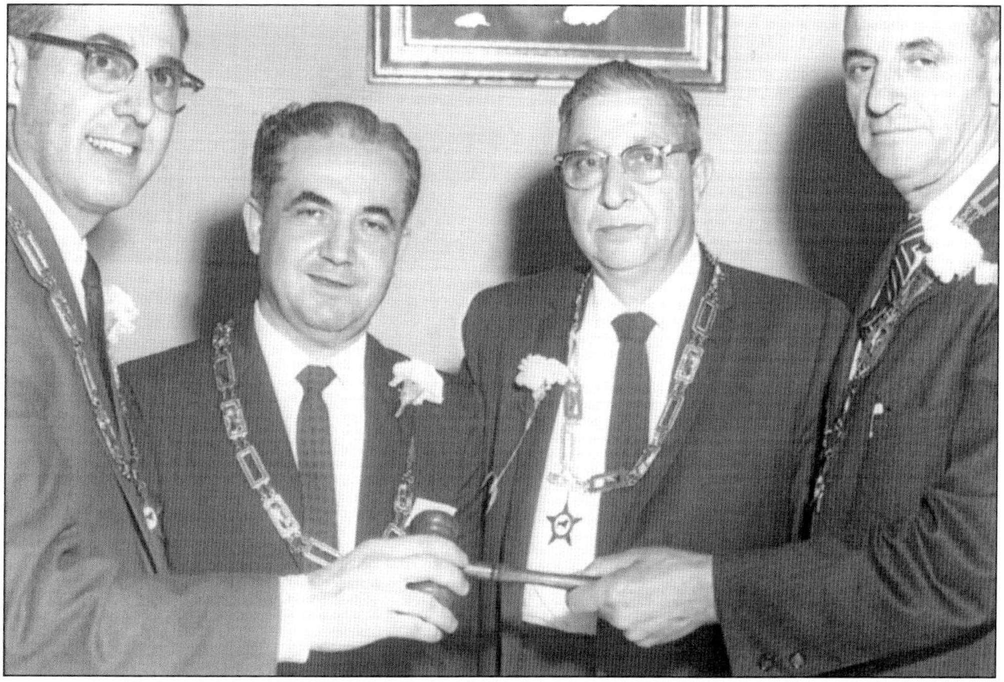

At an installation ceremony of the Cristoforo Colombo Regina Elena Lodge #169 in Fitchburg are, from left to right, new President John Pacetti, State Trustee Nick DeConza, Orator Tony Quatrale, and outgoing President Peter Lavanti, who is handing over the gavel.

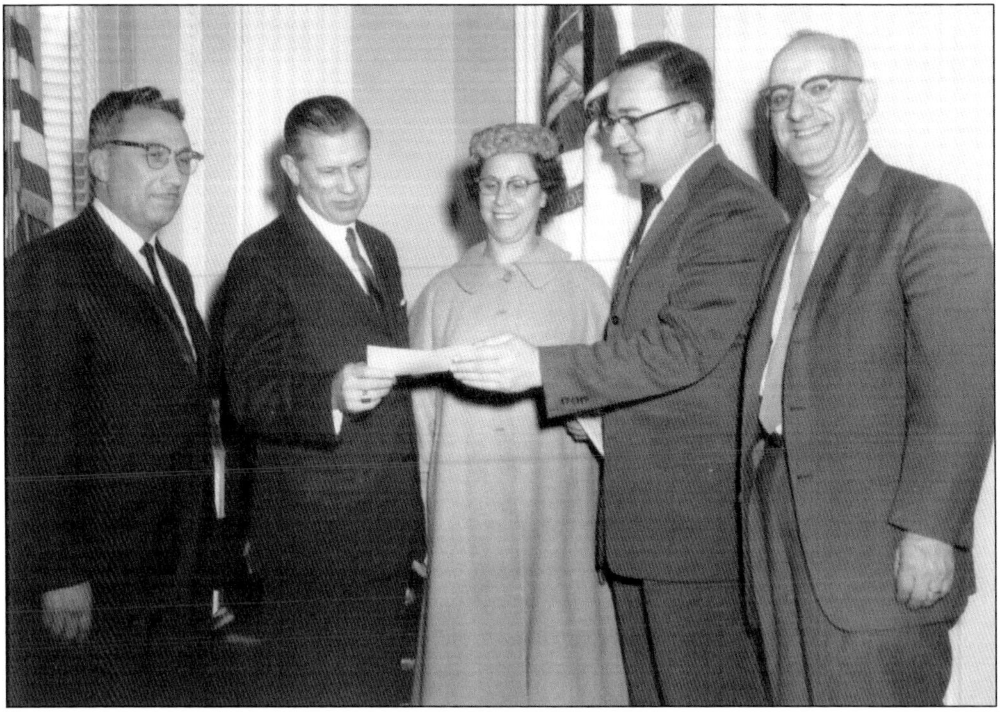

The Bandiera e Concordia Lodge #240 in Marlborough presents an award to successful businessman John A. Volpe in 1953 for his dedicated service and continued interest in the Sons of Italy in Massachusetts; that year, he had been appointed by Gov. Christian A. Herter as a commissioner of the Massachusetts Department of Public Works. From left to right are Dr. Peter Cottone, Volpe, Ann Trolla, Dante Masciarelli, and Joseph Trolla.

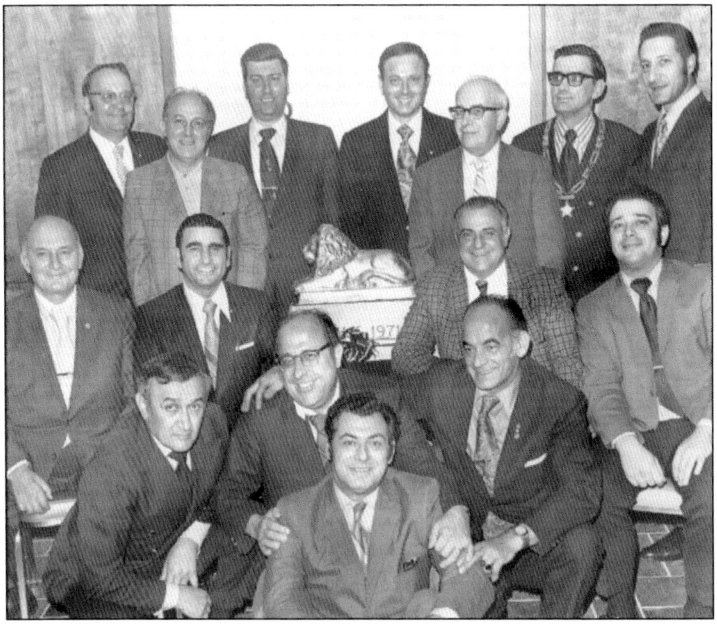

Members of the Sons of Italy, surrounding a golden lion of the Order Sons of Italy in America in 1971 include Peter E. Donadio, Aldo A. Caira, Rocky Bounvinco, Edmund Mattes, James Mastrantonio, John Fantucchio, Alfred DelCupolo, Sebastian Papagno, Joe Mattarazzo, Nick Fantasia Sr., John Bersani, Domenic D'Arcangelo, Louis Salvatore, Nick Fantasia Jr., and Agrippino "Rocky" Roccuzzo.

Three

Charities and Community Outreach

Associazioni e Comunità

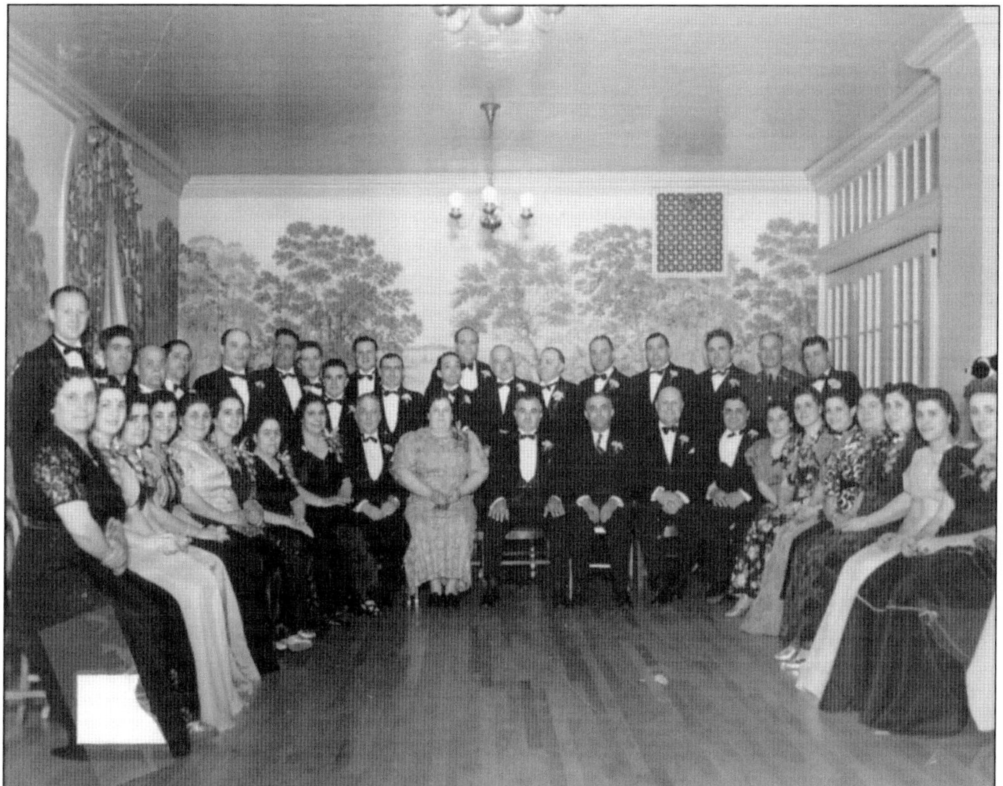

The installation in 1939 of Judge Joseph Gorrasi as Grand Venerable of the Grand Lodge of Massachusetts, seen in the center beside Sophie Gorrasi, was a gala affair in the pre–World War II days. These installations were often followed by a dinner and dance that became one of the highlights of the year for the Lodge; the installations also included the annual reports of the charitable contributions made by the Lodge to charities such as the Home for Italian Children, the Italian Red Cross, the Don Orione Home, and the war bonds program during World War II. Today, there are many supported charities including Casa Monte Cassino, Cooley's Anemia Foundation, Doug Flutie Foundation for Autism, and the Alzheimer's Association.

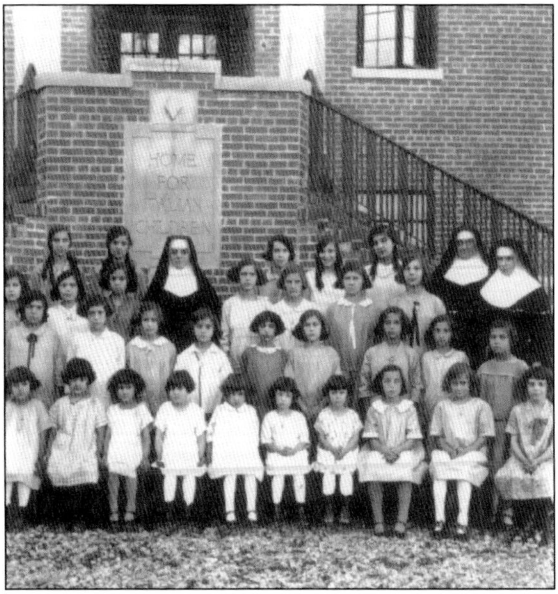

Some of the children of the Home for Italian Children on Centre Street in Jamaica Plain pose in front of the new building that was opened in 1927. The Franciscan Sisters admirably cared for the children, some of whom were orphans; others were placed in the home by their parents for a period of time from a few months to a decade. During the 1930s, the Grand Lodge of Massachusetts raised funds to assist with the ongoing support and operation of the home.

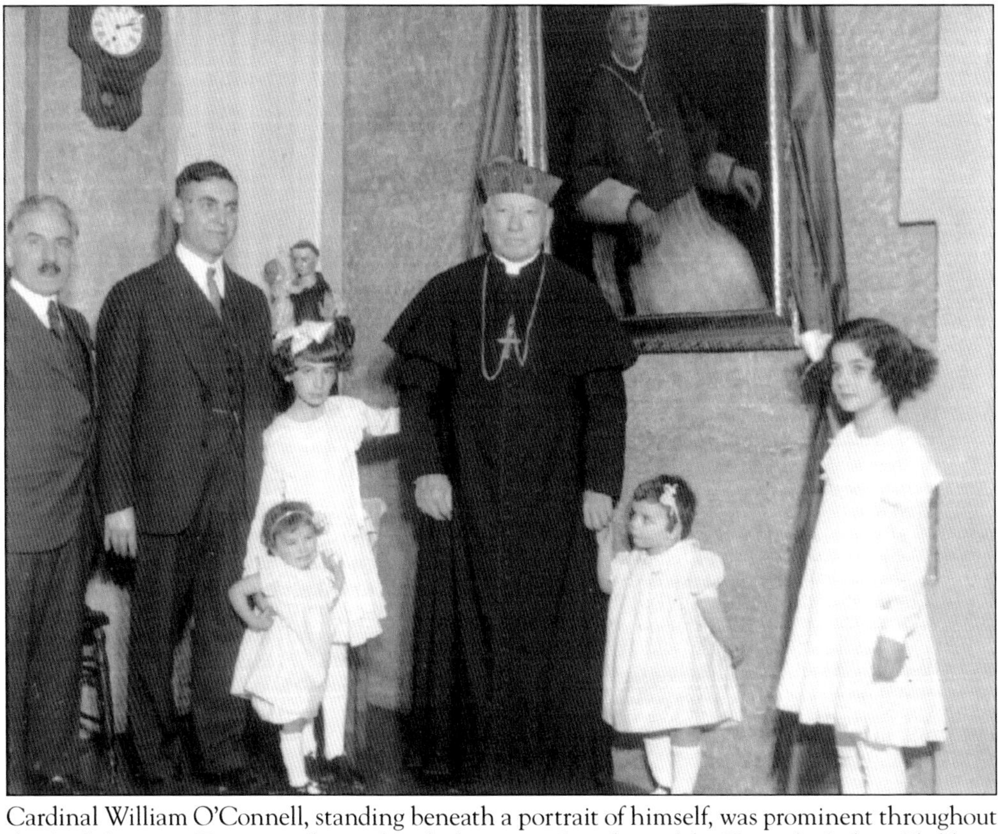

Cardinal William O'Connell, standing beneath a portrait of himself, was prominent throughout the Archdiocese of Boston and served as the honorary President of the Home for Italian Children. On the left are Ernest Martini and Paul Cifrino, cofounder of the Upham's Corner Market and the Supreme Market chain, whose generosity made the portrait of the cardinal possible, posing with girls living at the home during the unveiling in 1931.

Officers and members of the board of directors of the Home for Italian Children flank Cardinal O'Connell. From left to right are (first row) Ernest Martini, an unidentified priest, Louisa DeFerrari, Cardinal O'Connell, Principio Santosuosso, Michael Troiano, and Judge Felix Forte; (second row) Paul Cifrino, an unidentified priest, the President of the home Msgr. Richard J. Haberlin, Gaetano LaMarca, and two unidentified priests.

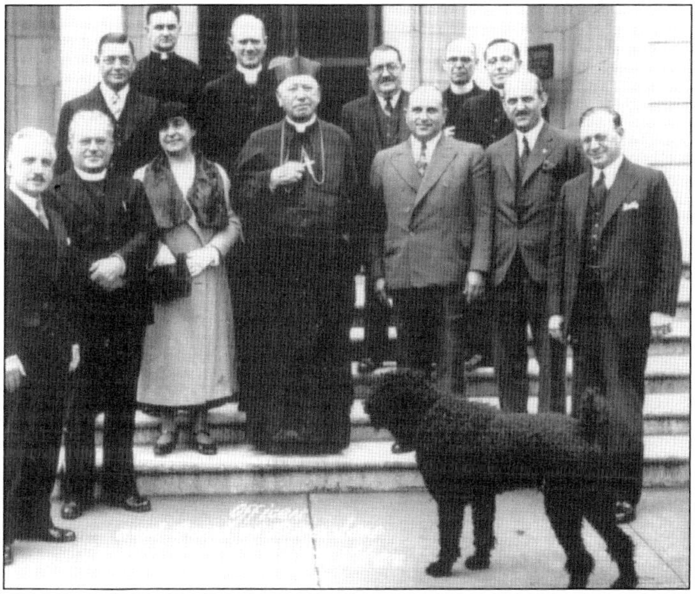

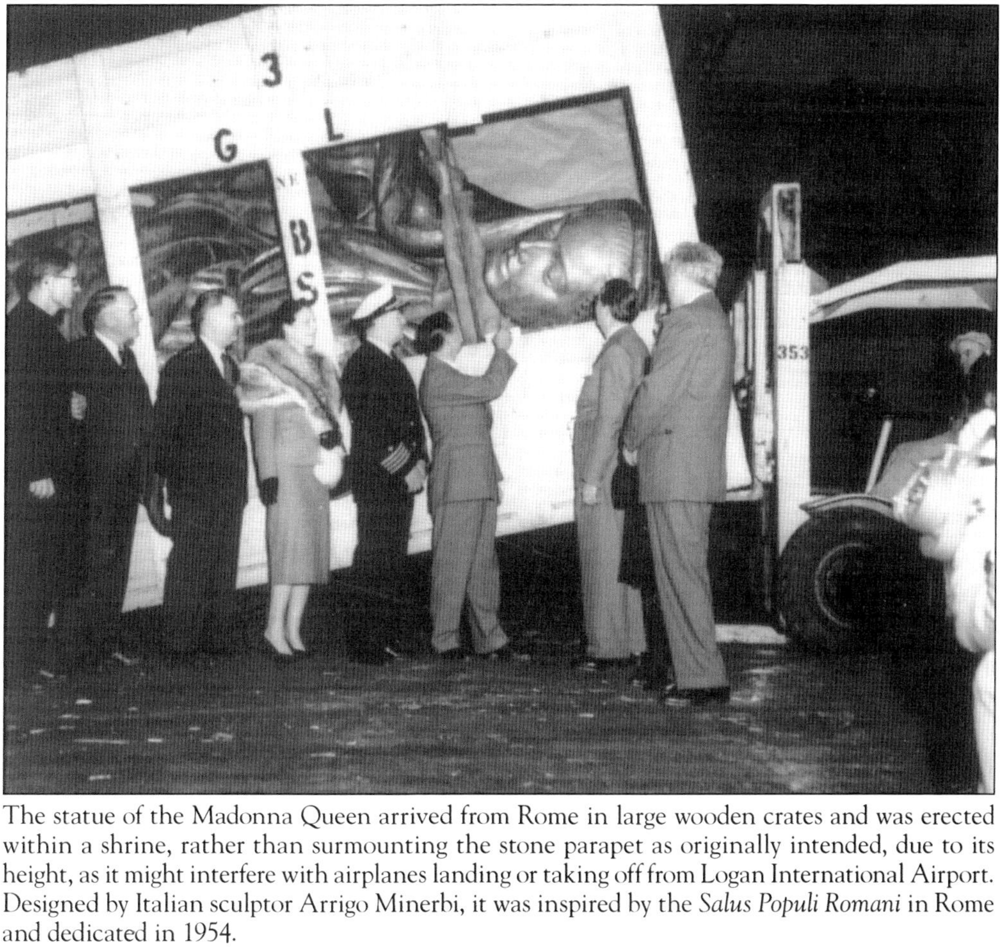

The statue of the Madonna Queen arrived from Rome in large wooden crates and was erected within a shrine, rather than surmounting the stone parapet as originally intended, due to its height, as it might interfere with airplanes landing or taking off from Logan International Airport. Designed by Italian sculptor Arrigo Minerbi, it was inspired by the *Salus Populi Romani* in Rome and dedicated in 1954.

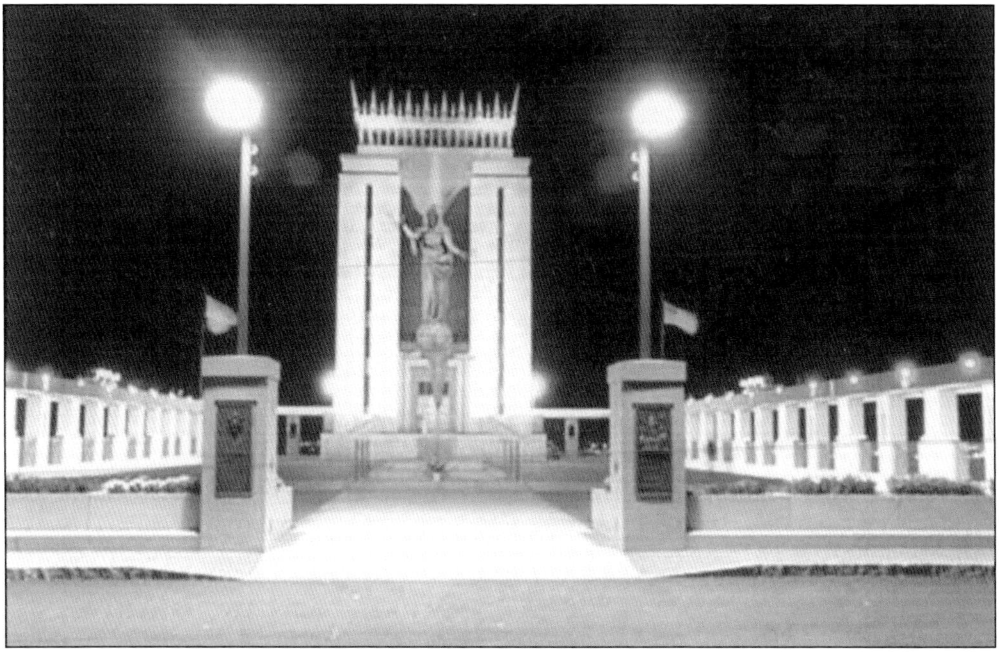

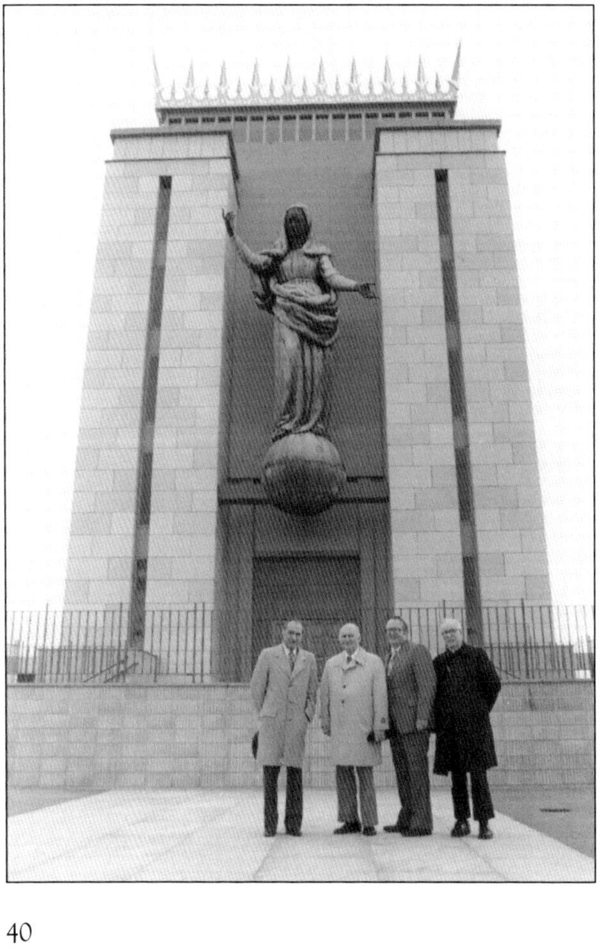

The Madonna Queen Shrine Chapel in East Boston was erected on a portion of the Don Orione Home to pay homage and reverence to the Virgin Mary. Designed by Mario Bacciocchi, the shrine is a replica of the Don Orione Shrine in Rome. Seen here in the evening during the early 1960s, it was a reverential shrine that could be seen from both East Boston as well as Winthrop.

Standing in front of the 35-foot *Madonna Queen of the Universe* statue and Madonna Queen Shrine Chapel are, from left to right, Guy Arigo, Peter Donadio, Aldo Caira, and Fr. Rocco Crescenzi from the Don Orione Shrine. The Grand Lodge of Massachusetts was a supporter of the Don Orione Home for over three decades.

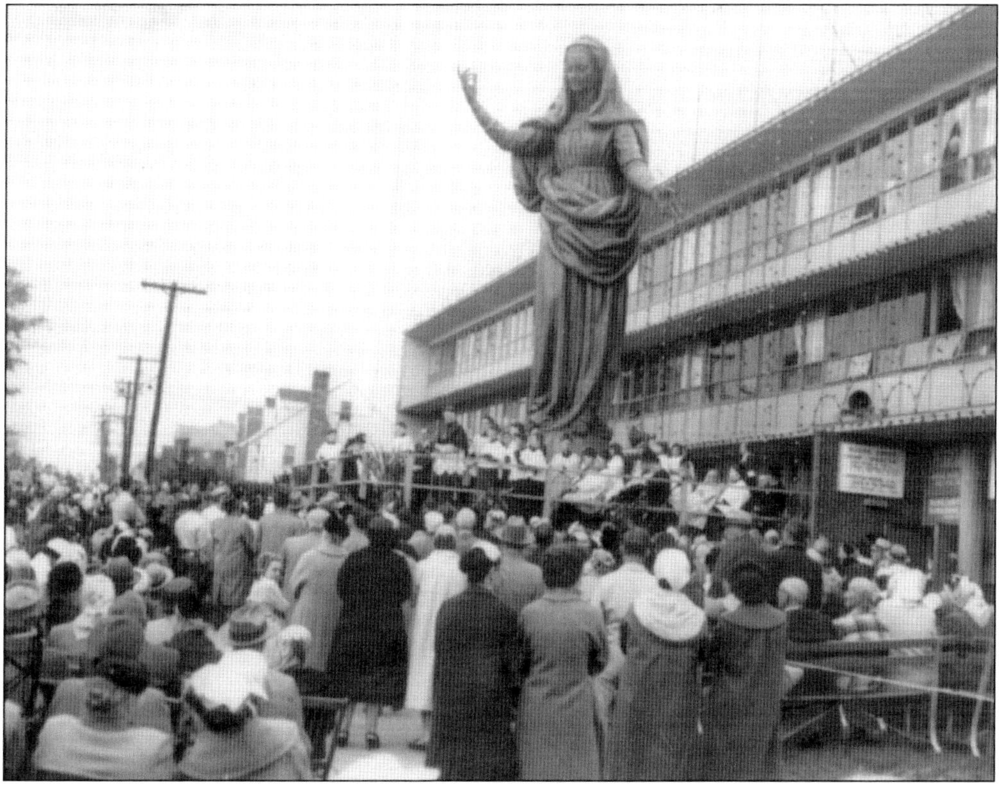

Cardinal Richard Cushing dedicated the *Madonna Queen of the Universe* statue upon its arrival from Italy with a very large group of people, including members of the Sons of Italy who had contributed to the statue by Arrigo Minerbi. (Author's collection.)

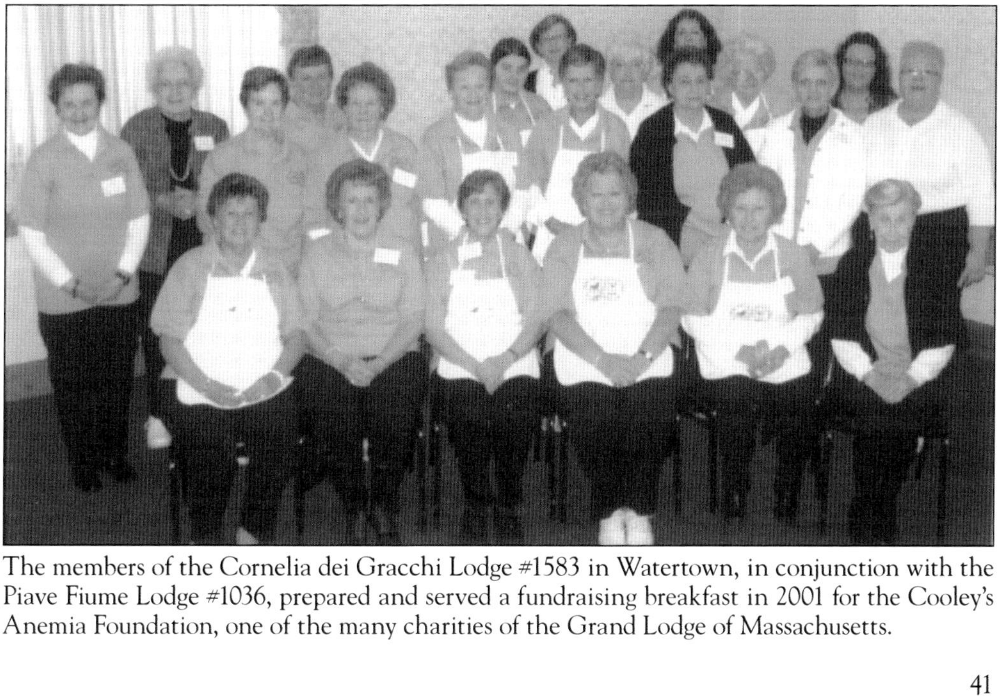

The members of the Cornelia dei Gracchi Lodge #1583 in Watertown, in conjunction with the Piave Fiume Lodge #1036, prepared and served a fundraising breakfast in 2001 for the Cooley's Anemia Foundation, one of the many charities of the Grand Lodge of Massachusetts.

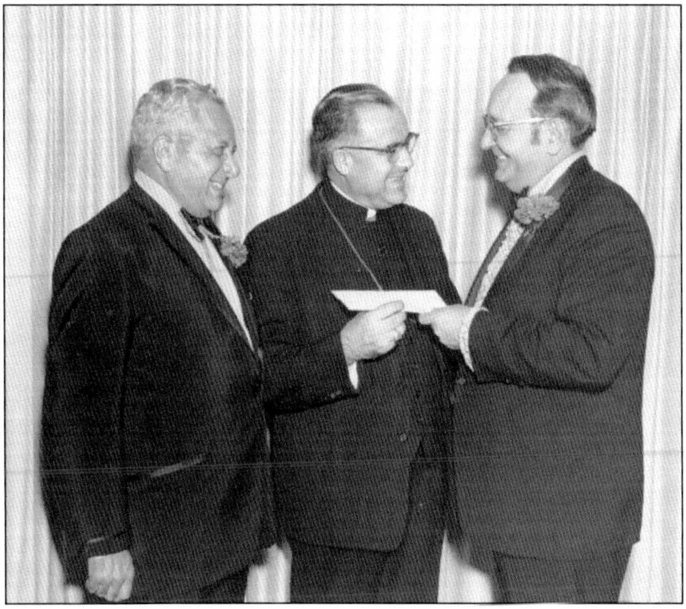

The Grand Lodge of Massachusetts was also a supporter of Catholic charities. Seen presenting a check from the Grand Lodge of Massachusetts to Cardinal Humberto Madeiros in 1970 is Aldo A. Caira. On the left is John Guarino, who had served as Grand Venerable on two occasions (1955–1959 and 1965–1969).

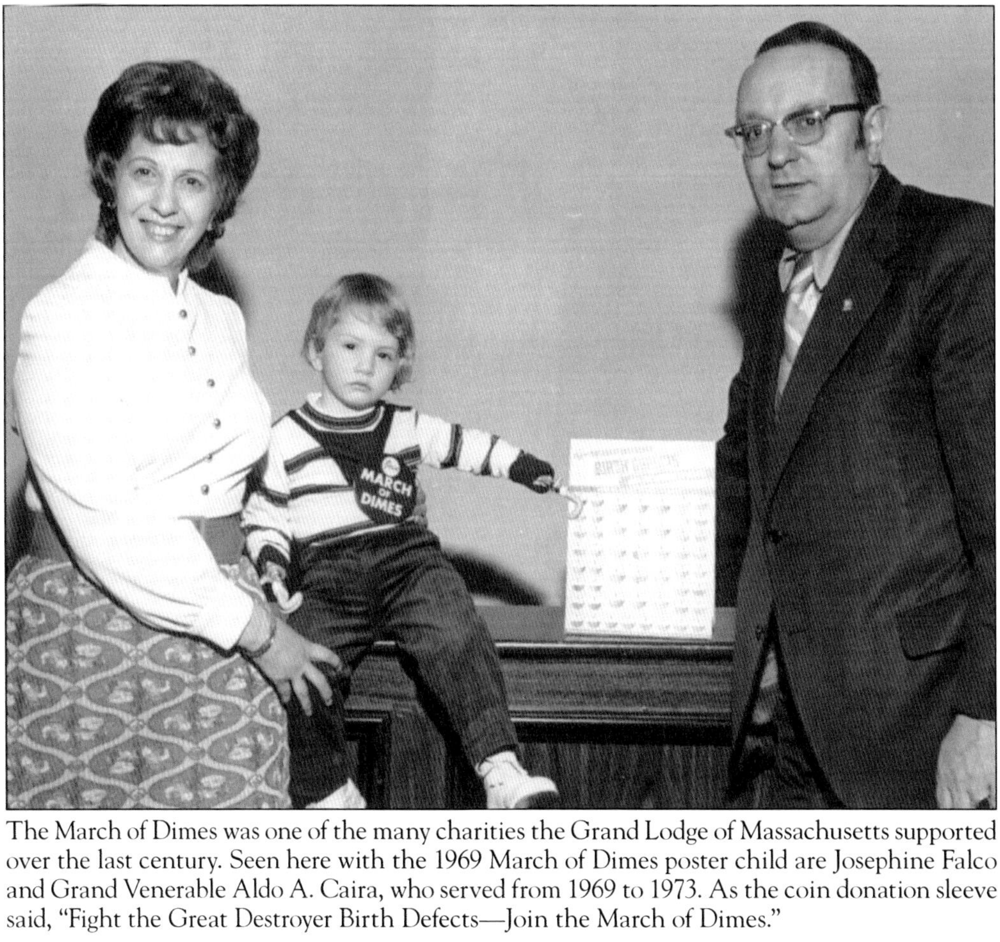

The March of Dimes was one of the many charities the Grand Lodge of Massachusetts supported over the last century. Seen here with the 1969 March of Dimes poster child are Josephine Falco and Grand Venerable Aldo A. Caira, who served from 1969 to 1973. As the coin donation sleeve said, "Fight the Great Destroyer Birth Defects—Join the March of Dimes."

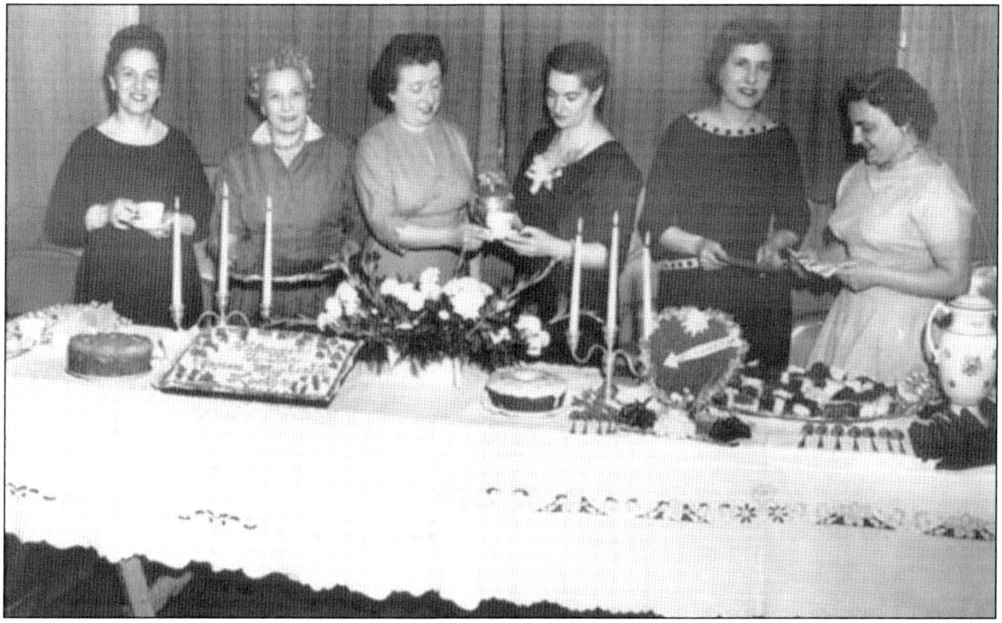

A Valentine's Day tea in 1956 at the Regina Margherita Di Savoia Lodge #1402 in Waltham, Massachusetts, helped raise funds for charities. With homemade cookies, pies, and a cake that reads "Welcome to the Regina Margherita Lodge," one can readily imagine how pleasant these ladies made the event.

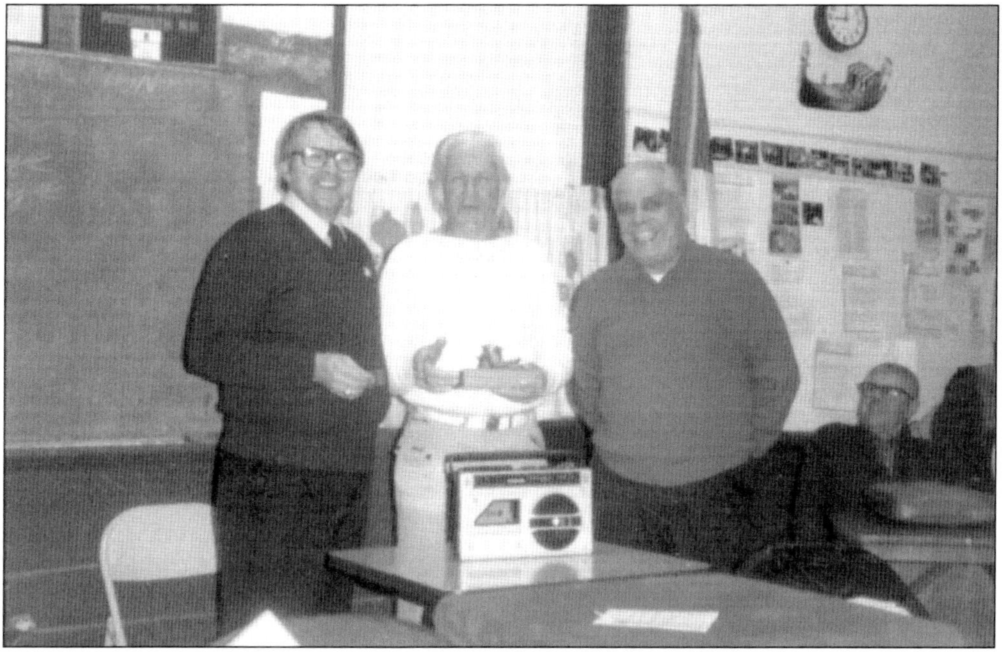

The Seacoast Area Lodge #2303 was proud to have raised the most pledges for the March of Dimes in 1987. Pictured are Brad Trafton, Dominick Karlo, and Carl Anania with the "Battered Boot," which is a reference to Walk America. Walk America began in 1970 as the first charitable walking event in the United States. According to the March of Dimes, proceeds help fund research to prevent premature births, birth defects, and infant mortality.

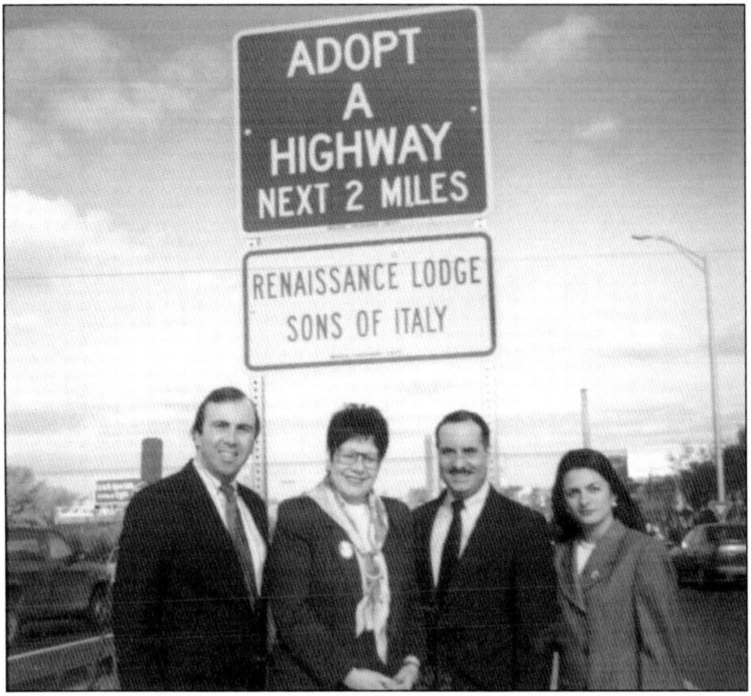

Two Massachusetts state transportation department officials flank Marjorie Cahn and Dr. Dean Saluti as the Greater Boston Renaissance Lodge #2614 "Adopts a Highway" on the expressway in Quincy. By raising funds for the upkeep of this two-mile stretch of Route 3, they create through this prominently displayed sign a reminder of the many charitable contributions of the Sons of Italy.

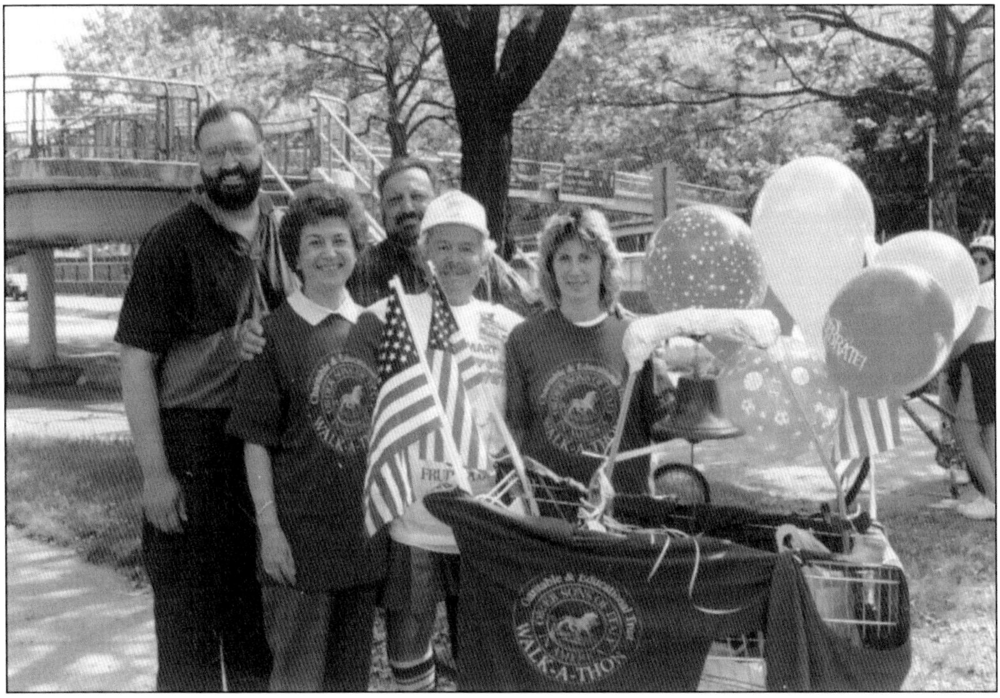

Members of the Sons of Italy participated in the walk-a-thon that was held in Boston along the Esplanade to raise funds for the Charitable and Educational Trust of the Grand Lodge of Massachusetts. From left to right are Kevin A. Caira, President of the Grand Lodge from 2003 to 2007; Antoinette Papagno; two unidentified; and Florence Ferullo Kane, who served as President of the Grand Lodge of Massachusetts from 2007 to 2009.

Four

PARADES FOR ALL OCCASIONS

CORTEI PER TUTTE LE OCCASIONI

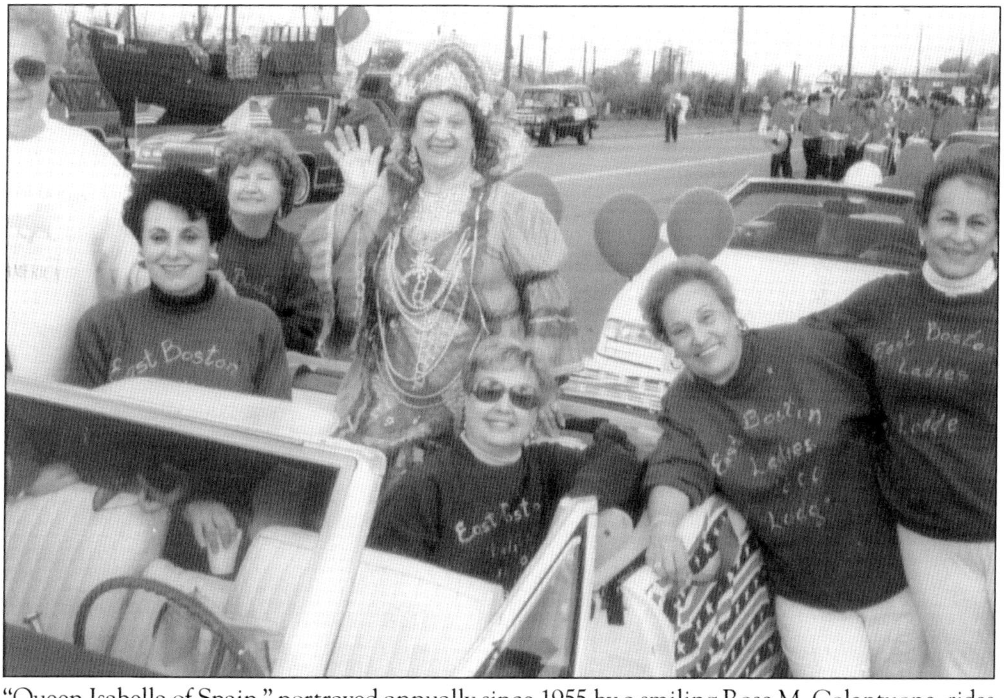

"Queen Isabella of Spain," portrayed annually since 1955 by a smiling Rose M. Colantuone, rides in her convertible in the Columbus Day Parade in Boston's North End in 1993. Surrounding her are members of her court, members of the East Boston Ladies Lodge #1600, of which she was founder; she served as a State Delegate for over four decades and was a member of the Sons of Italy for 60 years.

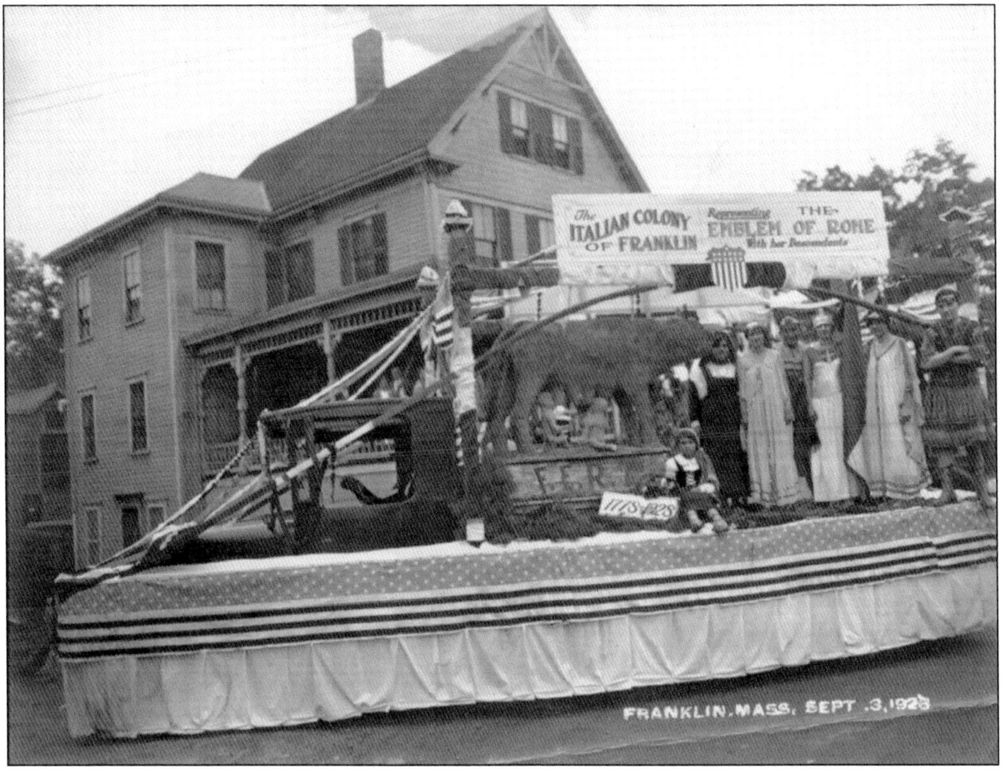

In 1928, members of the Quattro Eroi Lodge #1414 in Franklin participate with a float of "The Italian Colony of Franklin" in the 150th anniversary parade of the town of Franklin, Massachusetts. The float, with Romulus and Remus beneath the Capitoline Wolf of Rome, was said to represent the "Emblem of Rome with her Descendants."

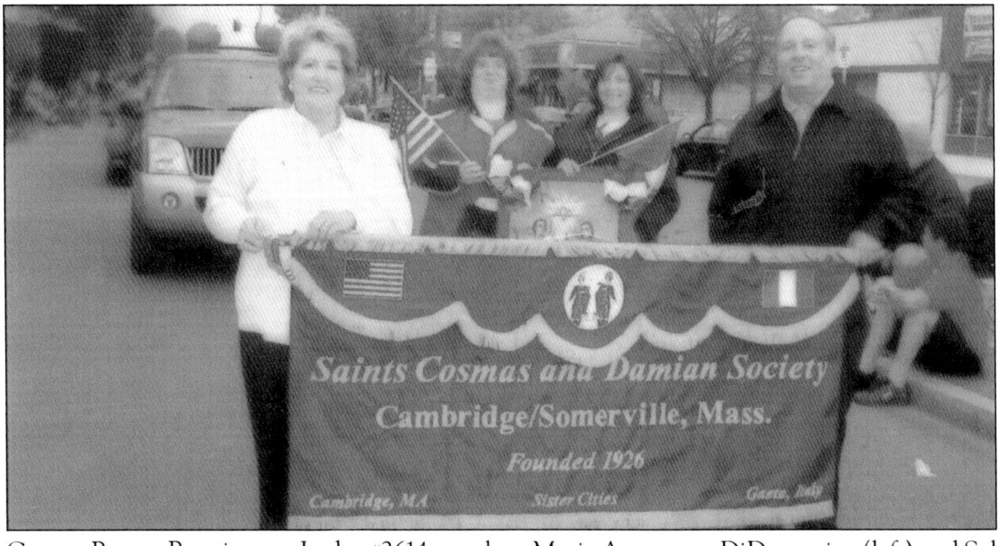

Greater Boston Renaissance Lodge #2614 members Marie Apruzzesse DiDomenico (left) and Sal DiDomenico are carrying the banner of the Saints Cosmas and Damian Society at the Columbus Day Parade in 1995. The two women behind the banner hold not only flags of the United States and Italy but also a banner of the two saints.

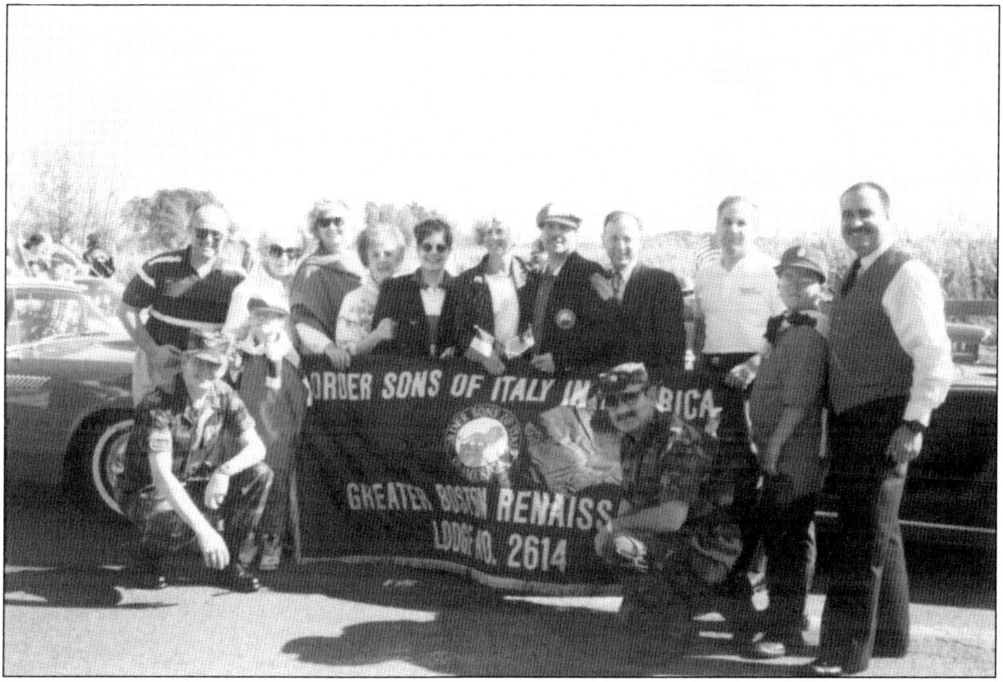

At the Columbus Day Parade in East Boston in 1992, Brig. Gen. William Bennett Hurley is crouched to the left of the banner, surrounded by members of the Greater Boston Renaissance Lodge #2614. Bill Hurley was the parade grand marshal that year, having served for 40 years in the Army and Massachusetts National Guard, retiring as a brigadier general; in 2005, he founded the Commonwealth Clinical Services Home Health Care Agency.

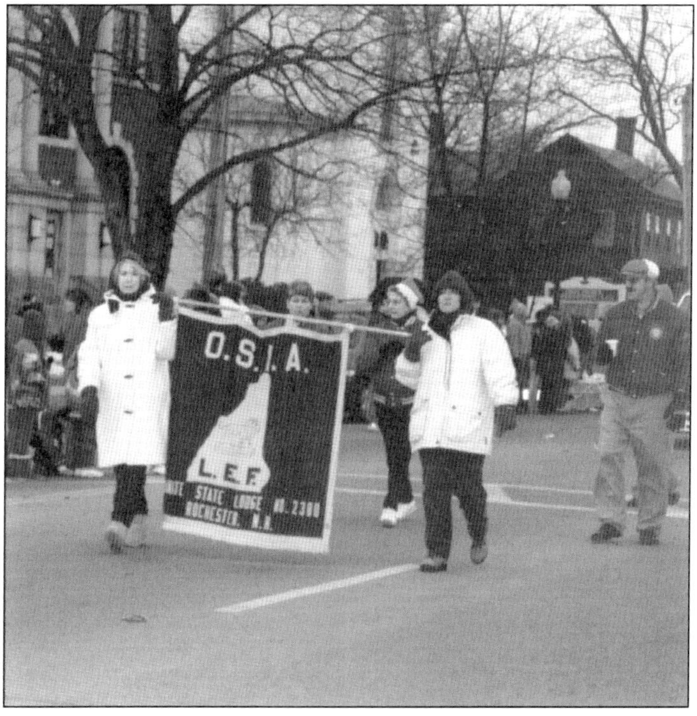

Members of the Granite State Lodge #2380 in Rochester, New Hampshire, hold aloft the banner of the Order Sons of Italy in America as they march in the Rochester Christmas Parade in 1985. Participating are Ruthann Mammone, Laurie Vandenhecke, Marie Maggio, Celia Vrevioli, and John Krekorian.

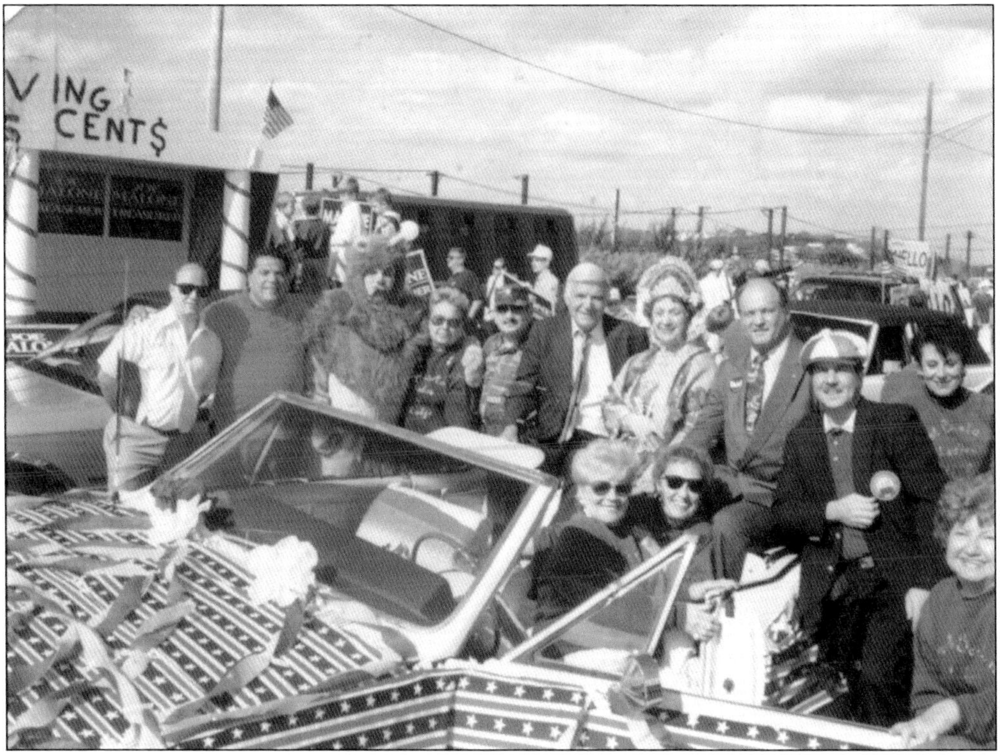

At the Columbus Day Parade in East Boston, Rose M. Colantuone depicts Queen Isabella of Spain. To the left are Greater Boston Renaissance Lodge #2614 members Col. John Silva; Chipper Riley, dressed as the Sons of Italy Lion; Dr. John Christoforo; and Doug Ness, among many members and friends of the Sons of Italy. Note that the convertible is papered with the stars and stripes of the United States, a decidedly patriotic touch.

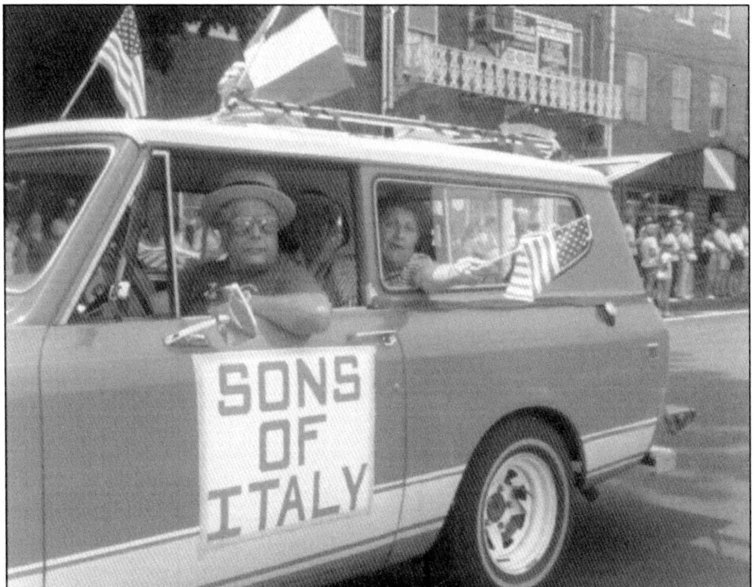

Seen in the Fourth of July Parade in Portsmouth, New Hampshire, are Carl Anania and Mary Anania, members of the Seacoast Area Lodge #2303, waving flags of both the United States and Italy.

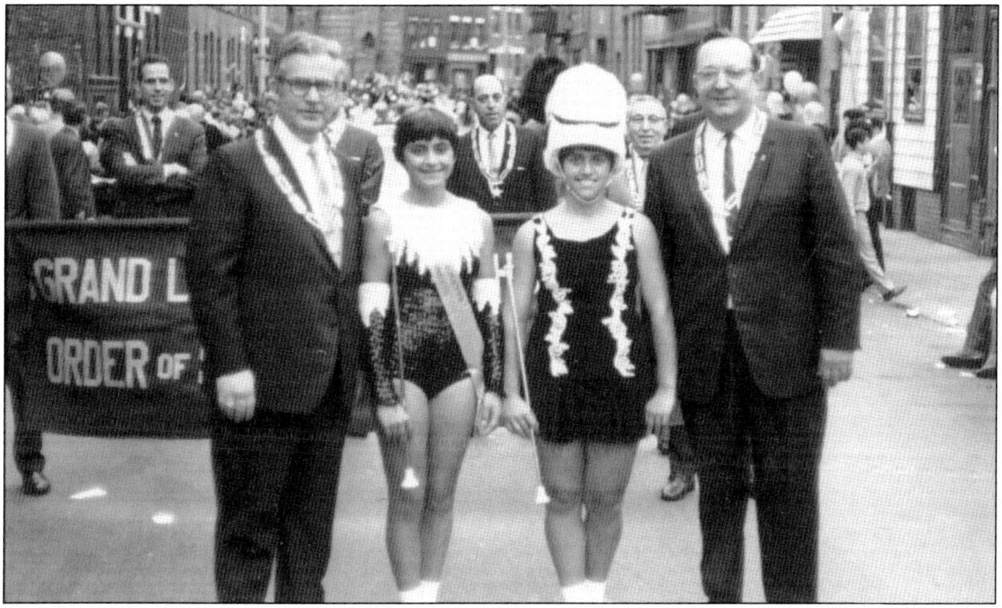

Two majorettes, with their batons at the ready, participated in the Columbus Day Parade in East Boston. Behind the banner are John Saladino, Bob Fiore, and Ignazio Columbo, and flanking the majorettes are Jack Cinnotti on the left and Aldo A. Caira on the right.

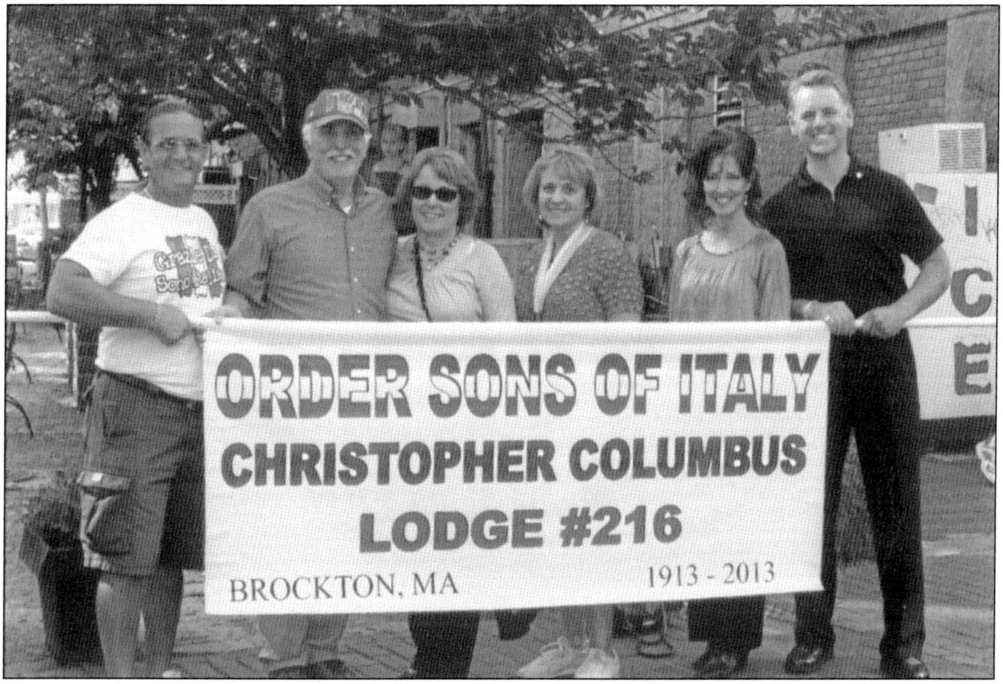

Here, members of the Christopher Columbus Lodge #216 are pictured marching in the Columbus Day Parade. From left to right are Lance Petti, Richard Alfonso, Lois Alfonso, Jacquelyn Bonarrigo, Kathy Petti, and Todd Petti.

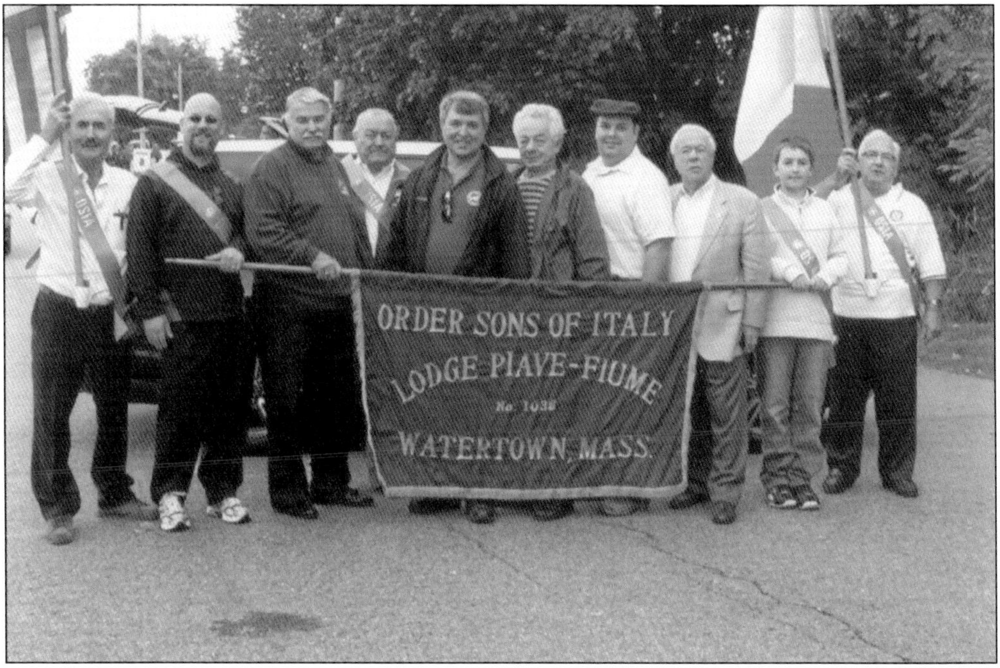

Members of the Piave Fiume Lodge #1036 from Watertown, Massachusetts, marched in the Columbus Day Parade.

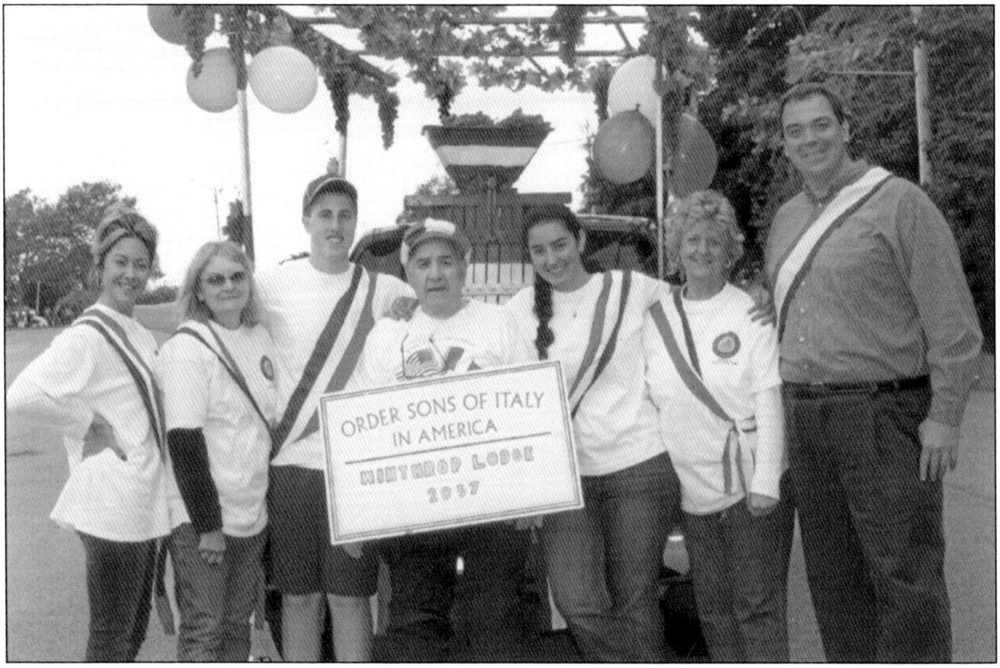

Members of the Winthrop Mixed Lodge #2057, bedecked with sashes of the colors of the Italian flag, marched in the Columbus Day Parade. Their float was decorated with tricolor balloons and had a pergola with hanging grape leaves and clusters of grapes.

Five

Italian Festas, Dances, and Songs

Italiano Feste, Balli, e Canti

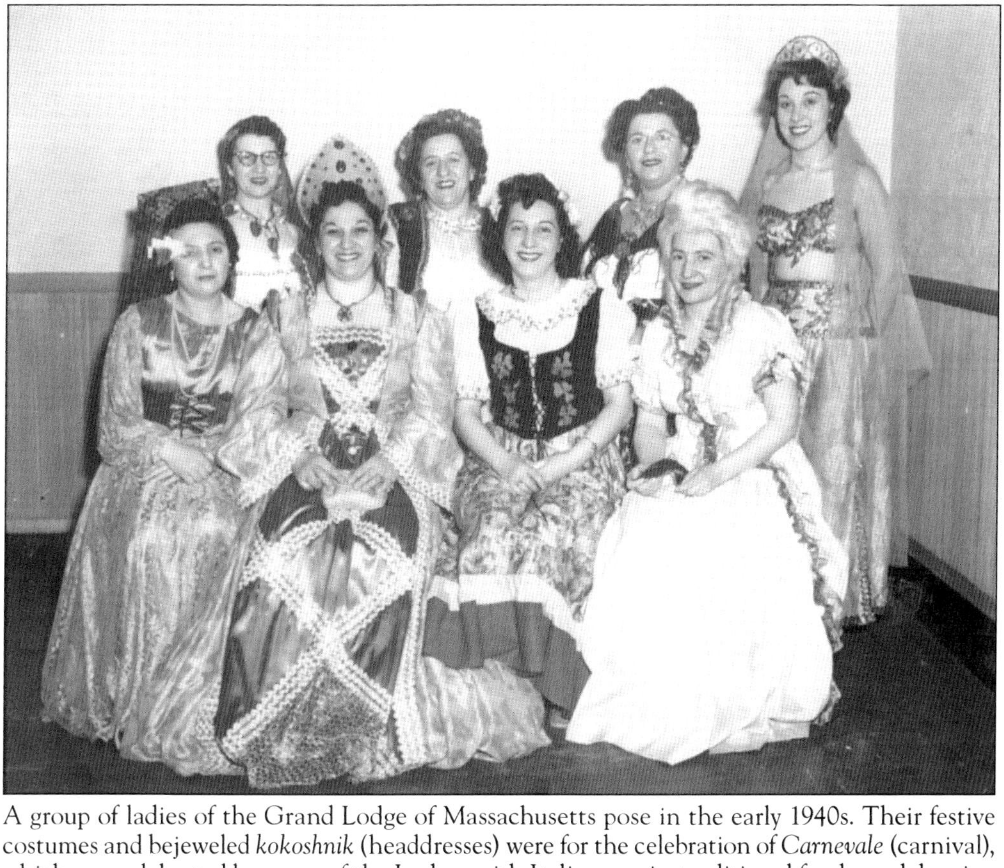

A group of ladies of the Grand Lodge of Massachusetts pose in the early 1940s. Their festive costumes and bejeweled *kokoshnik* (headdresses) were for the celebration of *Carnevale* (carnival), which was celebrated by many of the Lodges with Italian music, traditional foods, and dancing in the 40 days before Easter. One last overindulgence of traditional foods is followed by a Lenten fast.

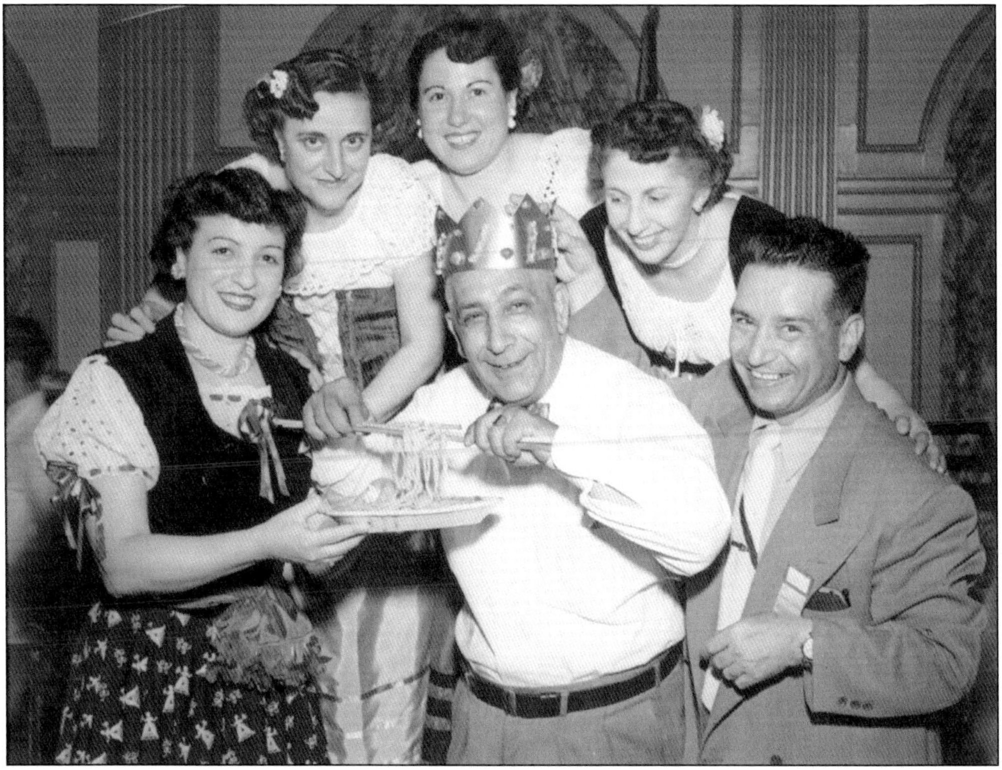

A crowned king of Carnevale smiles as a plate of spaghetti is proffered. From left to right, Jennie Polcari of Belmont, Olga Pientrantonio of Everett, Toni Mosca of Watertown, and Josephine Falco of Waltham surround Carnevale king Phil Cacciatore of Newton and Alfred Campisi of Waltham. Carnevale comes from the words *carne*, which means meat, and *leavare*, which means to remove. During Lent, which begins on Ash Wednesday, one fasts from eating meat and overindulging.

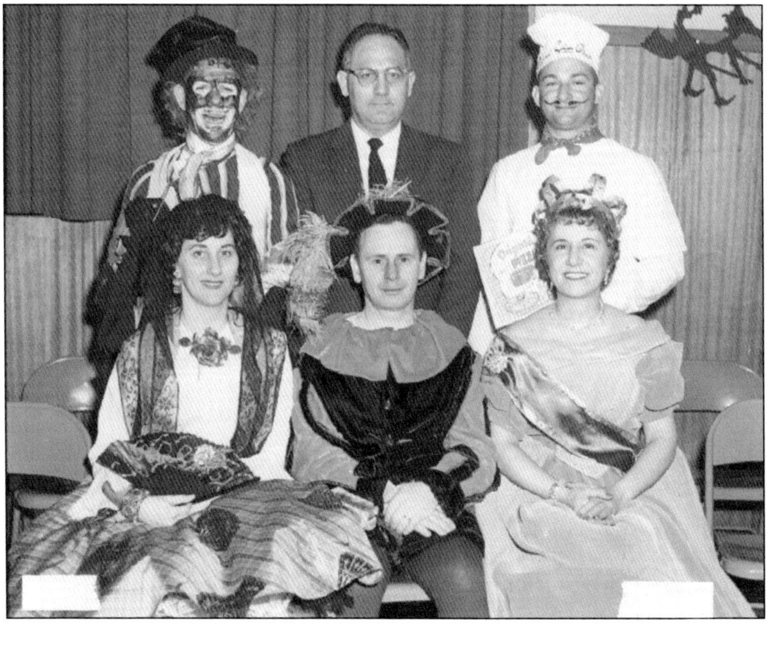

At the Waltham Carnevale in the early 1950s are Ed Tarallo and Tony Mosca, among other members of the Sons of Italy who wore fancy dress to the event, from an Italian signorina and queen of Carnevale, to a decidedly ragged hobo and a pizza maker, complete with chef's hat and a cardboard pizza box.

Adele Malone poses in traditional Italian dress at the Waltham Sons of Italy in 1969. Malone is the mother of Joe Malone, the former State Treasurer and Receiver-General of Massachusetts. On the left is Adolph Caso, and on the right is Msgr. Joseph J. Rocco, who served as the Lodge Chaplain and was later to become an auxiliary bishop of Boston.

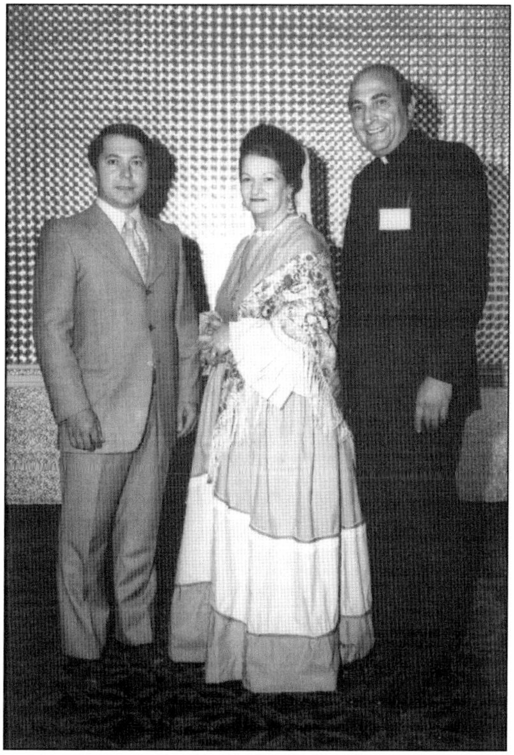

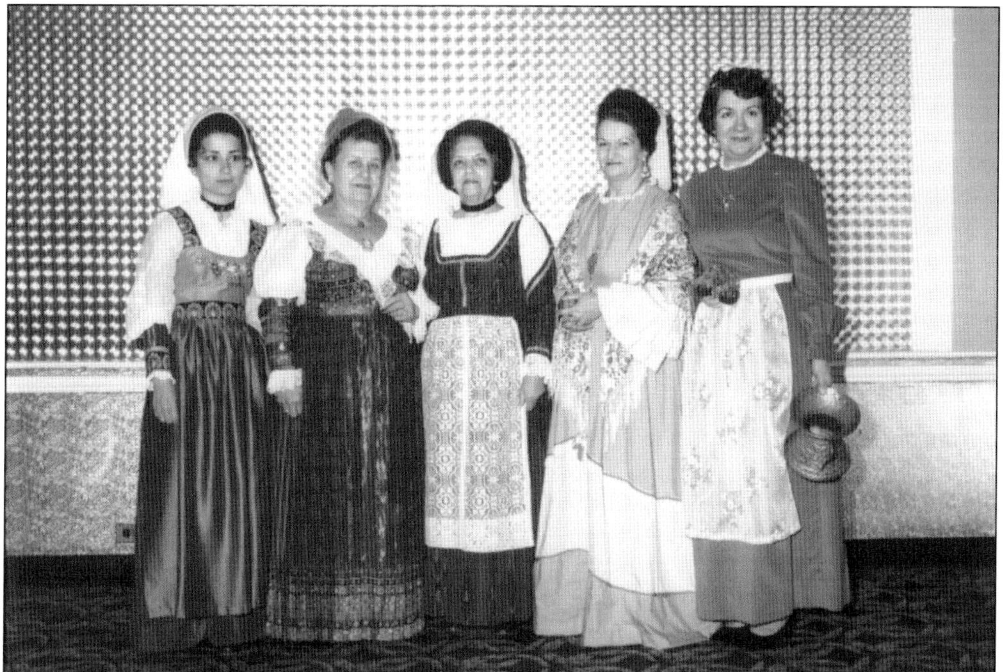

The ladies of the Waltham Sons of Italy, including Adele Malone and Maria Pia, both on the right, pose in the traditional dress of late-19th-century Italy during a combined evening event of the Dante Alighieri Lodge #648 and the Regina Margherita Di Savoia Lodge #1402.

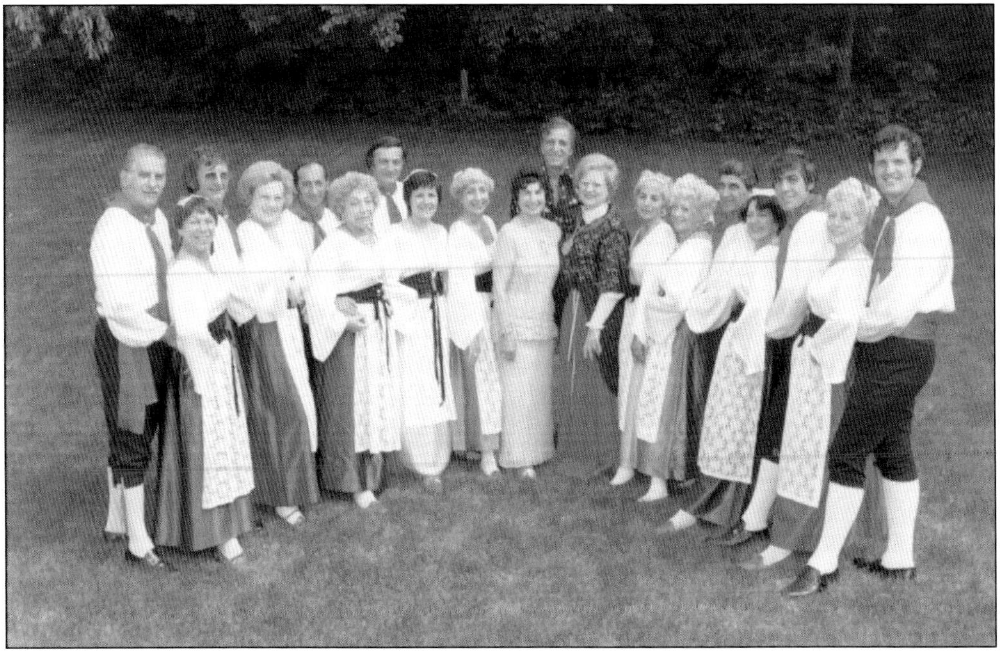

The Italian Serenaders is a mixed group of performers who preserve the traditional songs of Italy and present concerts to not just entertain, but to also preserve and hopefully pass down a part of the cultural heritage of Italy through song. Dressed in colorful costumes, the members perform songs and dances of Italy that are enjoyed by descendants of Italian immigrants.

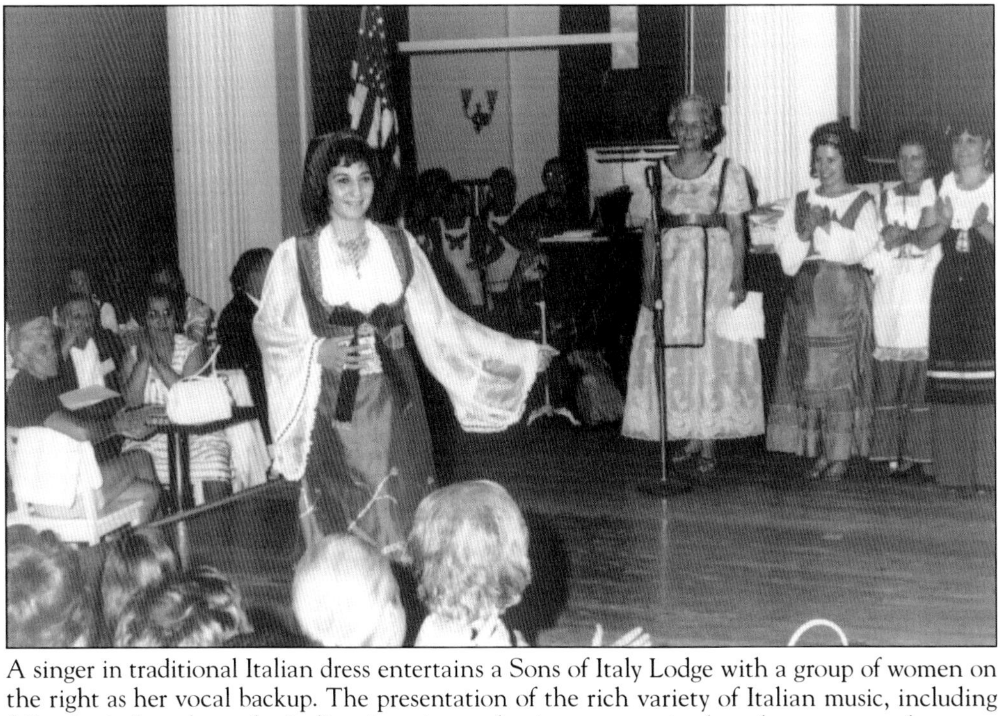

A singer in traditional Italian dress entertains a Sons of Italy Lodge with a group of women on the right as her vocal backup. The presentation of the rich variety of Italian music, including folk, classical, and popular Italian American selections, entertains but also preserves the songs for future generations.

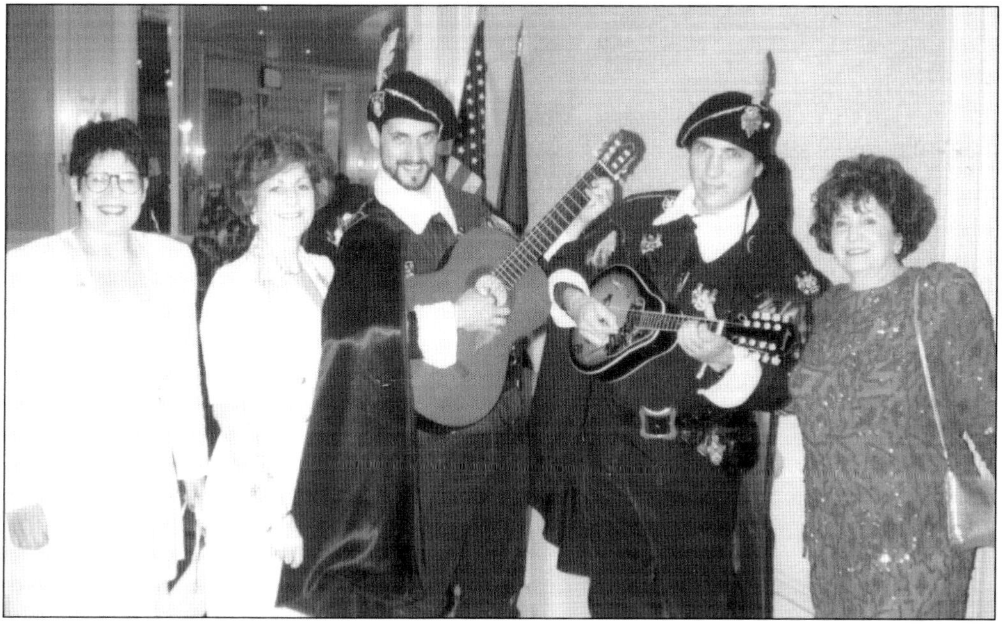

Two Italian Serenaders with their traditional Italian guitars are seen at the Parkman House on Beacon Hill in Boston. Thelma Hawkins, on the right, brought in these performers in traditional dress to entertain at a Greater Boston Renaissance Lodge #2614 reception. On the far left is Marjorie Cahn.

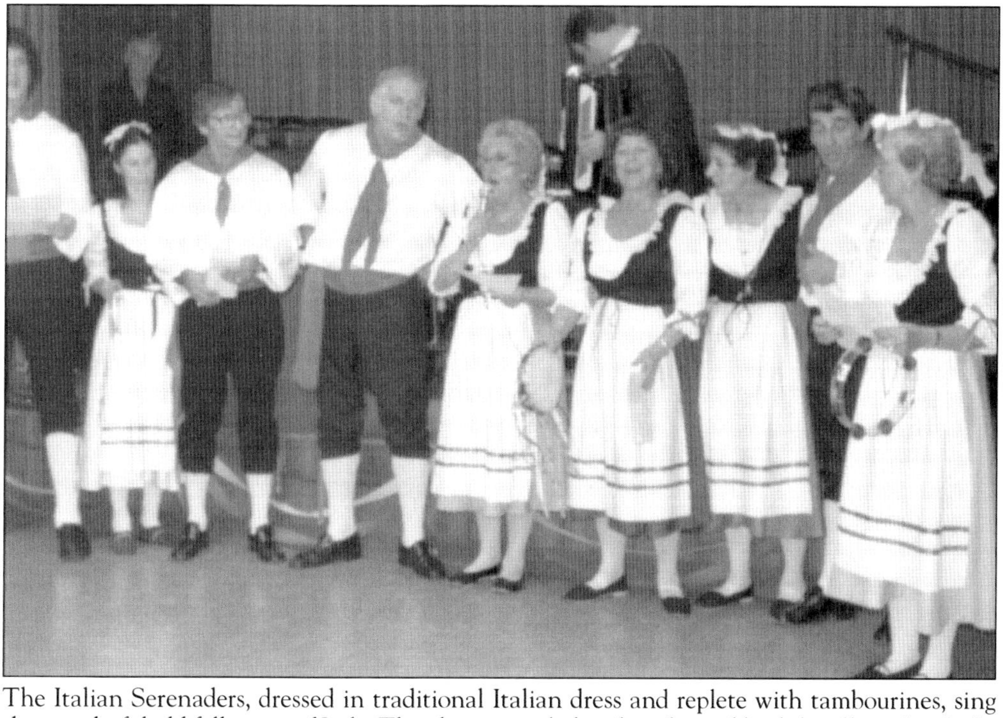

The Italian Serenaders, dressed in traditional Italian dress and replete with tambourines, sing the wonderful old folksongs of Italy. They have traveled and performed both locally and in Italy, where they were welcomed when singing familiar provincial melodies like "Santa Lucia," "O Marenariello," and "O Surdato."

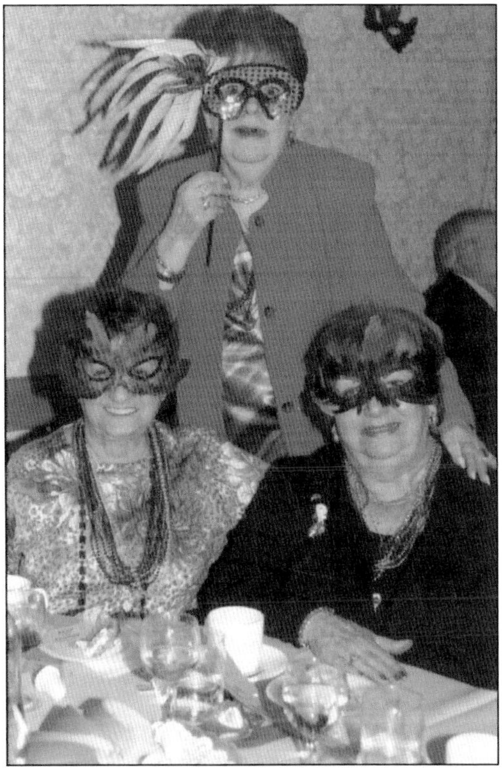

Carnevale was sponsored by the Italian Culture Commission of the Grand Lodge of Massachusetts and was a fun time, with those attending wearing fanciful masks that hide the identity of the reveler. Carnevale is celebrated throughout Italy, especially in Venice, where people don masks and costumes to party through the streets in the days leading up to Ash Wednesday. Here, three friends pose with colorful feathered masks.

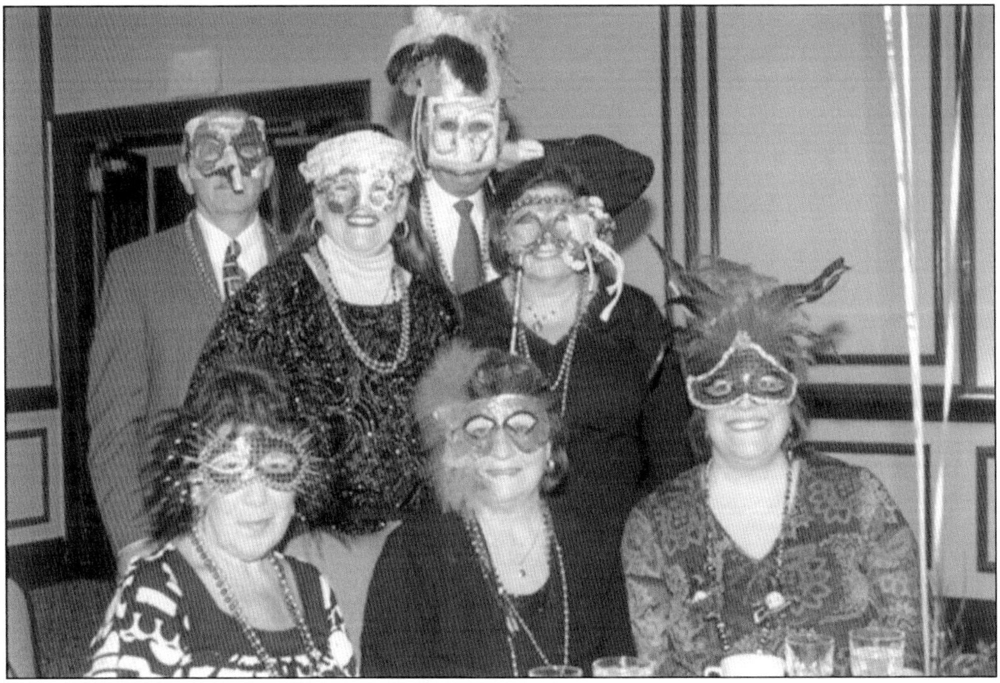

A group of Carnevale revelers pose with their fanciful masks. These events, which the Italian Culture Commission sponsors, bring members and friends of the Grand Lodge of Massachusetts together not just for an enjoyable evening but to preserve the traditions of our ancestors.

Six

Prominent Members and Friends

Personalità e Amici

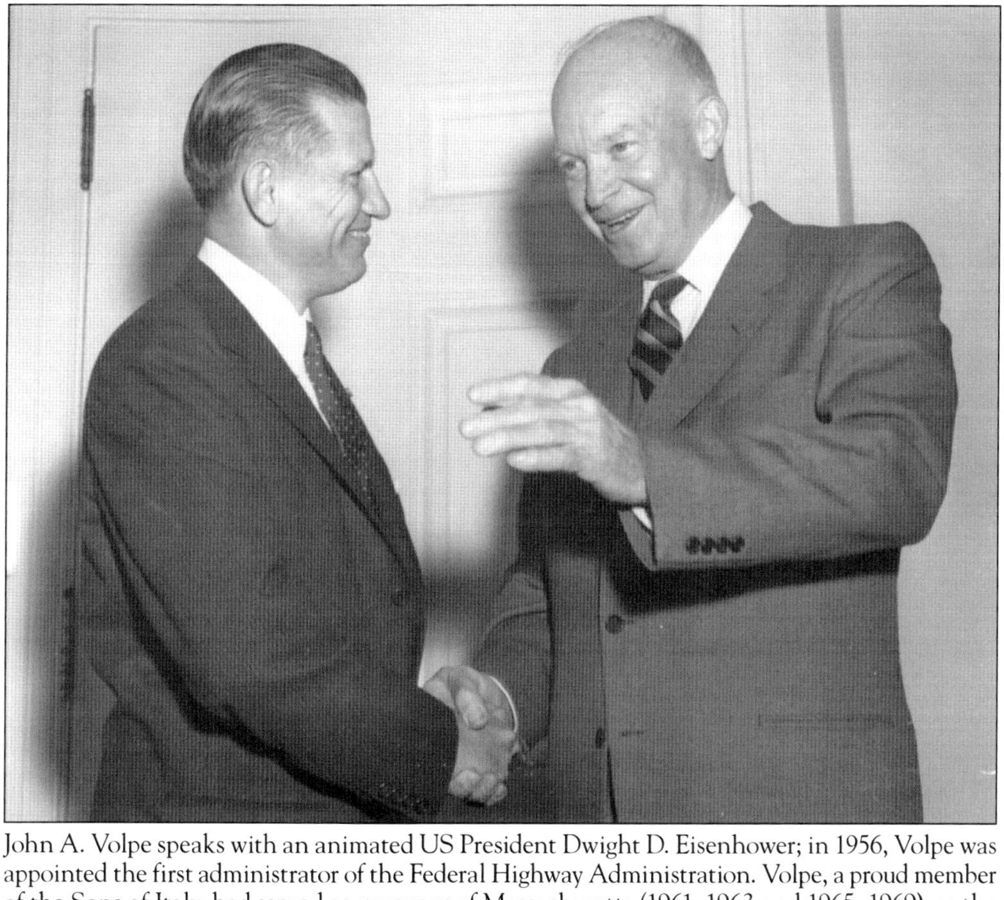

John A. Volpe speaks with an animated US President Dwight D. Eisenhower; in 1956, Volpe was appointed the first administrator of the Federal Highway Administration. Volpe, a proud member of the Sons of Italy, had served as governor of Massachusetts (1961–1963 and 1965–1969), as the US secretary of transportation (1969–1973), and as the US ambassador to Italy (1973–1977).

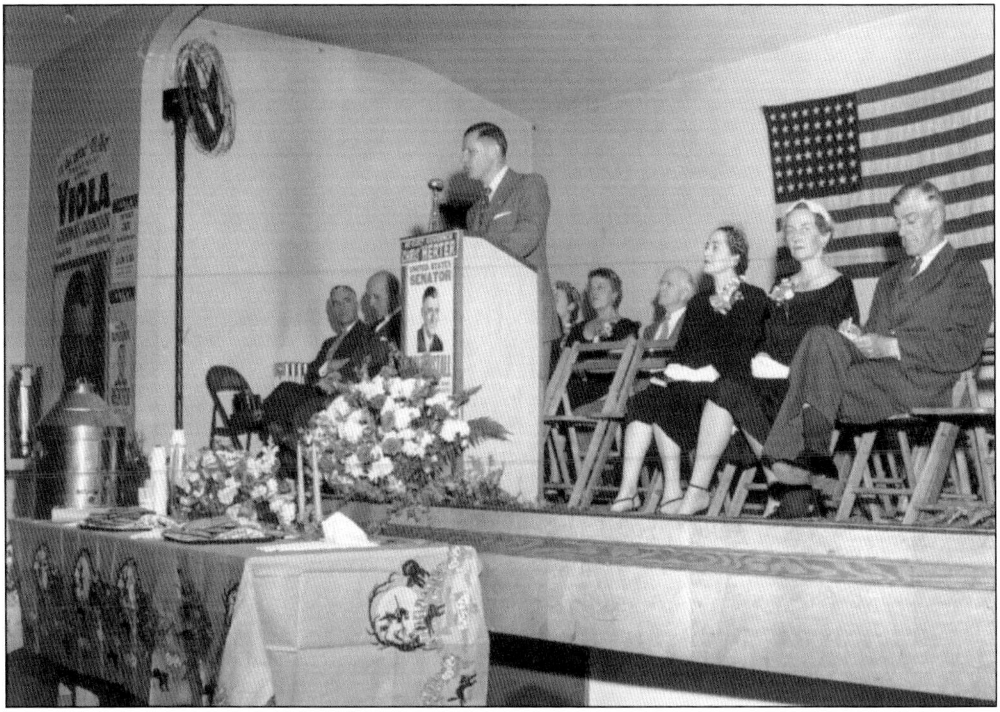

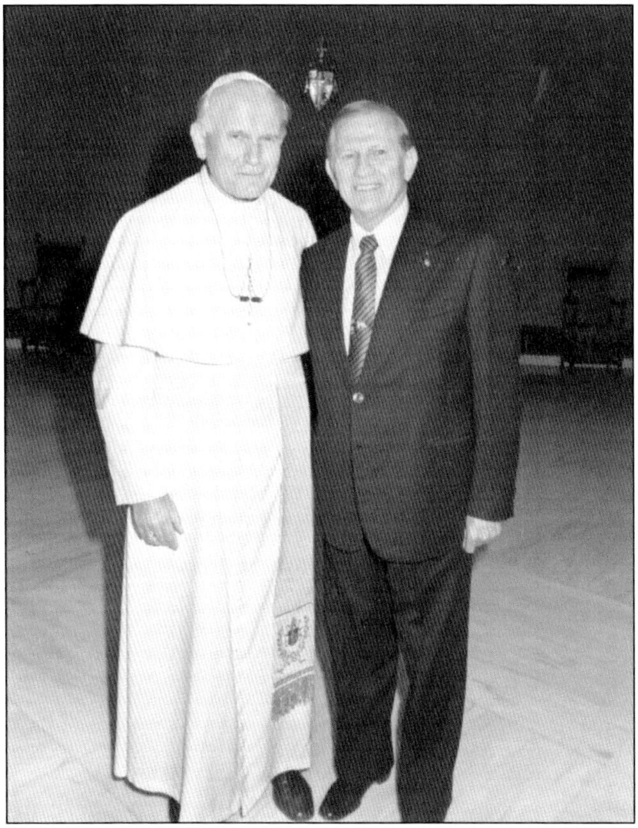

A well-respected politician and member of the Winchester Men's Lodge#1580, John A. Volpe spoke in 1948 from the podium on behalf of the reelection campaigns of Leverett Saltonstall for US Senate and Christian A. Herter for the US House of Representatives. Seated on the right are Giovaninna Benedetto Volpe, Alice Wesselhoeft Saltonstall, and Leverett Saltonstall. On the far left with his hands crossed is Christian A. Herter.

In 1973, John A. Volpe was nominated by Pres. Richard M. Nixon and confirmed by the US Senate as the US ambassador to Italy, a position he held until 1977. Here, he poses with Cardinal Karol Józef Wojtyła, later to become Pope John Paul II, who was canonized in 2014 as Blessed Pope John Paul II.

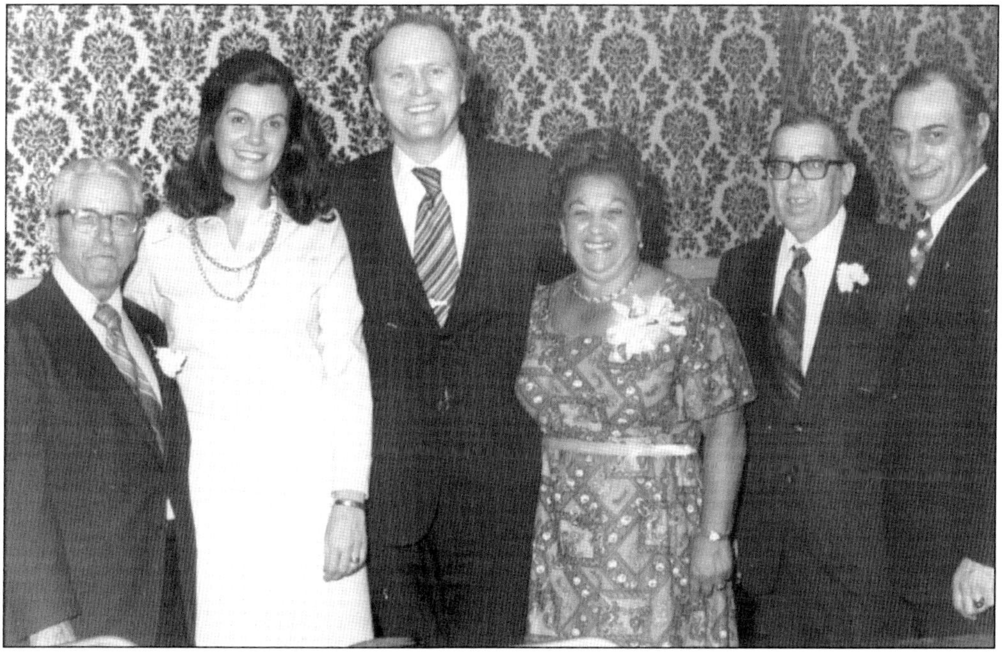

In 1974, then Massachusetts state attorney general Robert H. Quinn visited the Corporal Barberini Lodge in Chelsea, Massachusetts, as he was campaigning for the Democratic nomination for governor. From left to right are Mr. Pucci, Claudina Quinn, Robert H. Quinn, Rose M. Colantuone, Dom Pegnato, and Guy Arigo, President of the Grand Lodge of Massachusetts from 1977 to 1981.

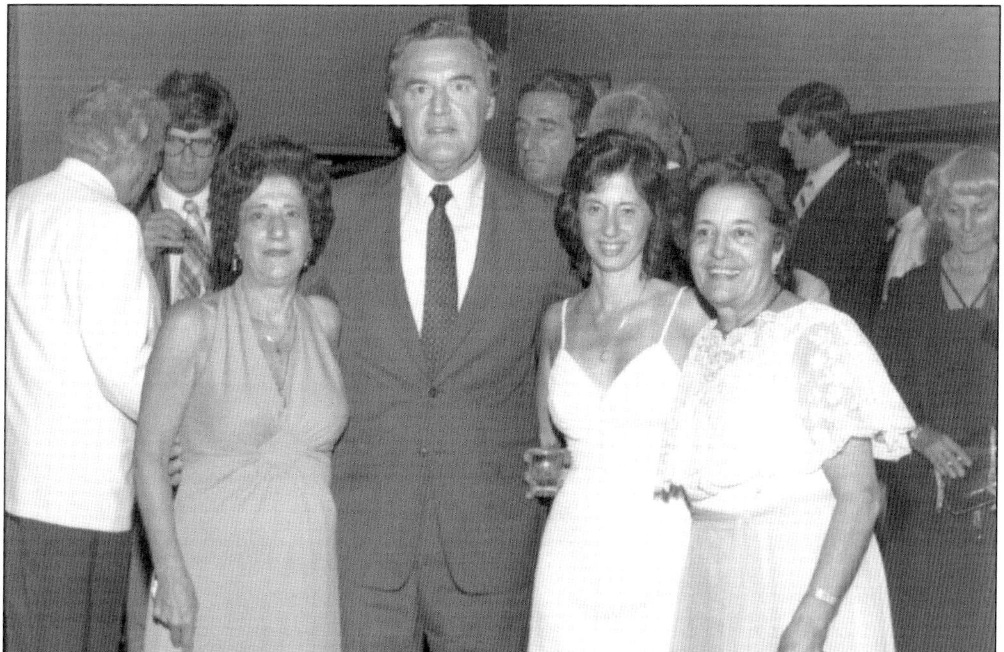

Gov. Edward J. King, who served as the governor of Massachusetts from 1979 to 1983, attended a Sons of Italy event in 1980. From left to right are Gloria Ferullo, Governor King, Florence Ferullo Kane, who later served as President of the Grand Lodge from 2007 to 2009, and Ann Marmai.

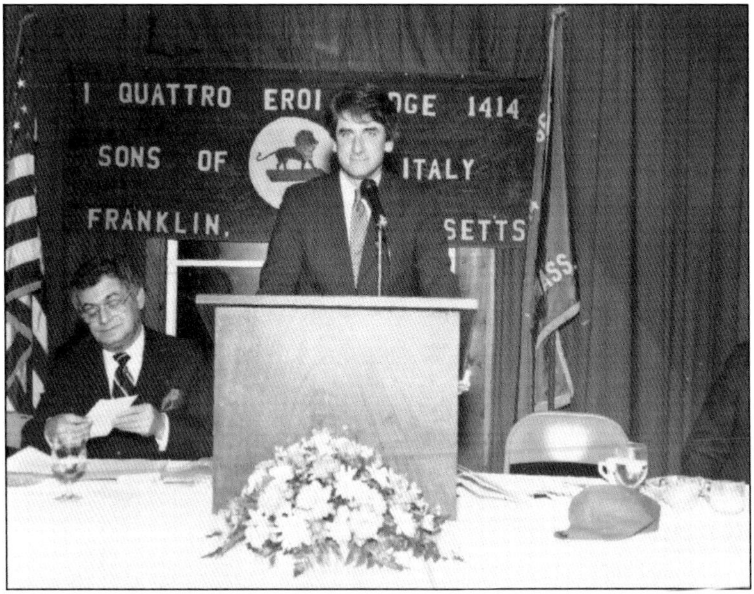

At the 56th anniversary banquet of the founding of Quattro Eroi Lodge #1414 in Franklin, the guest speaker was Lt. Gov. Thomas P. O'Neill. Seated on the left is National Trustee Sebastian Papagno.

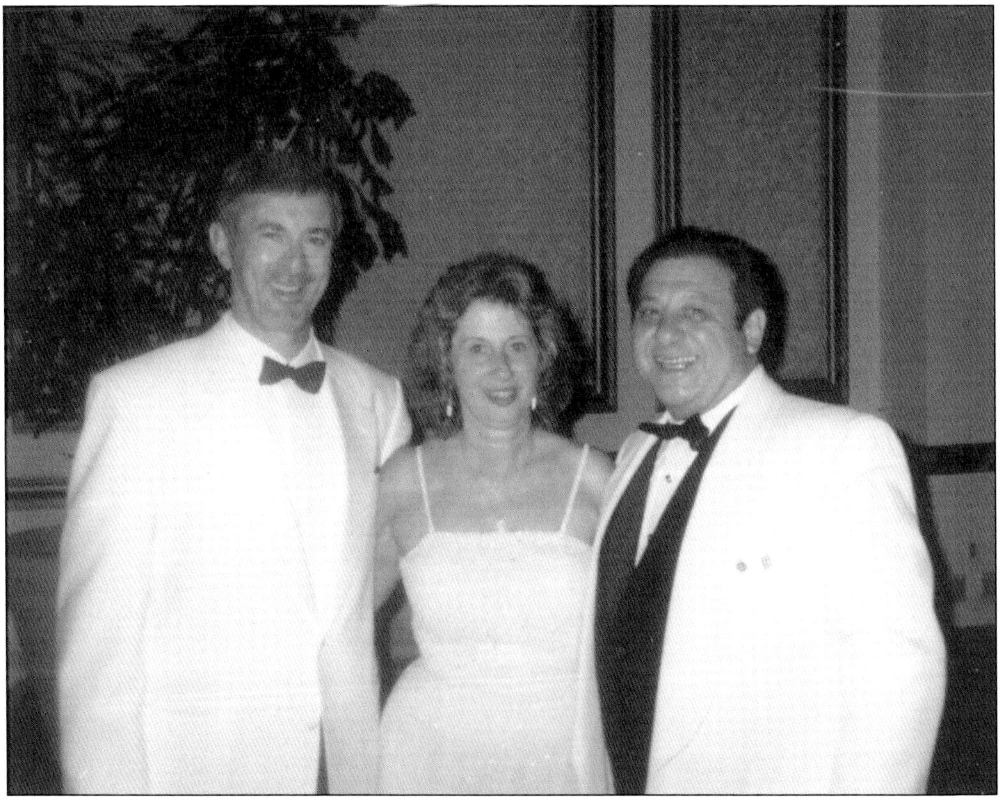

From left to right, Gov. Paul A. Celucci, Florence Ferullo Kane, and Philip Boncore pose in 1996. Kane served as President of the Grand Lodge from 2007 to 2009, and Boncore was President of the Grand Lodge from 1993 to 1995. Celucci became acting governor when William Weld resigned in 1997; he was elected governor in 1998 and served until 2001, when he resigned to become US ambassador to Canada.

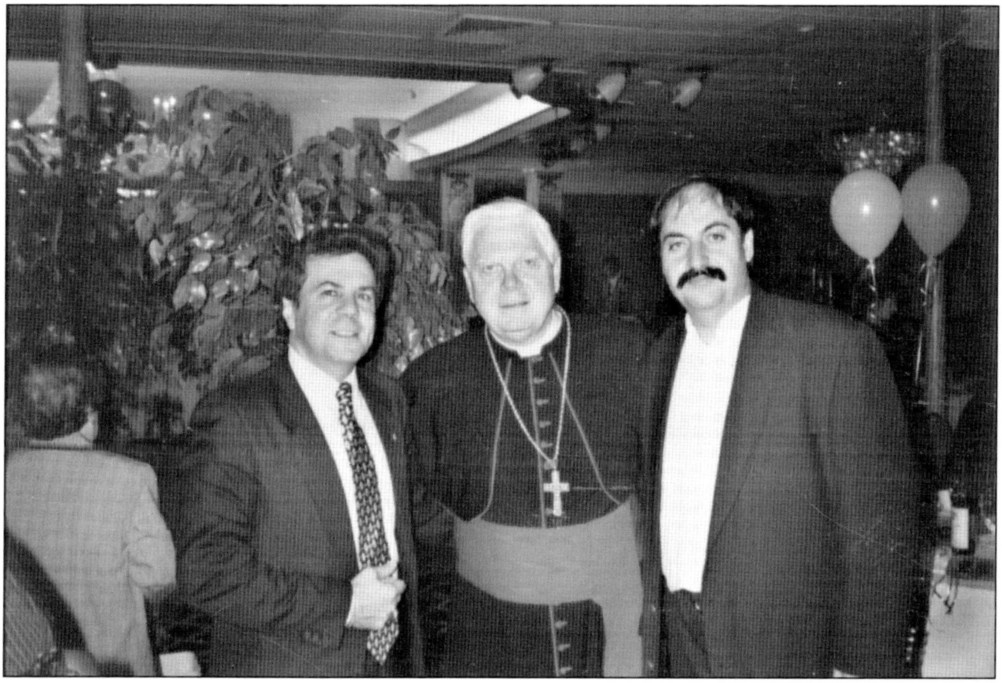

At a Saints Cosmas and Damian Society banquet, Cardinal Bernard Law is flanked by Carmen Cardillo on the left and Bobby Nicolosi on the right.

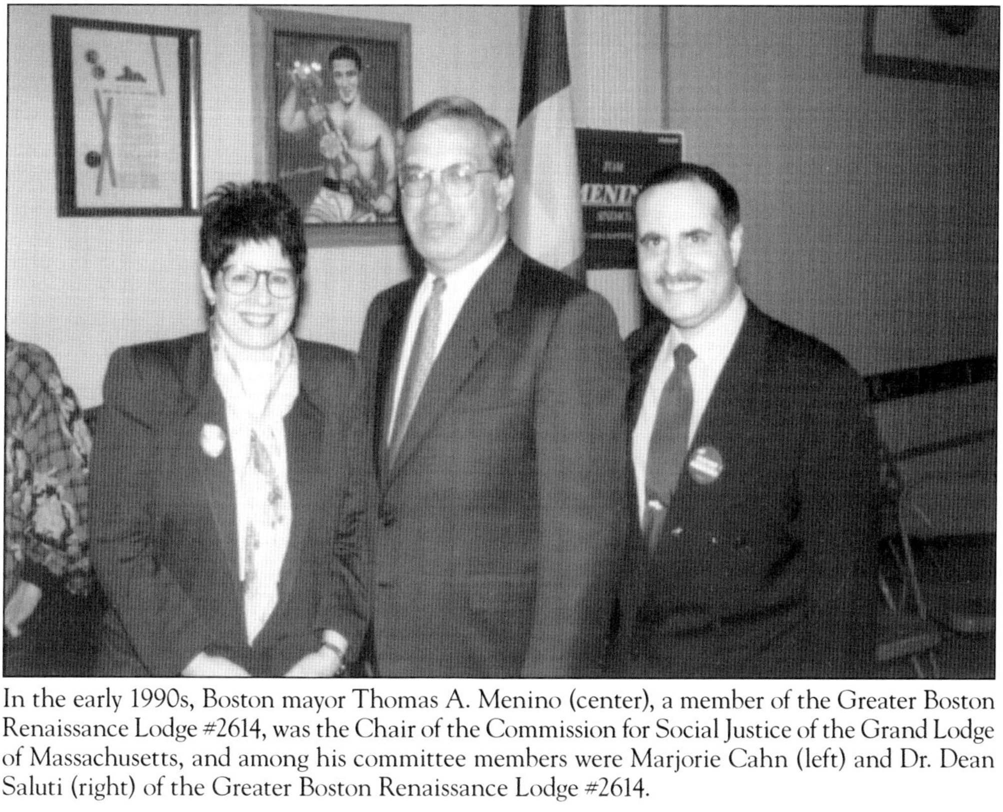

In the early 1990s, Boston mayor Thomas A. Menino (center), a member of the Greater Boston Renaissance Lodge #2614, was the Chair of the Commission for Social Justice of the Grand Lodge of Massachusetts, and among his committee members were Marjorie Cahn (left) and Dr. Dean Saluti (right) of the Greater Boston Renaissance Lodge #2614.

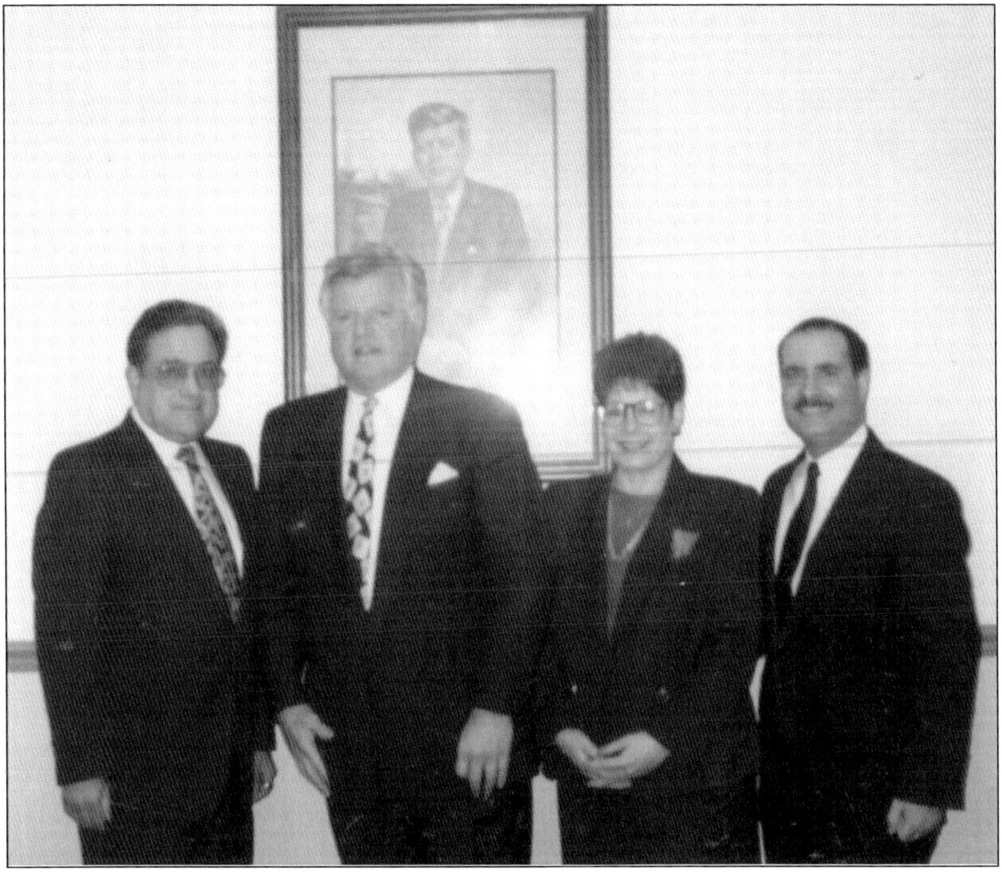

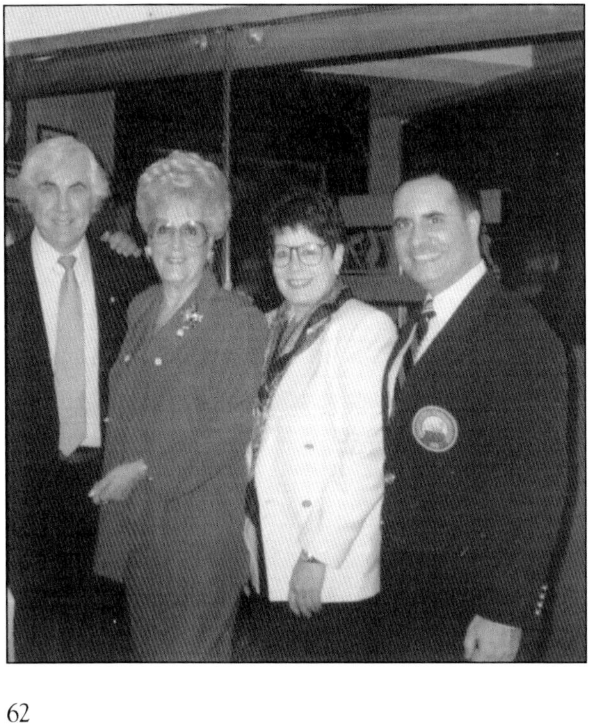

Here, Sen. Edward M. Kennedy (second from left) becomes a member of the Greater Boston Renaissance Lodge #2614. State President Angelo Furnari, who served as President from 1989 to 1993, is on the left, and Marjorie Cahn and Dr. Dean Saluti are on the right as they pose beneath a portrait of President John F. Kennedy.

At a presentation sponsored by the Greater Boston Renaissance Lodge #2614 in the North End of Boston are, from left to right, the legendary Boston-area radio personality Ron Della Chiesa, Irene Granara, Marjorie Cahn, and Dr. Dean Saluti.

Seven

Lodge Events, Dinners, and Fun

Lodge Eventi, Feste, e Divertimento

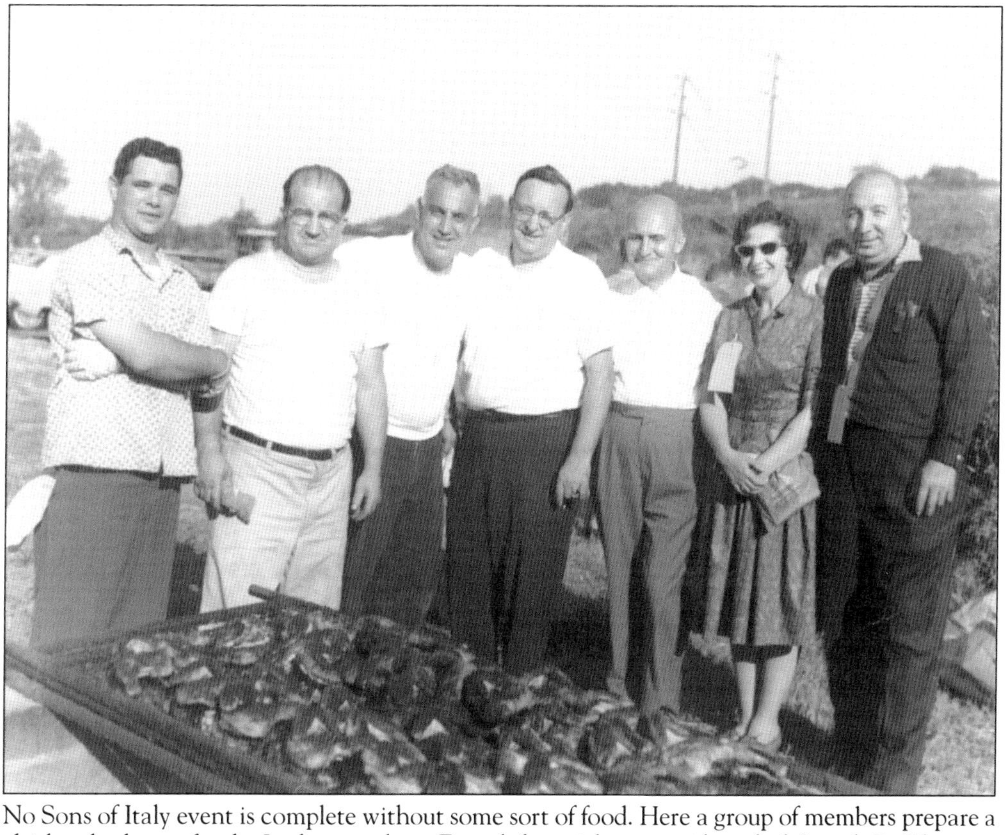

No Sons of Italy event is complete without some sort of food. Here a group of members prepare a chicken barbecue for the Lodge members. From left to right are unidentified, Joseph B. Silvestro, Anthony Julian, Aldo A. Caira, Peter E. Donadio, Josephine Falco, and Mario Columbo overseeing the makeshift barbecue grill.

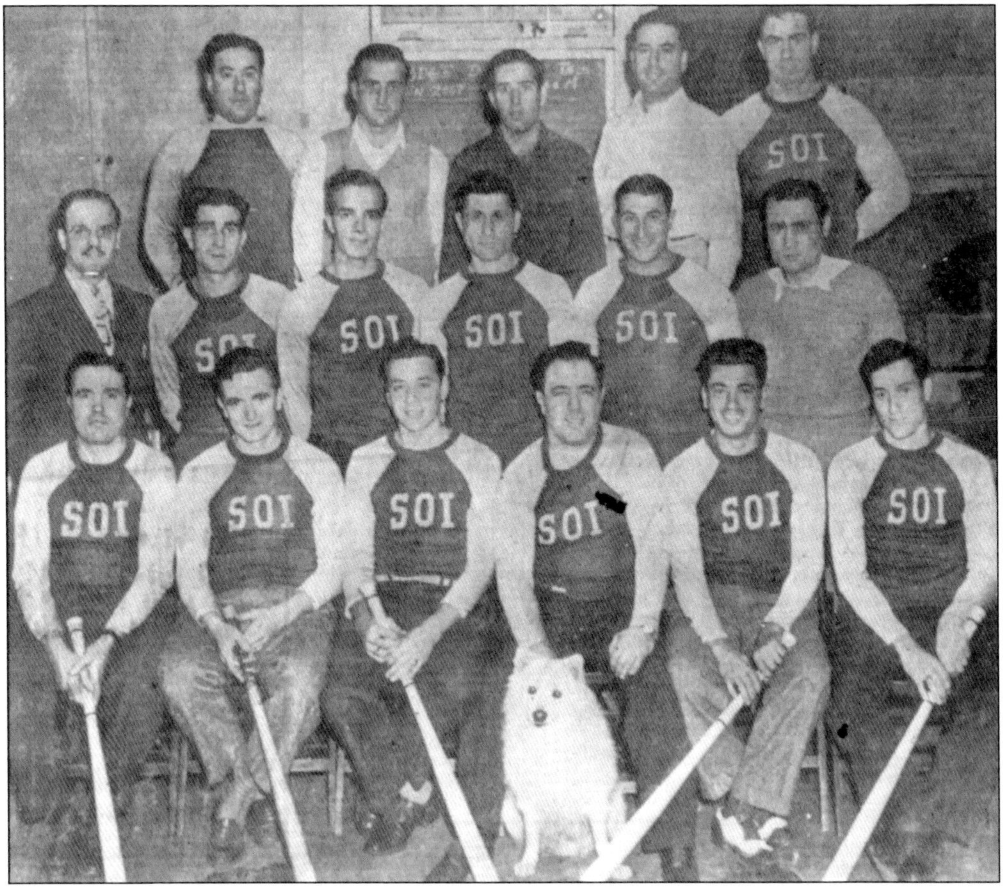

The Winchester Sons of Italy had a popular softball team that, in 1946, had 35 wins, 4 losses, and 1 tie game. Members are, from left to right, (first row) Henry Chefalo, Joseph Ciarcia, Nick Molea, Anthony Cefalo, Ralph DiMambro, and William Fiore; (second row) Venerable Anthony Ficociello, Gaspar Muraco, Sam DiBenedetto, Frank Procopio, Robert DelGrasso, and manager Andrew Diapells; (third row) Angelo Tufuri, Michael Saraco, Alfred DeMinico, Frank DeMinico, and Paul Lentine. Alas, the name of the canine mascot is not recorded.

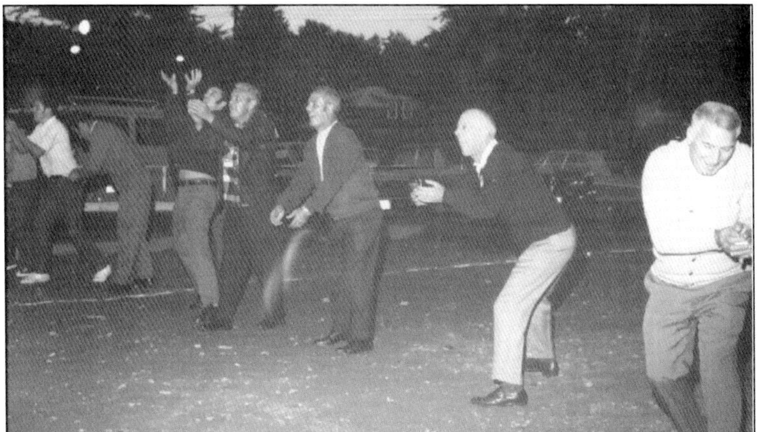

Seeing adult men participating in an egg toss might look odd, but the mess that could be made from flying eggs was certainly not fun. This Sons of Italy event had some dapperly dressed members, whose clothing was not yet egg stained.

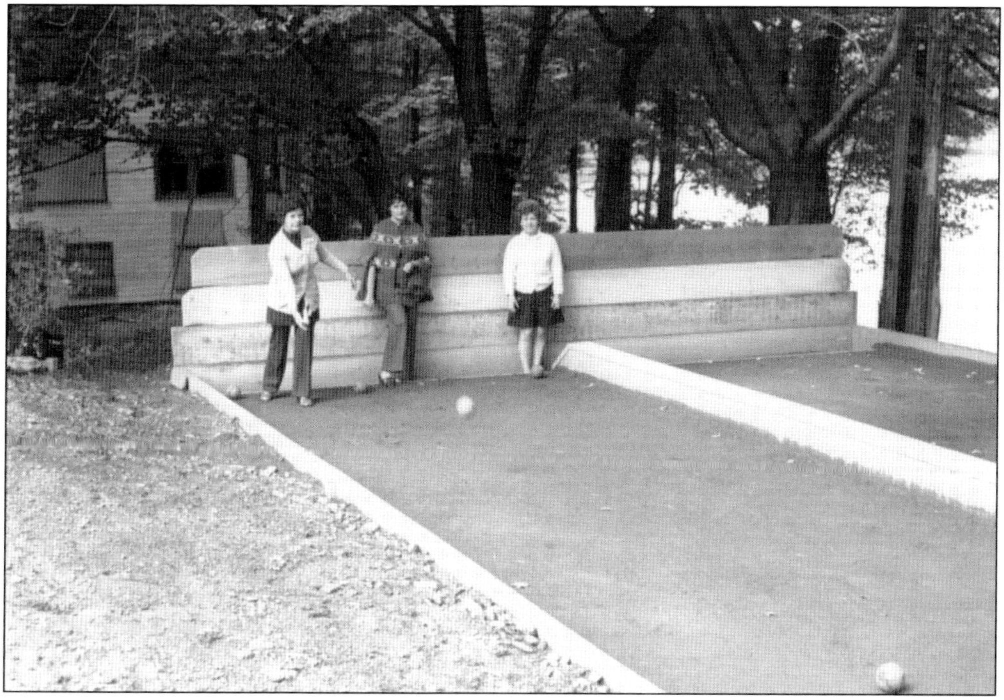

Antoinette Papagno, seen on the right, waits her turn at the bocce court. This game was as popular in Italy as it has become in Massachusetts.

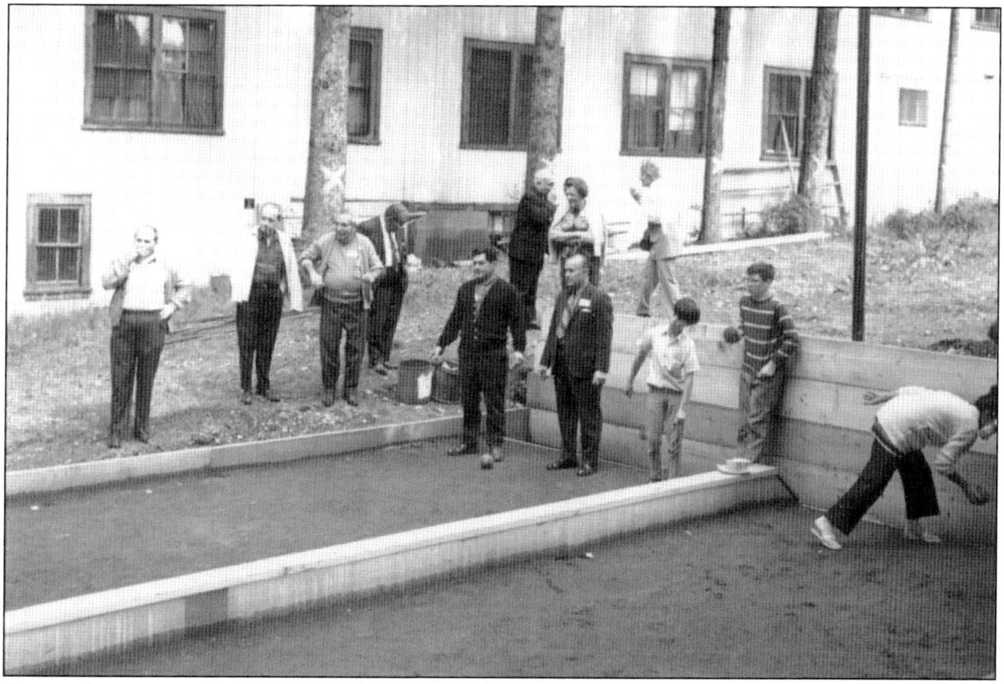

Bocce players come in all ages, as both young boys and members of the Sons of Italy participate in a game. Bocce was initially played among the Italian immigrants but has slowly become more popular with their descendants and the wider community.

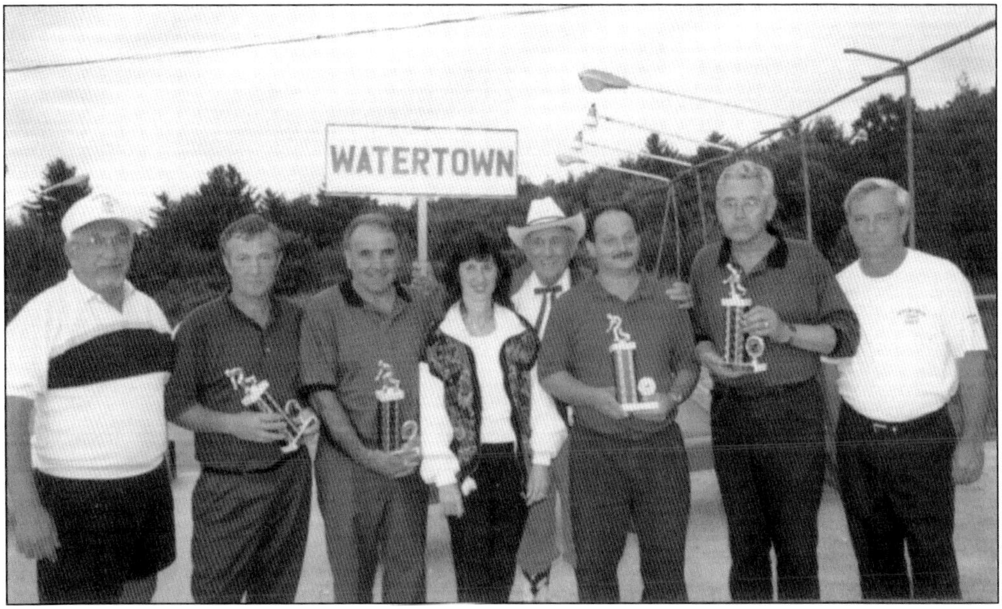

The winners of the Grand Lodge Bocce Tournament, Piave Fiume Lodge #1036, pose with their trophies. From left to right are Chairman Dick Cirrone, Constanzo Baccari, Giulio Coppola, Florence Ferullo Kane (who acted as cheerleader), Vinnie Massa, Luciano Camilli, Antonio DeLuca, and Sports Commission member Bob Cassette.

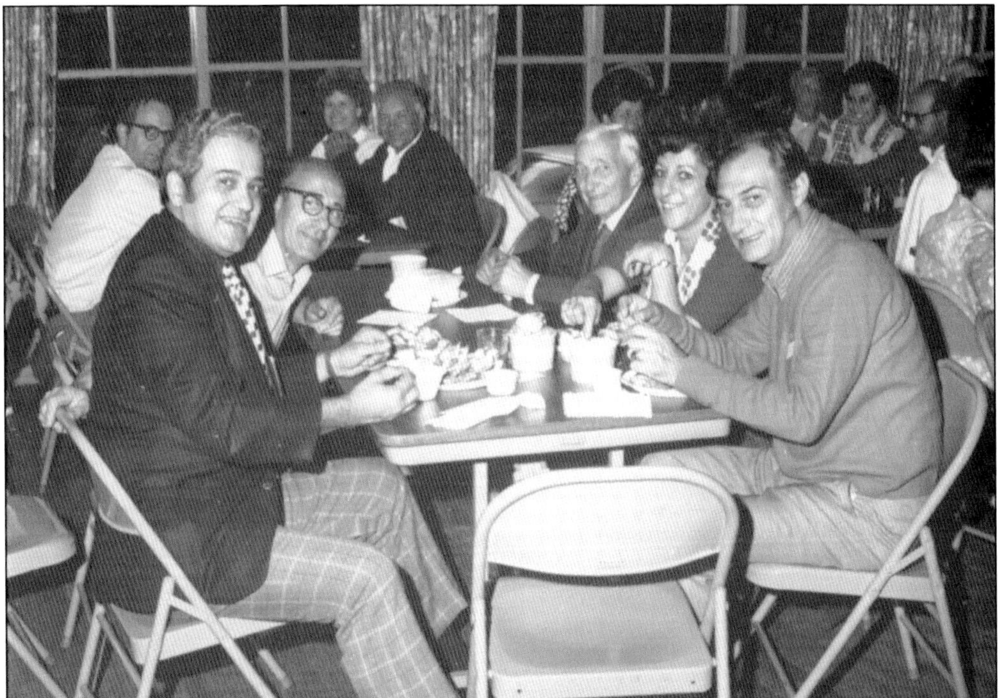

After an afternoon bocce game, there was nothing better than dinner with fellow members of the Sons of Italy. From left to right at the front table are Joe Furnari, Tony Paratori, Guy Arigo, Claire Arigo, and unidentified.

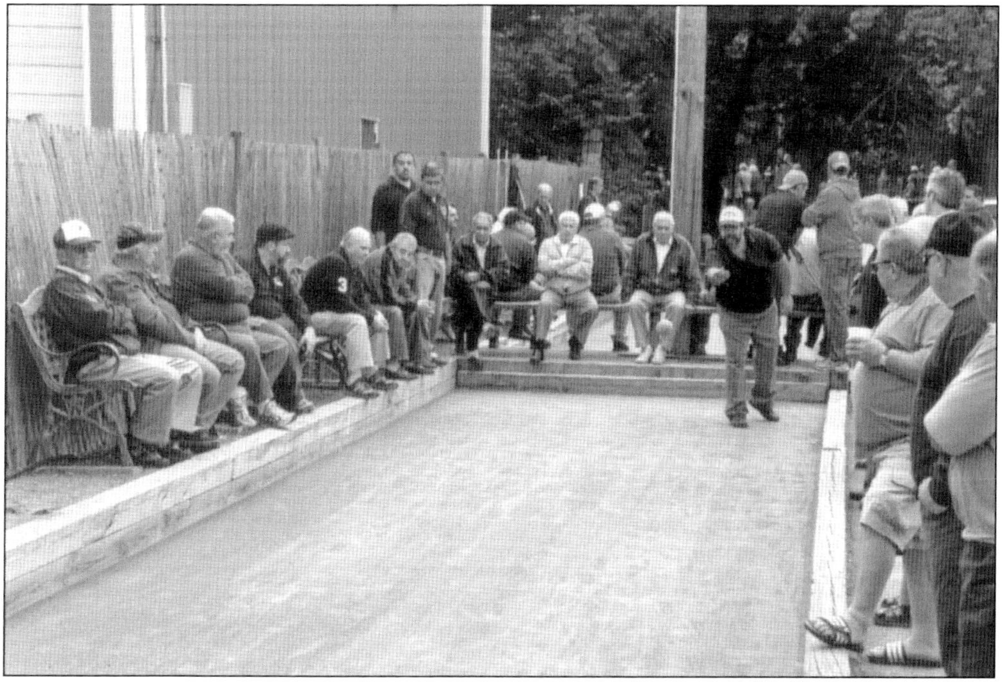

The bocce court brought members of the Sons of Italy for the Grand Lodge Bocce Tournament in 2014 at the Watertown Sons of Italy. The first-place team members in the men's division were Joe Cacia, Vito Varano, Vincenzo Sammartino, and Sal Pinzone. The first-place team members in the women's division were Teresa Iodice, Gerri Cimino, and Donna Mazzola.

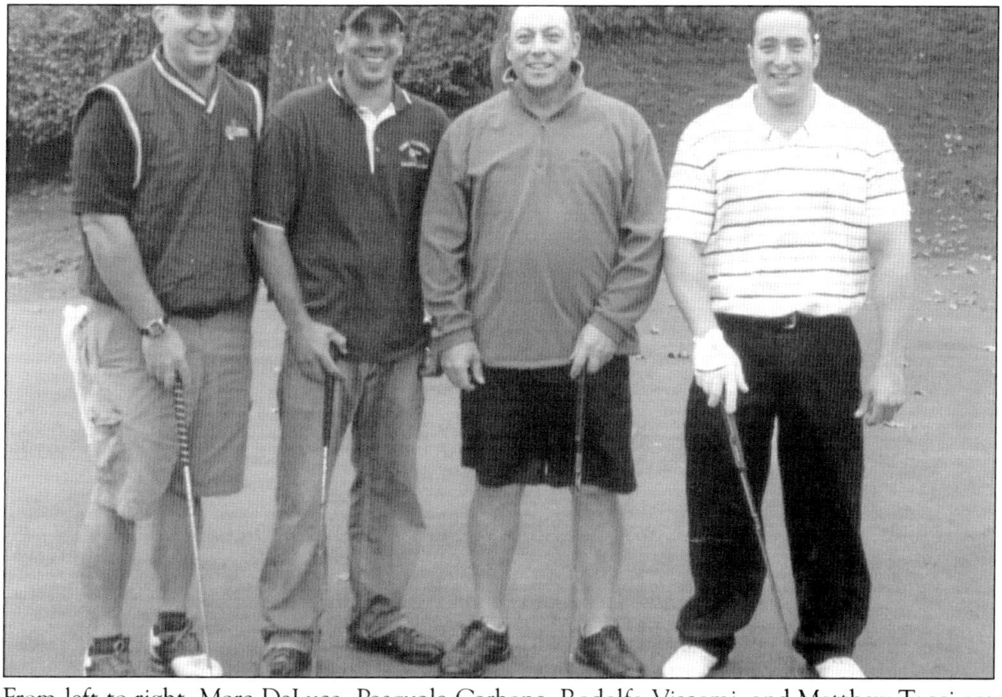

From left to right, Marc DeLuca, Pasquale Carbone, Rodolfo Viscomi, and Matthew Tocci are pictured at the Piave Fiume Lodge #1036 of Watertown's Scholarship Golf Tournament in 2012.

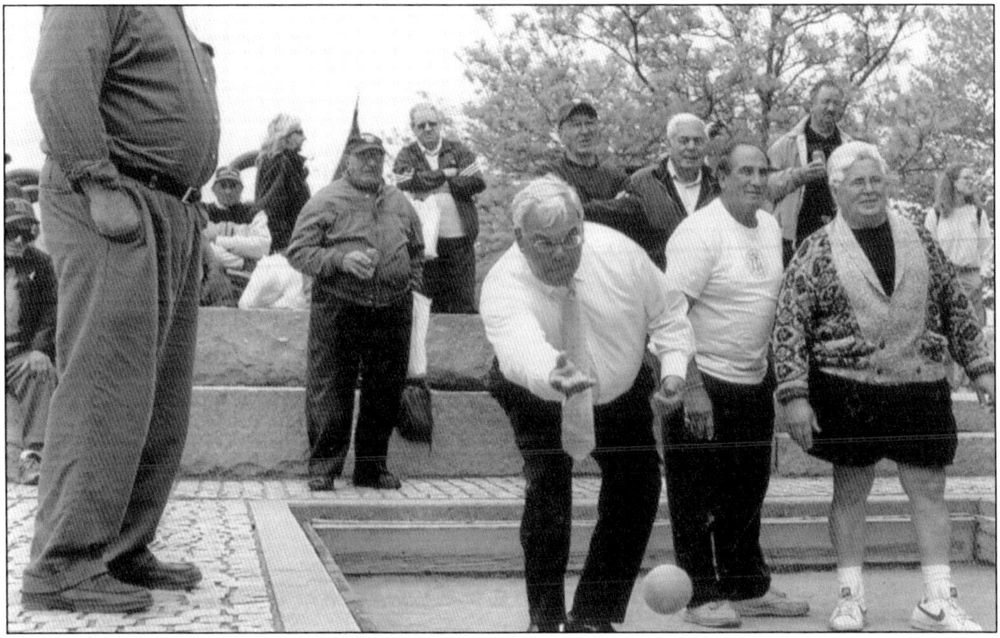

Thomas M. Menino, then mayor of Boston, plays bocce in a tournament in 2009 for senior citizens at Langone Park in Boston's North End. On the left is Giovanni Mucci, along with fellow members of the Piave Fiume Lodge #1036 in Watertown. A member of Greater Boston Renaissance Lodge #2614, Mayor Menino was the recipient of the Commission for Social Justice of the Grand Lodge of Massachusetts Public Service Award in 1999.

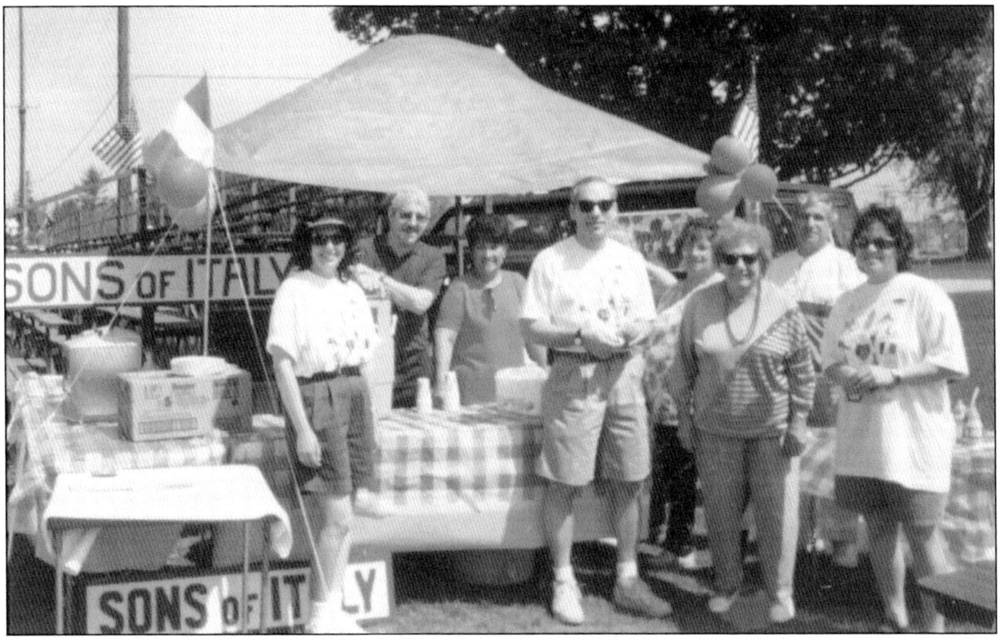

The Lilac Festival in 2000 brought members of the Granite State Lodge #2380 in Rochester, New Hampshire, together in May during Lilac Weekend. From left to right are Theresa Farina, John Krekorian, unidentified, Richard Farina, Angela Krekorian, Mary Arigo, John Mammone, and unidentified.

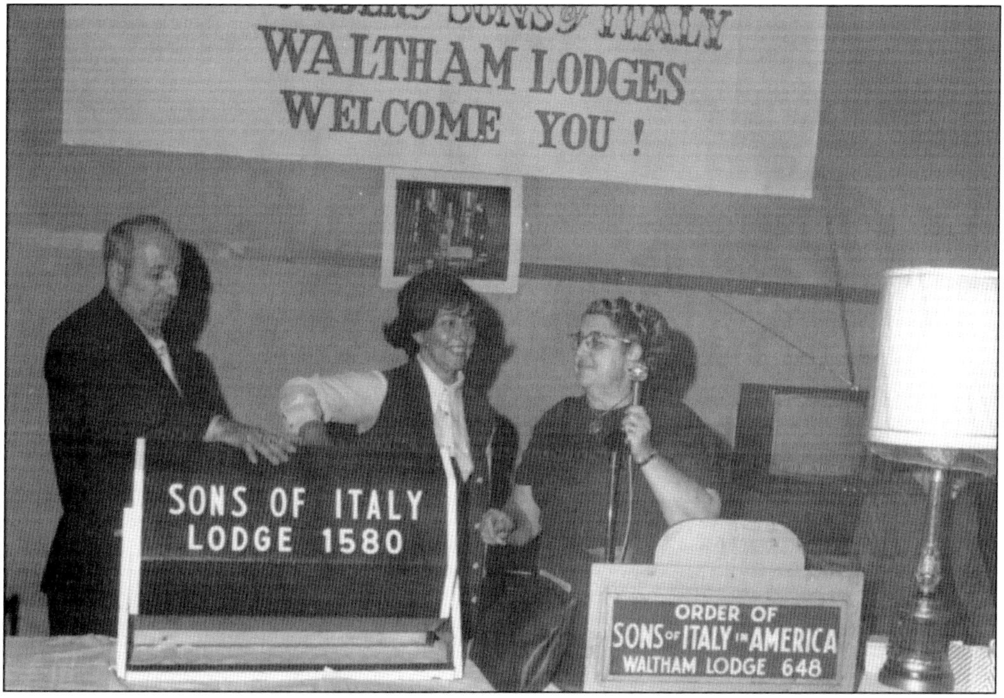

Raffles have always been a popular way to raise money, and the Winchester Men's Lodge #1580 and Dante Alighieri Lodge #648 of Waltham joined together to sponsor one. Laura Caira is seen in the center picking the number of a raffle winner. On the left is Mario Columbo, and on the right is Madeline Miceli.

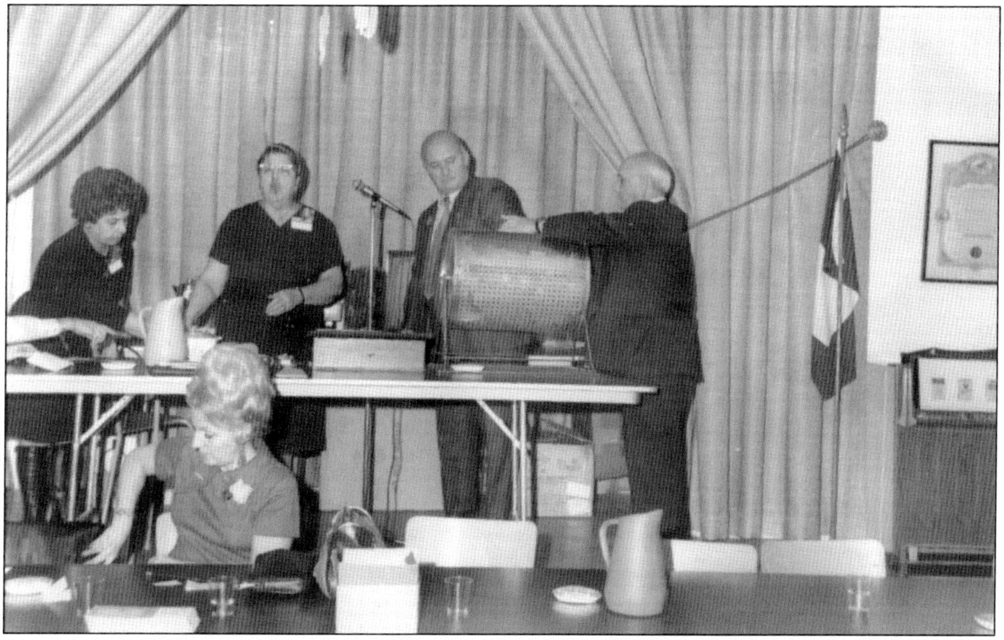

Bingo has always been popular, but with a caller who entertained as well as called the number, it was fun. Seen calling numbers is Madeline Miceli with Peter Donadio pulling the numbers from the roller. In the foreground is Irene Granara.

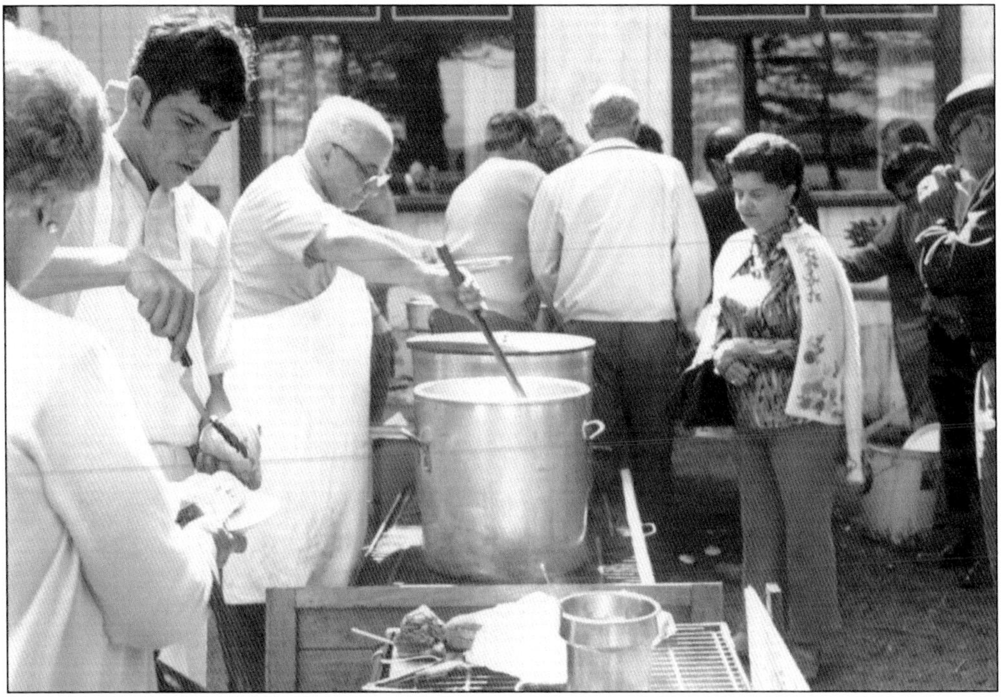

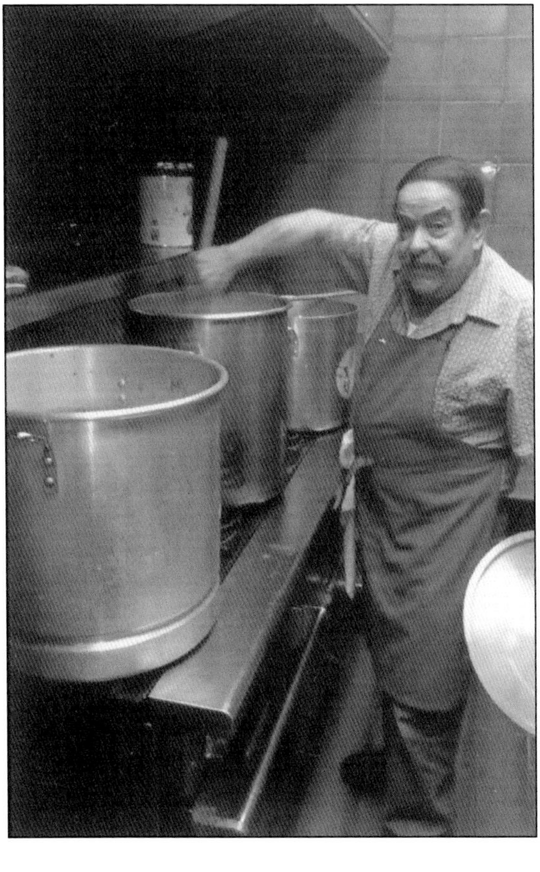

Nate Binacuzzo is seen stirring a huge pot of macaroni to feed the hungry members of the Piave Fiume Lodge #1036 in Watertown. These events were eagerly looked forward to, and the traditional Italian foods that were prepared were greatly enjoyed by the Lodge members.

Chef Joe Marchio cooks tripe on an annual Thanksgiving open house in 2013 at the Piave Fiume Lodge #1036 in Watertown. Tripe is an edible offal and is prepared by boiling and then cooking it with such traditional ingredients as tomatoes, olive oil, garlic, and herbs to create a dish that evokes the cuisine of our Italian ancestors.

Renato DiStefano, Julio Coppola, and Luciano DeAngelis stir an enormous pot of polenta at one of the Piave Fiume Lodge #1036 polenta nights. Polenta, a staple in many Italian American homes, is simply cornmeal boiled into a thick porridge, sometimes mixed with bitter greens, which is then poured on oiled wooden boards and dressed with tomato sauce, meats, and grated cheese. Various regions in Italy prepare it in their own unique way, but it is always a delicious and filling meal.

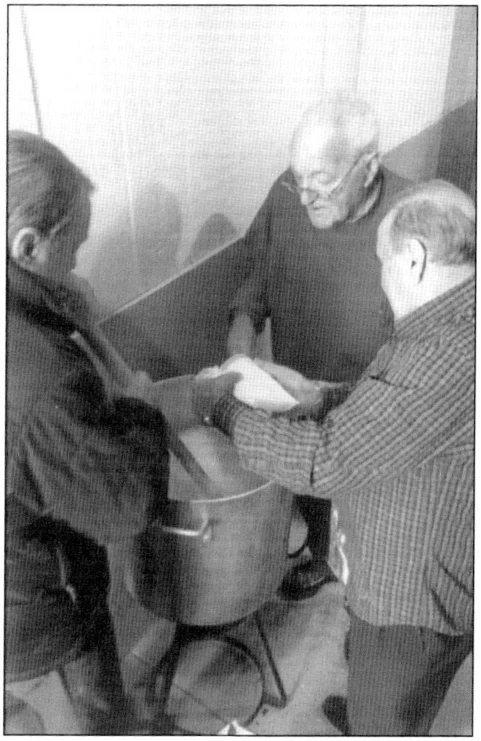

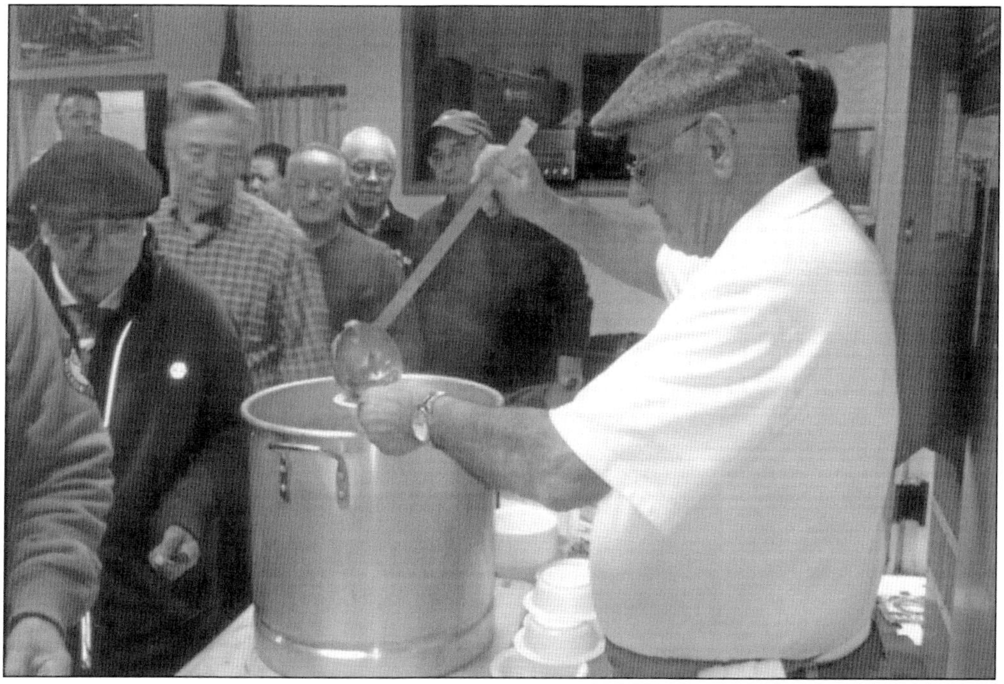

Joe DiMambro, with a large metal ladle in hand, feeds the hungry members of the Piave Fiume Lodge #1036 in Watertown who queue for bowls of tripe prepared in a homemade tomato sauce. The dish was once served in many homes, but today it is rarely seen on restaurant menus; on occasion, Lodges will prepare the traditional Italian foods their ancestors heartily enjoyed.

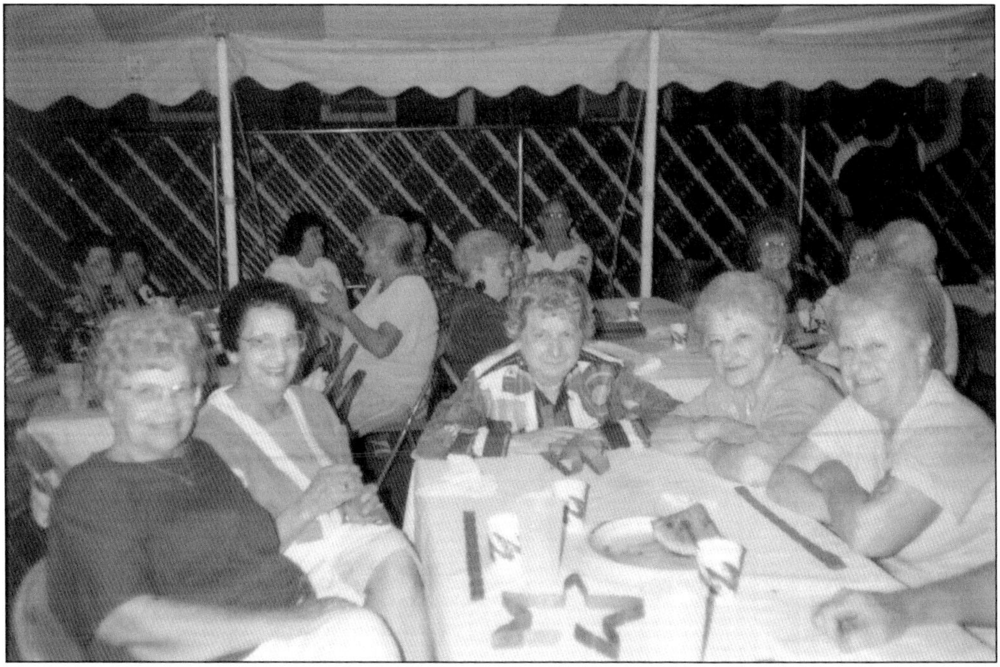

Members of the Braintree Ladies Lodge #1422 enjoyed a tented summer picnic in 1994 at the Newton Sons of Italy. From to right are Carmella Fiorentino, Carmella Milani, Dorothy Berlandi, Lucy Naples, and Louise Aiello.

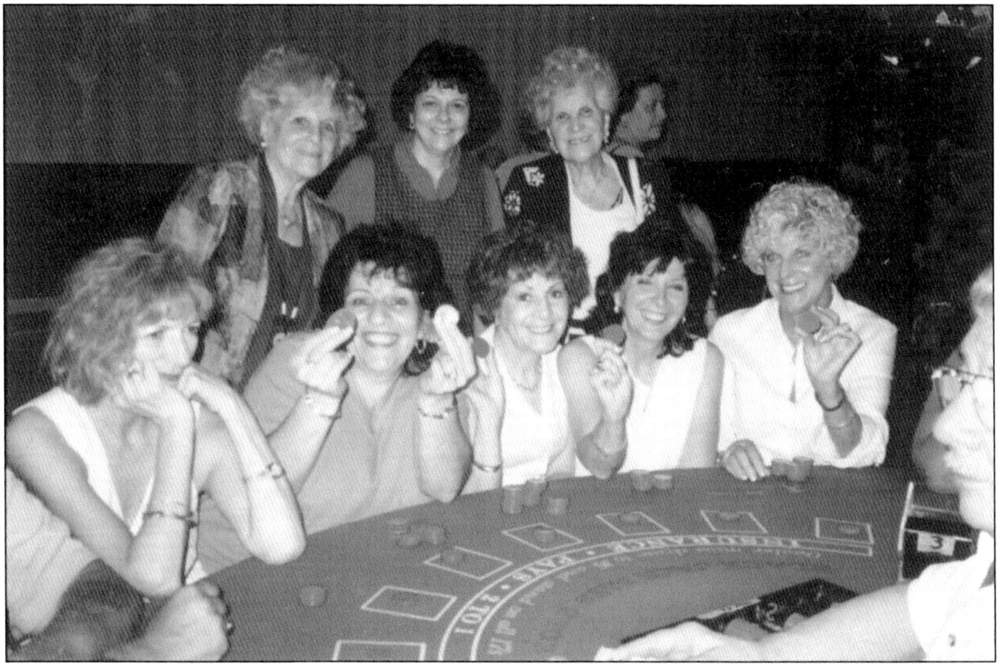

A group of Greater Boston Renaissance Lodge #2614 ladies attended the State Convention in the New York Catskills and seem to be enjoying the gambling table as they hold their chips aloft. Seated are, from left to right, Kathy Cammarata, Suzanne Mika, Annette Luongo, Pam Donnaruma, and Marie D'Eramo.

Eight

The Recent Activities of the Grand Lodge of Massachusetts

La Recente Attività dei Figli d'Italia in Massachusetts

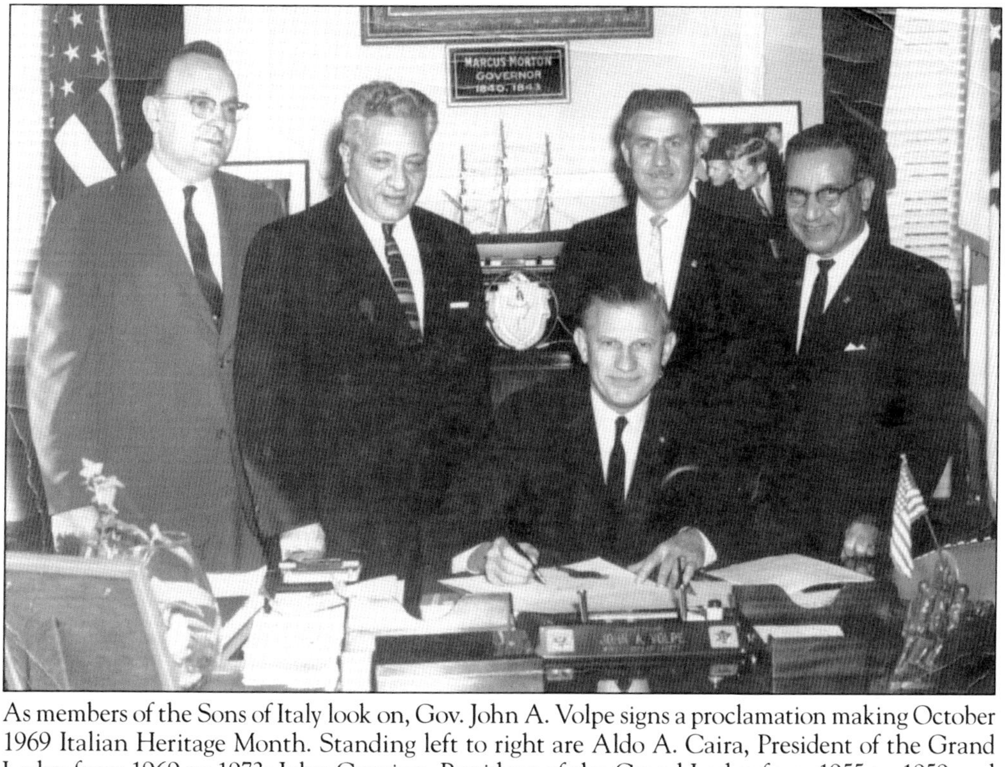

As members of the Sons of Italy look on, Gov. John A. Volpe signs a proclamation making October 1969 Italian Heritage Month. Standing left to right are Aldo A. Caira, President of the Grand Lodge from 1969 to 1973; John Guarino, President of the Grand Lodge from 1955 to 1959 and 1965 to 1969; John Concotti; and Al Campisi.

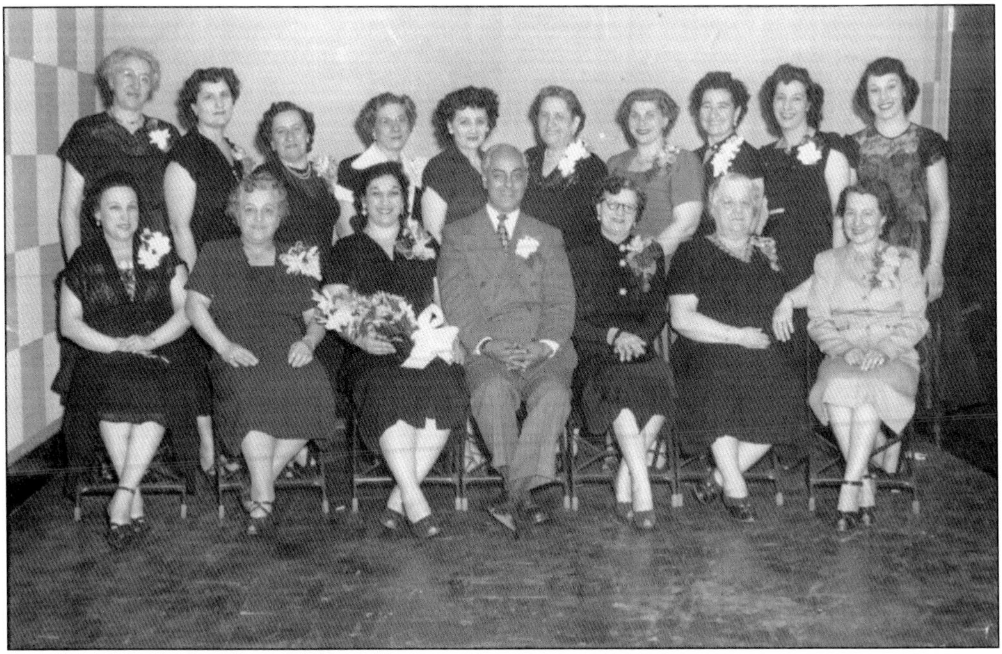

The members of Princess Pia Lodge #1895 pose in 1952. Holding a large bouquet of flowers is Rose M. Colantuone, an active member of the Sons of Italy for 60 years. Beside her is Anthony Julian, who served as President of the Grand Lodge of Massachusetts from 1946 to 1951.

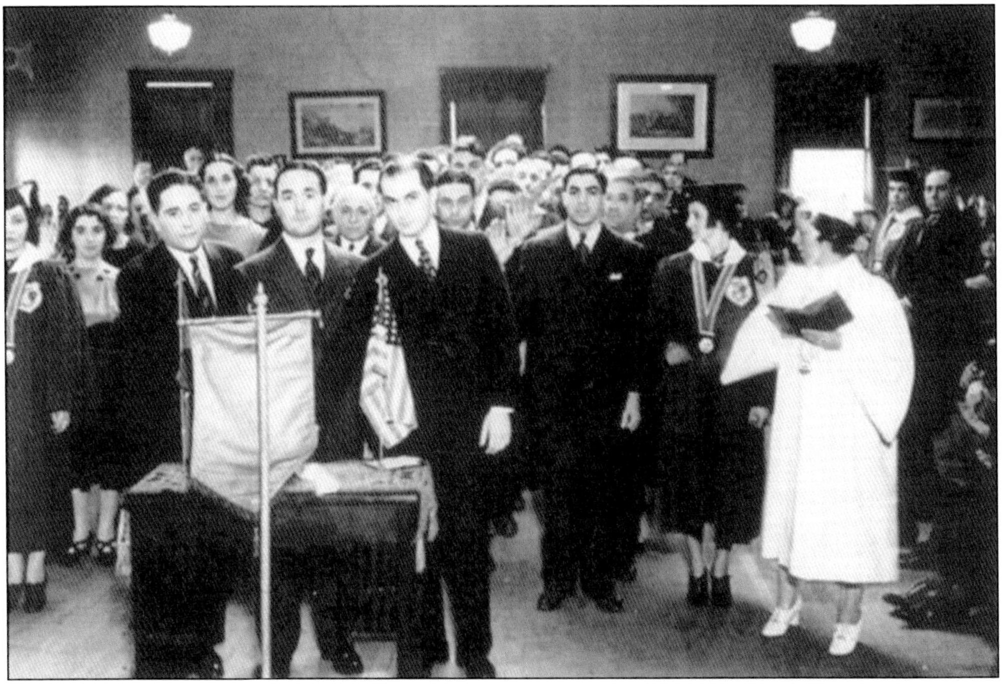

Members of the Veturia Romana Lodge #1200 in Salem, Massachusetts, participate in an installation of officers around 1935. These early Lodges created a support system for all Italian immigrants that assisted them in becoming citizens, attaining educational opportunities, and assimilating to American life.

These Junior Lodge members of the Stella Del Nord Lodge #1436 in Quincy are dressed in traditional costumes. Their installation was accompanied by the young man on the left with his accordion, which provided a lively bit of music.

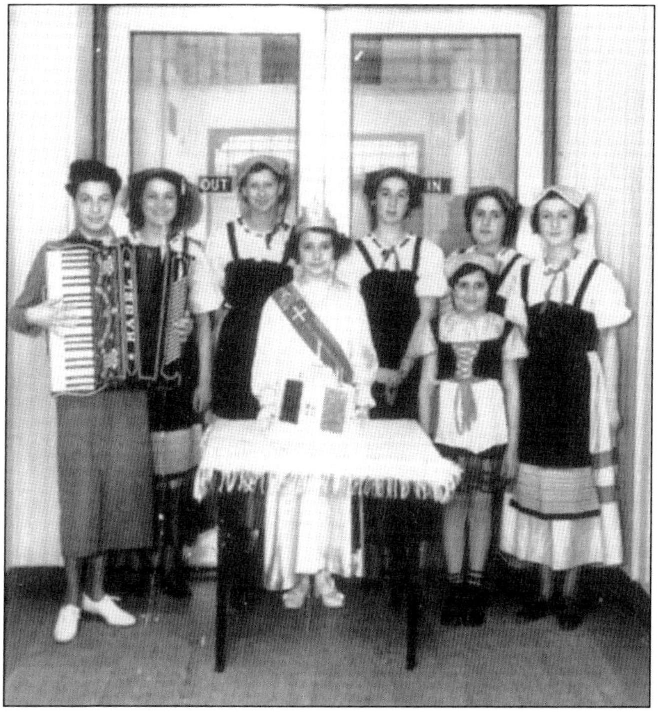

Members of the 1950 Watertown Girls' Degree Team are at the Santa Maria Lodge #1570 in Medford. With the American flag, the banner of the Sons of Italy, and their caped robes, they are the leaders of the future.

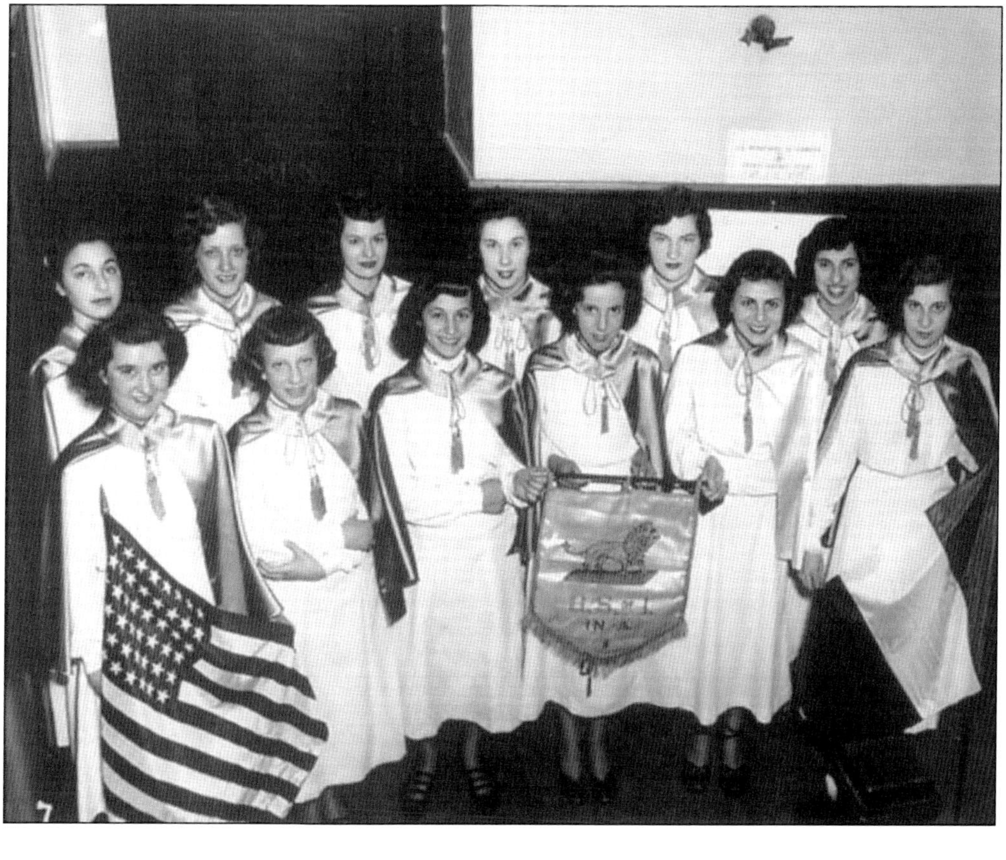

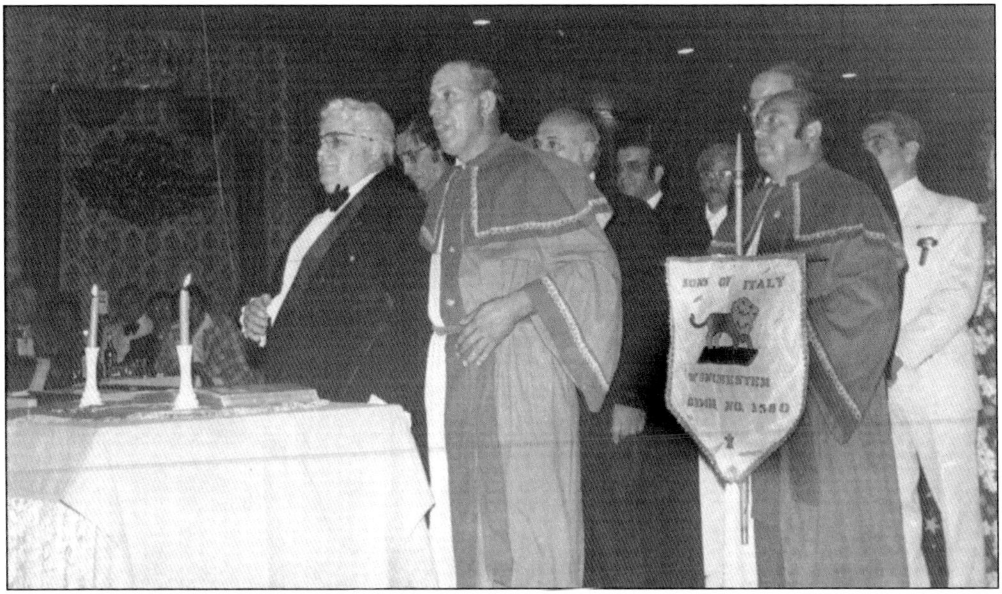

The 1975 installation of Joe Terzo as Grand Trustee was a traditional ceremony at the Brockton Manor, with members of the Winchester Degree Team bearing their banner on the right.

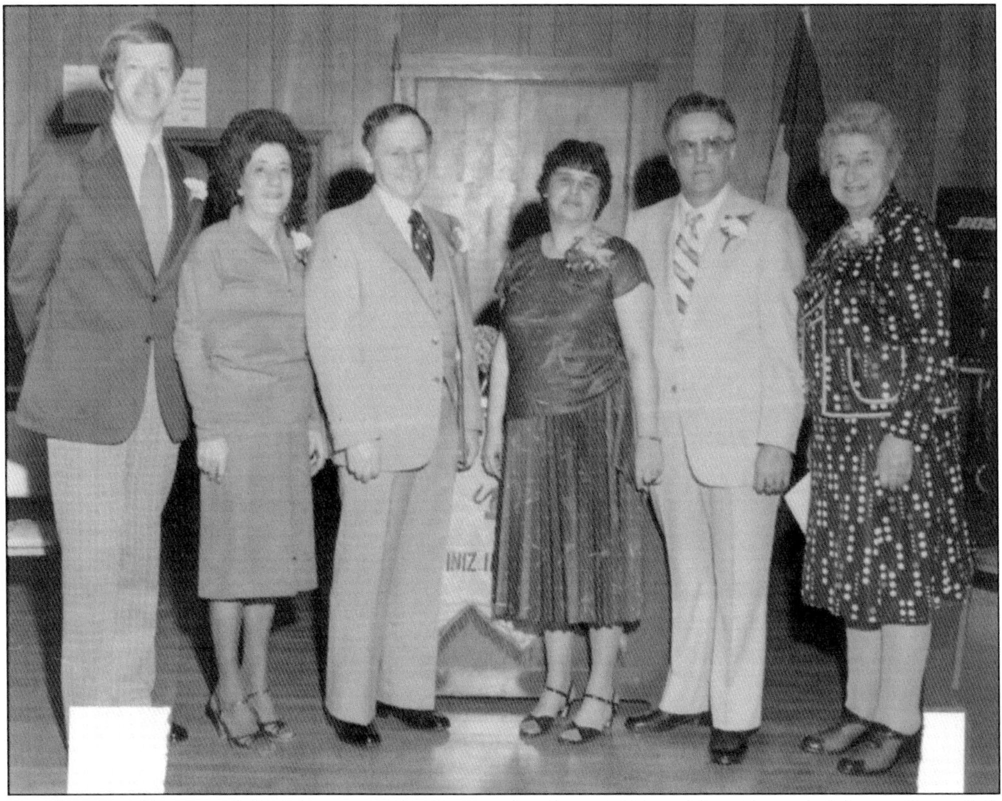

At the installation of the Francesco DeSanctis Lodge #1411 in Natick in 1980 are, from left to right, unidentified, Gloria Ferullo, Ed Tarallo, Cathy Bourassa, Armand Bourassa, and Rose McIntyre.

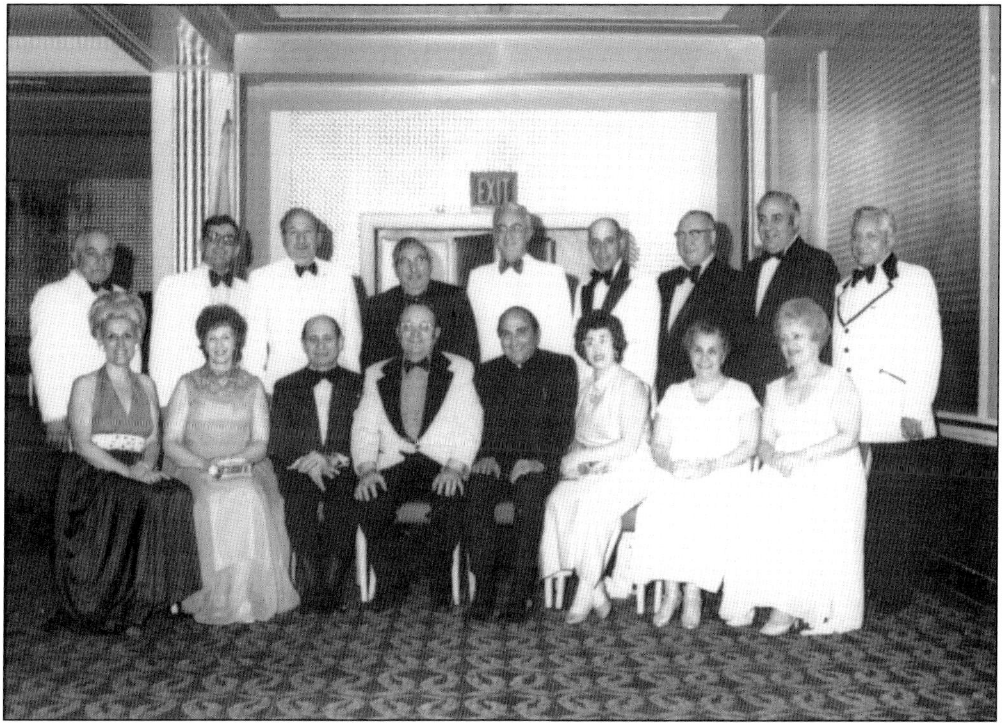

At a dinner dance in 1977 are, from left to right, (seated) Irene Granara; Josephine Falco; Nicholas Cipriani; Aldo Caira, President of the Grand Lodge from 1969 to 1973; Bishop Joseph Ruocco, the State Chaplain; June Alfano; Sophie Gorrasi; and unidentified; (standing) Nate Biancuzzo; Grand Venerable Louis Salvatore; Mario Columbo; Ignazio Colombo; Guy Pelligrinelli; Bob Fiore; Joe Zanghi; Henry Frissora, President of the Grand Lodge from 1981 to 1985; and John Guarino, President of the Grand Lodge from 1955 to 1959 and 1965 to 1969.

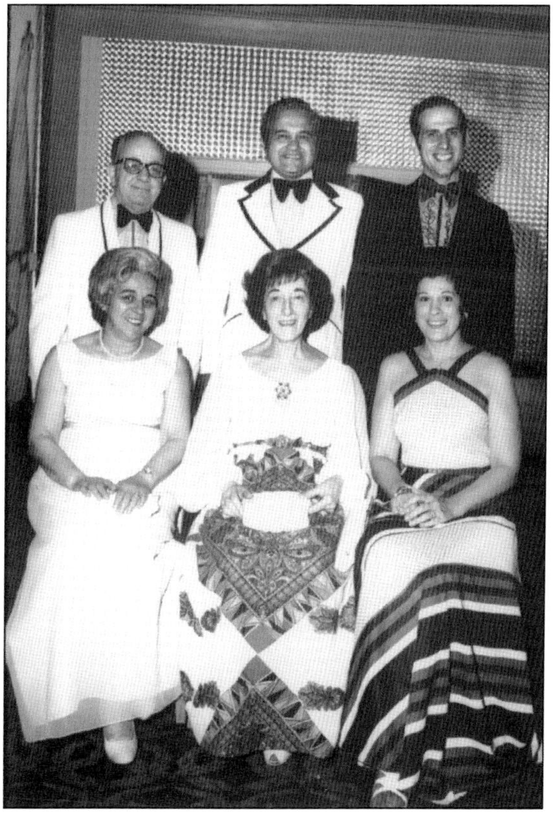

Pictured from left to right are (seated) Edith Messina, Edith D'Orozzio, and Mary Curro; (standing) Joe Pertrino, Joe Furnari, and John Saladino, members of the Benefit Insurance Commission.

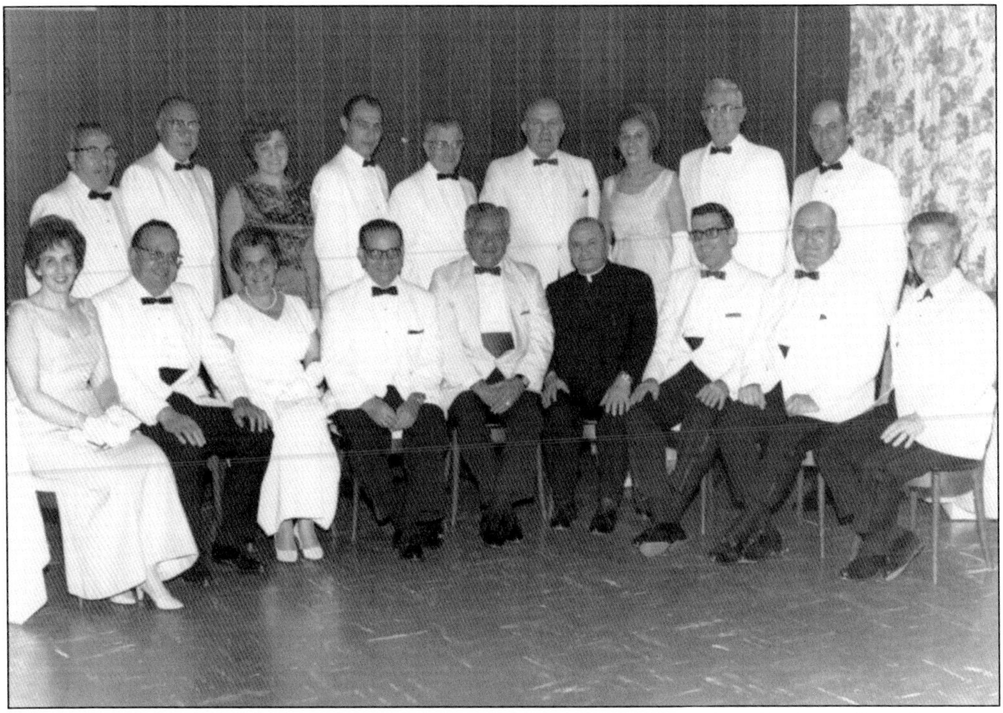

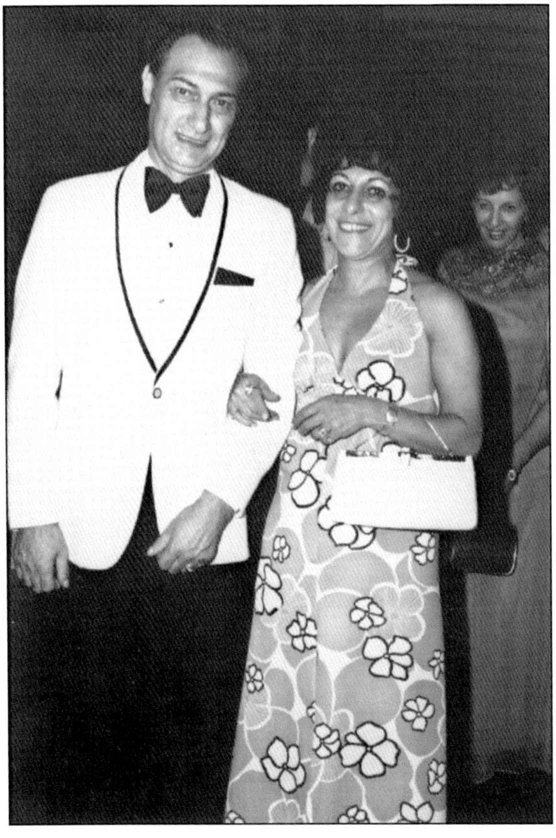

The Council under State President John Guarino in 1969 included, from left to right, (seated) Josephine Falco; Aldo Caira; Sophie Gorrasi; Al Campisi; John Guarino, President of the Grand Lodge from 1955 to 1959 and 1965 to 1969; Msgr. Albert Jacobbe; Louis Salvatore; Peter Donadio; and Jack Cincotti; (standing) Ignazio Columbo; Joe Zanghi; Jennie Polcari; Guy Arigo; Joe LoPresti; Matt DeLuca; Helen Cagno; Guy Pellegrinelli; and Bob Fiore.

Guy Arigo was the President of the Grand Lodge of Massachusetts from 1977 to 1981. He is pictured with his wife, Claire Arigo.

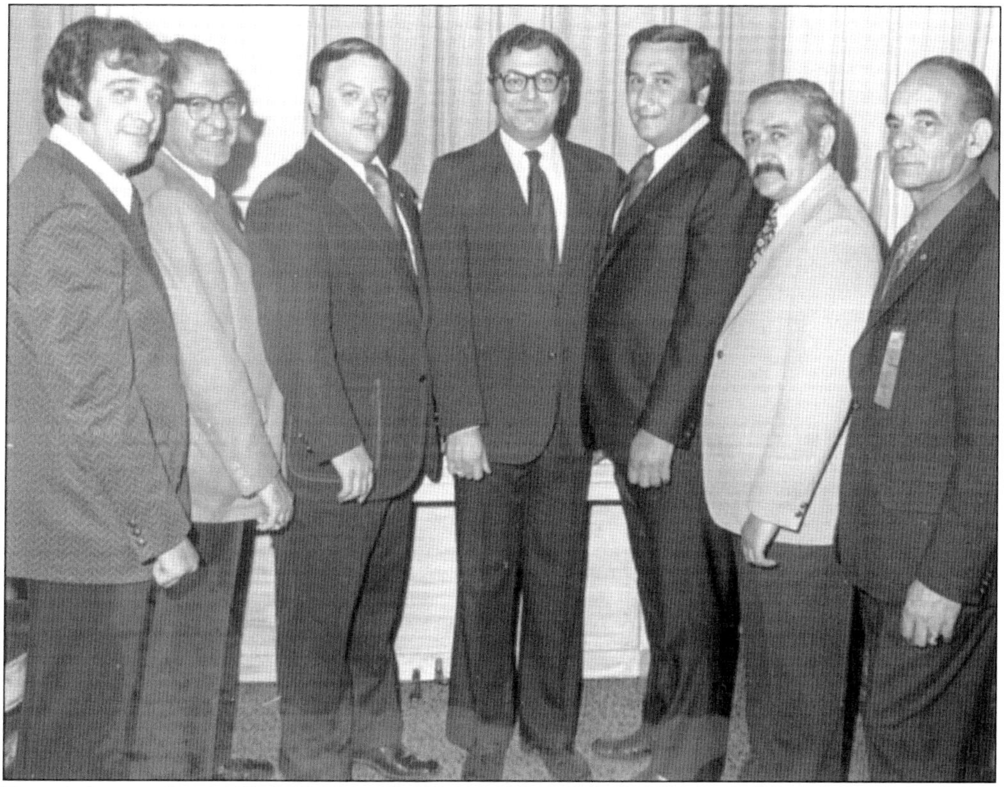

From left to right are Nick Fantasia Jr., Dante Mastro, Jack Brown, Sebastian Papagno, Peter Merlino, Rocky Buonavinci, and Domenic "Mimmo" D'Arcangelo.

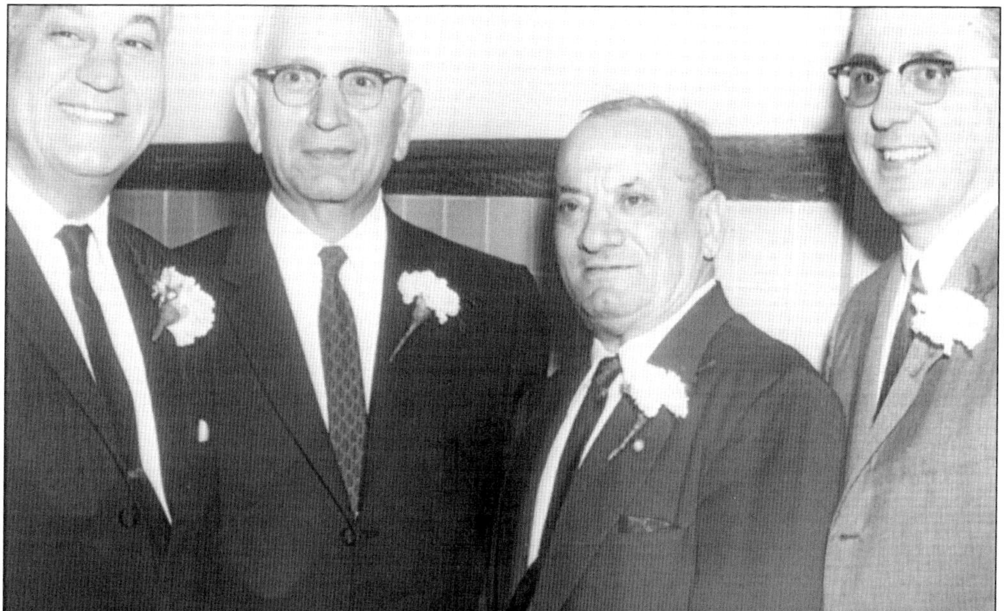

An installation of officers at the Cristoforo Colombo Regina Elena Lodge #169 in Fitchburg includes, from left to right, Bill Giadone, Joe Pandiscio, Patsy DiNardo, and John Pacetti.

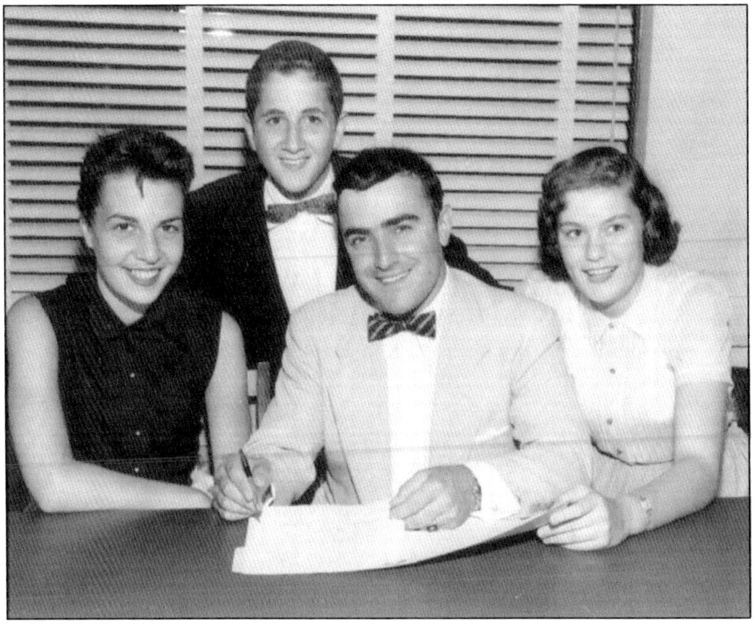

The Junior Division was planning a Moonlight Dance in 1954. Pictured are, from left to right, (seated) Camille Gravaliese of Medford, Russell Iuliano of Watertown, and Eleanor Vacca of Everett; (standing) Vincent Faille of Waltham.

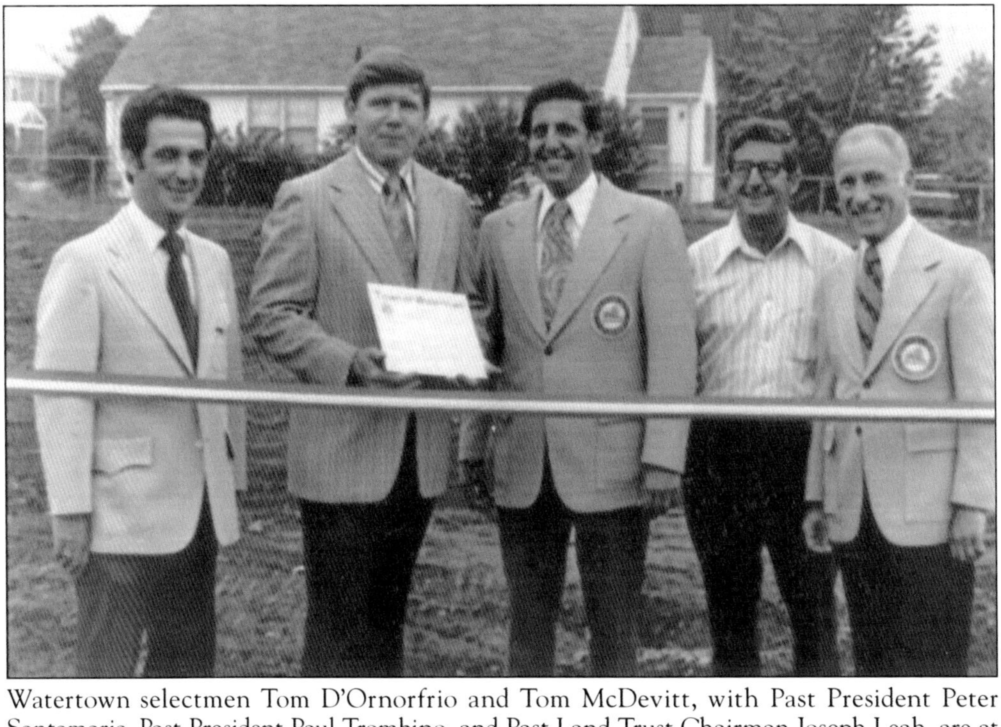

Watertown selectmen Tom D'Ornorfrio and Tom McDevitt, with Past President Peter Santamaria, Past President Paul Trombino, and Past Land Trust Chairman Joseph Leah, are at the groundbreaking ceremony of the new home of the Watertown Sons of Italy at 520 Pleasant Street in Watertown.

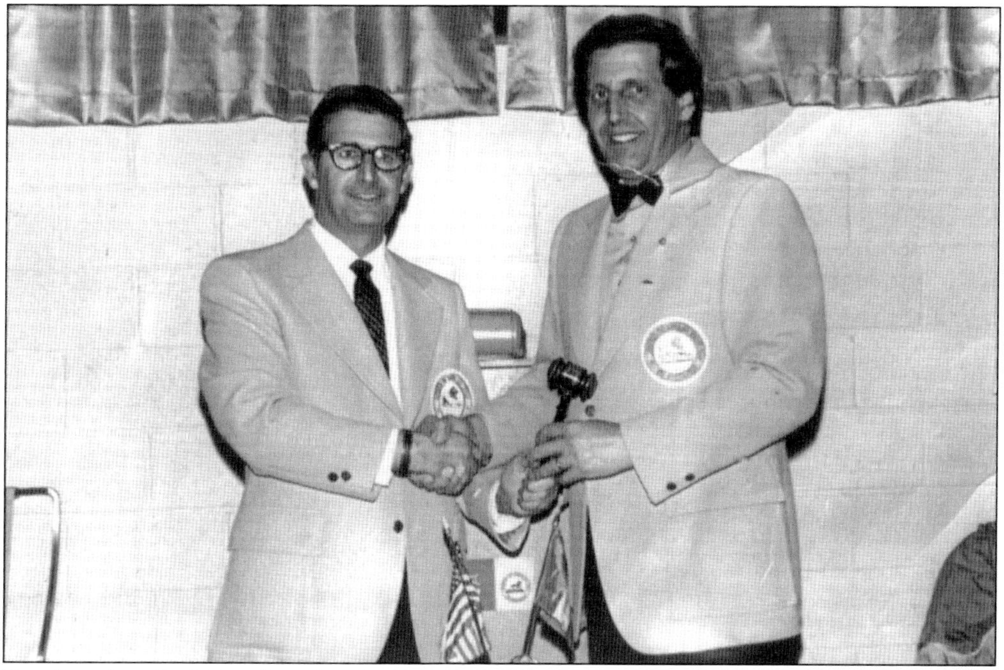

Past President Paul Trombino hands the gavel of the Piave Fiume Lodge #1036 in Watertown to new President Peter Santamaria in 1973.

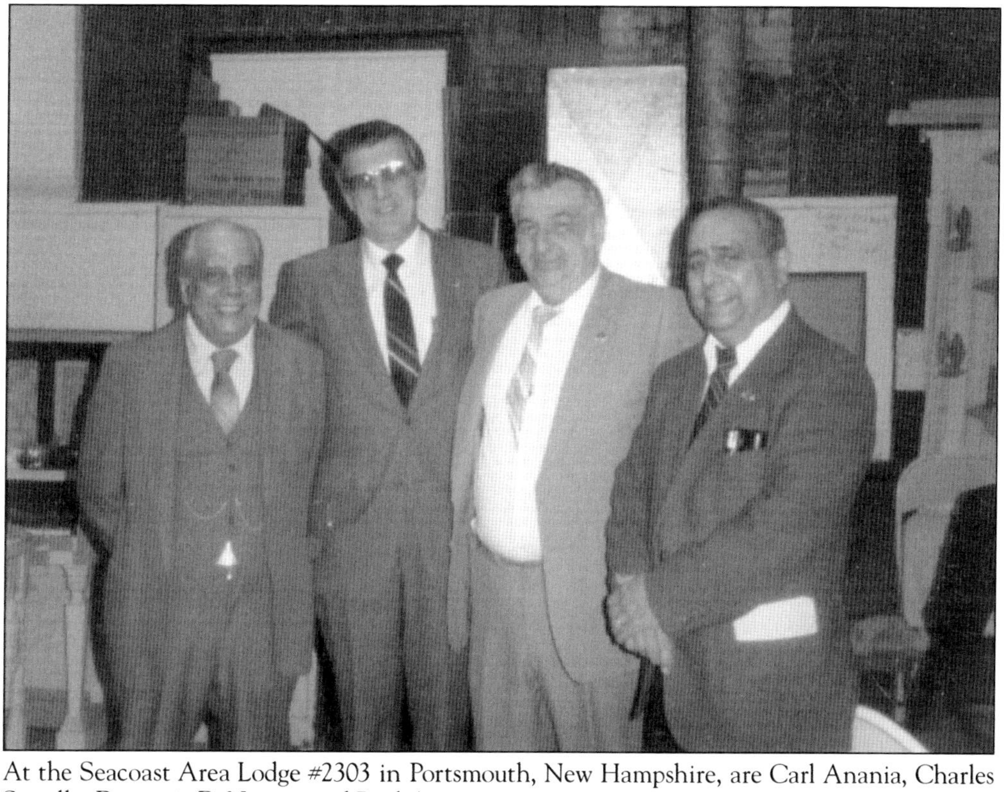

At the Seacoast Area Lodge #2303 in Portsmouth, New Hampshire, are Carl Anania, Charles Storella, Domenic DeNuzzio, and Paul Anania.

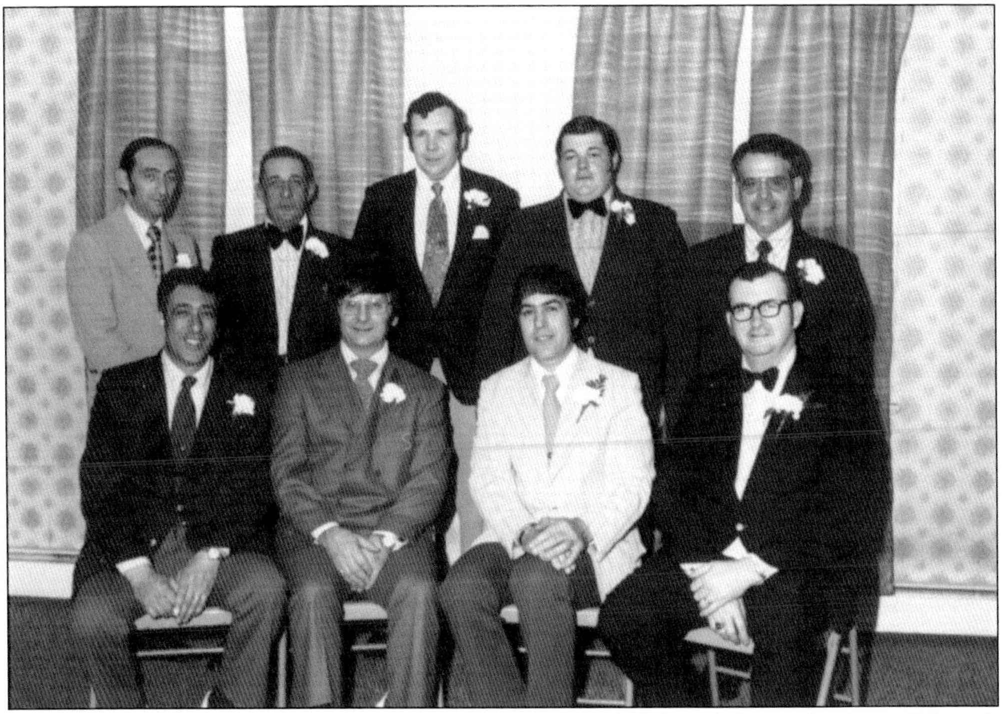

The Joseph Gorrasi Lodge #1406 installation in 1975 included, from left to right, (seated) Joseph Brann, James Garbino, John Balcastro, and Arthur Cumming; (standing) Pat Mogauro, Angelo Naticchioni, Francis Cahill, James Naticchioni, and Emilio Romano.

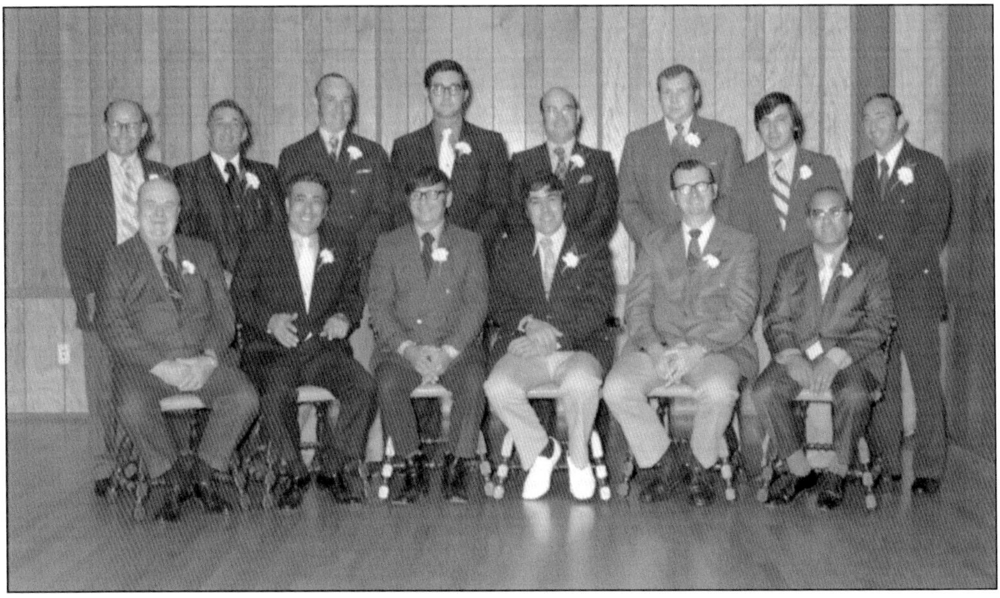

Members of the Joseph Gorrasi Lodge #1406 sponsored the Billerica Lodge's first installation and presented them with their regalia. From left to right are (seated) George Melcher, Joseph Bann, James Garbino, John Belcastro, Arthur Cumming, and Joseph Paonessa; (standing) Peter Lisacchi, Angelo Naticchioni, Anthony Lisacki, Leo Fama, Joe Sicari, Evan Cahill, Francis DiMambro, and Pat Mogauro.

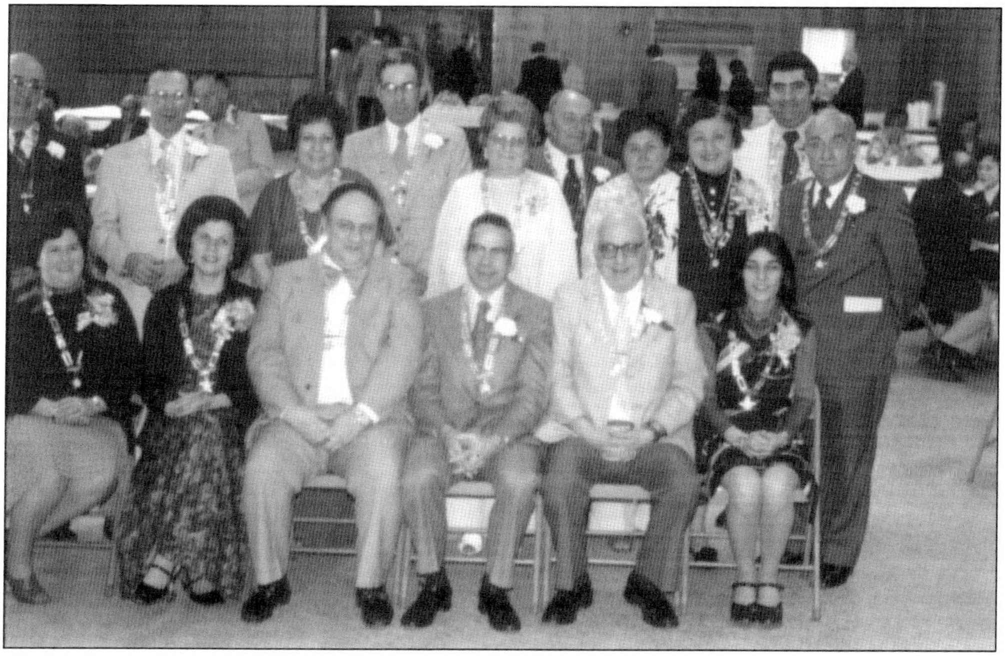

At the Granite State Lodge #2380 installation in 1980 are, from left to right, (seated) Yvonne Menegoni, Joyce Powles, Nicholas Grieco, Sal Farina, John Vinceguerra, and Mary-Ellen Margo; (standing) Vincent Luongo, Frank Menegoni, Mary Arigo, Nick Luongo, Catherine Fabiano, John DiPrizio, Rita Luongo, Evelyn Luongo, Anthony Lazzaro, and Michael Scala.

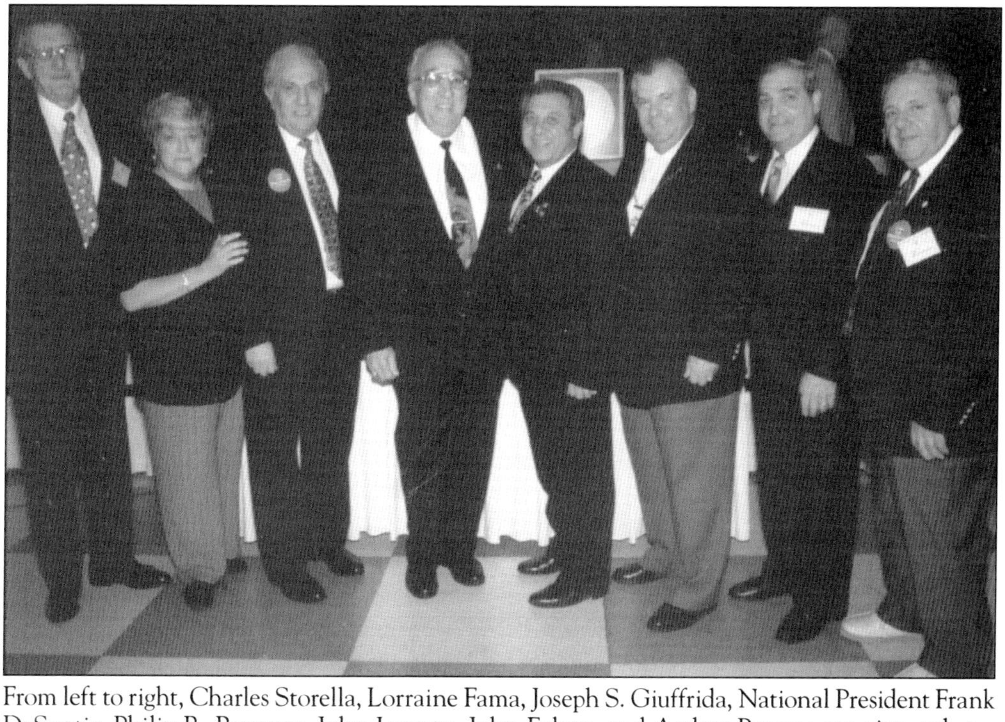

From left to right, Charles Storella, Lorraine Fama, Joseph S. Giuffrida, National President Frank DeSantis, Philip R. Boncore, John Larmey, John Falvey, and Arthur Porcaro are pictured at a National Convention.

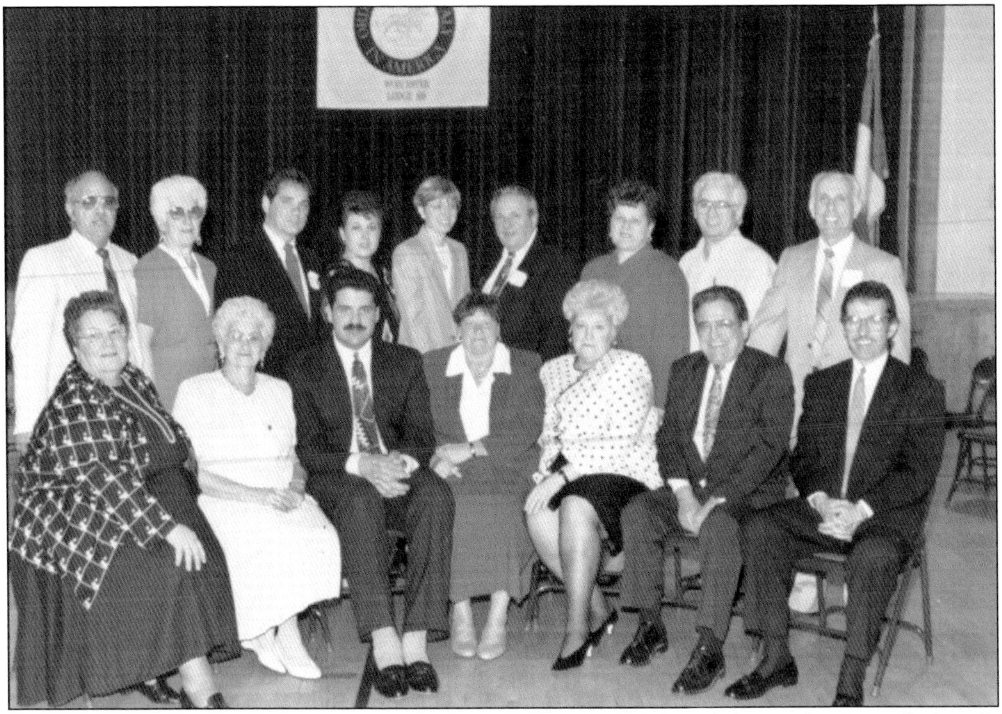

The installation of the Worcester Lodge #168 in 1991 included, from left to right, (seated) Angela DeMauro, Gladys Bello, Larry Trapasso, Carmelita Bello, Lorraine Fama, State President Angelo Furnari, and Tommy Colletta; (standing) Rubin Mikitarian, Rosemarie Mikitarian, Billy Capers, Gina Angella, Nancy Grimaldi, Arthur Porcaro, Aurora Fusaro, Louis Algeri, and Enzo Angilella.

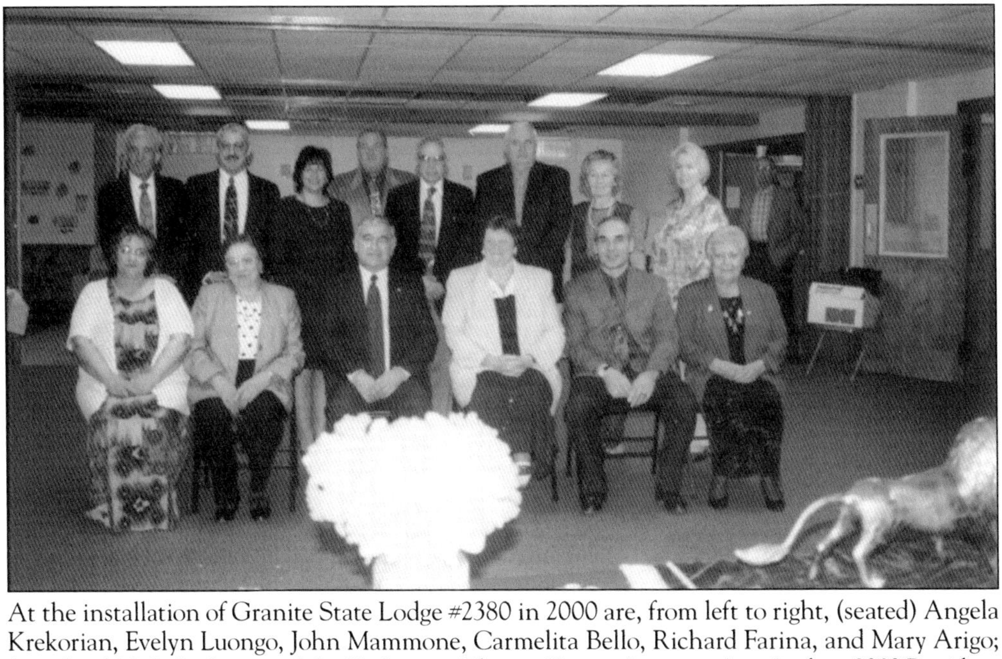

At the installation of Granite State Lodge #2380 in 2000 are, from left to right, (seated) Angela Krekorian, Evelyn Luongo, John Mammone, Carmelita Bello, Richard Farina, and Mary Arigo; (standing) Nicholas Luongo, John Krekorian, Theresa Farina, Seacoast Area Lodge #2303 President John Semprini, Salvatore Farina, Albert Cataldo, Celia Urcuioli, and Ruthann Mammone.

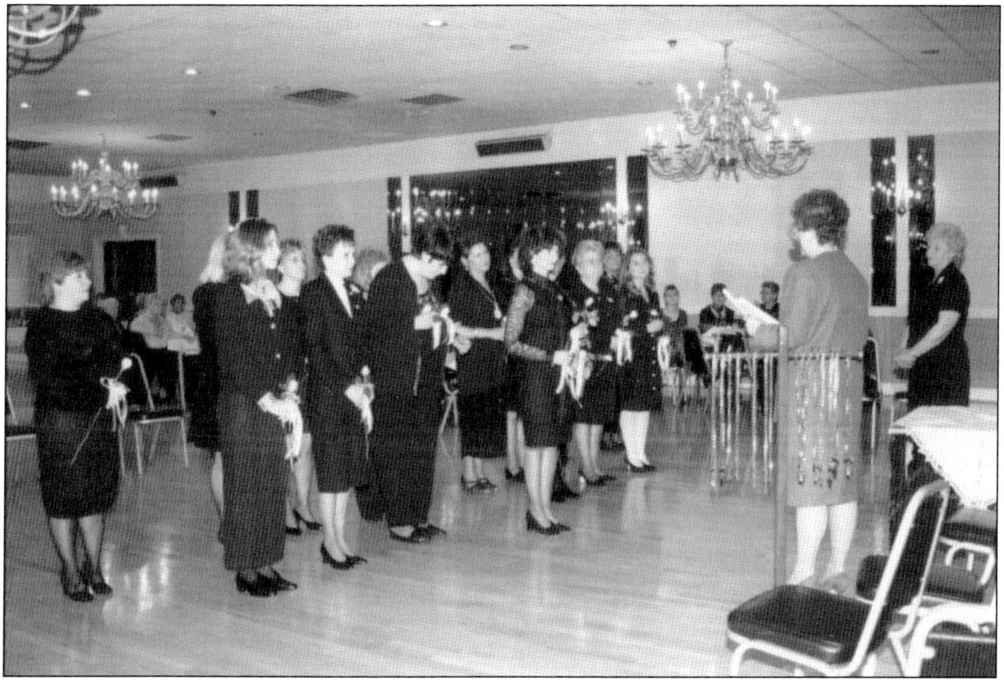

At the installation of the Braintree Ladies Lodge #1422 in 1999, the new President was Ruth-Ann Berlandi.

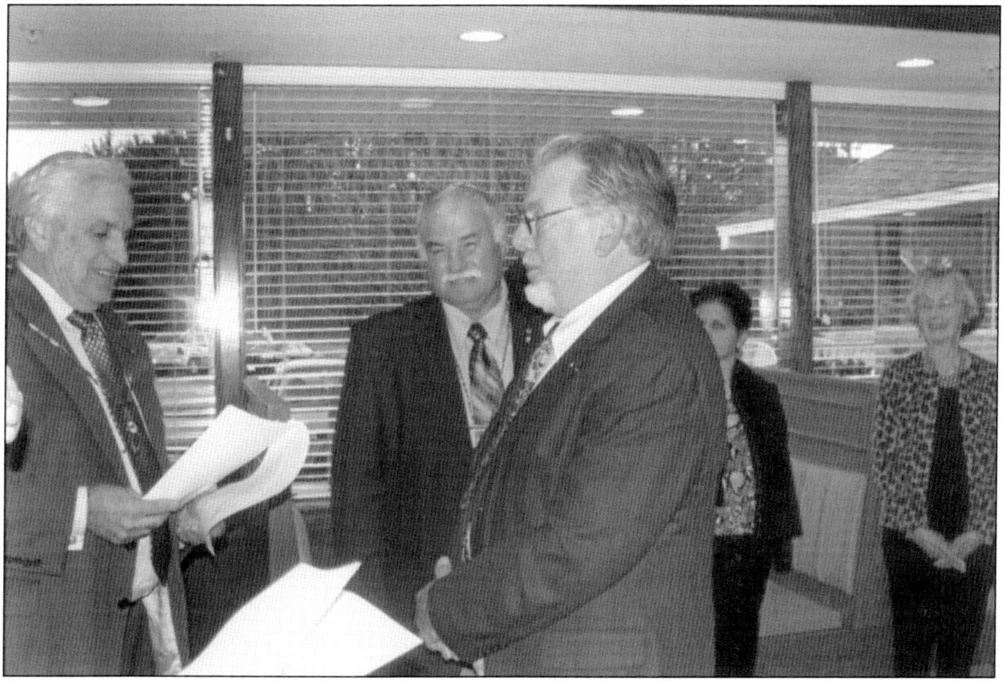

At the Granite State Lodge #2380 installation in 2013 are, from left to right, Joseph A. Russo, President of the Grand Lodge from 1999 to 2003; James DiStefano, President of the Grand Lodge from 2009 to 2013; and new President of the Granite State Lodge, Michael Dello Iacono.

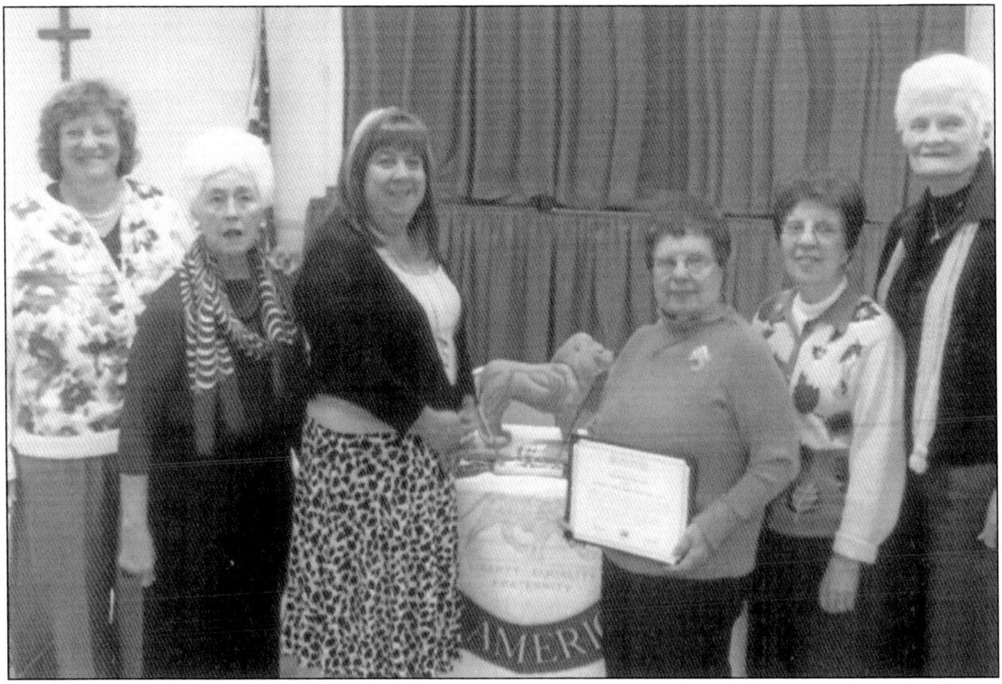

Celebrating the 100th anniversary of the Cristoforo Colombo Regina Elena Lodge #169 in 2013 are, from left to right, Grand Lodge of Massachusetts President Carmelita Bello, Phyllis LeBlanc, Cristoforo Colombo Regina Elena Lodge President Sylvia Pacetti-Poirier, Ann Pacetti, Florence Volpe, and Irene Brogna.

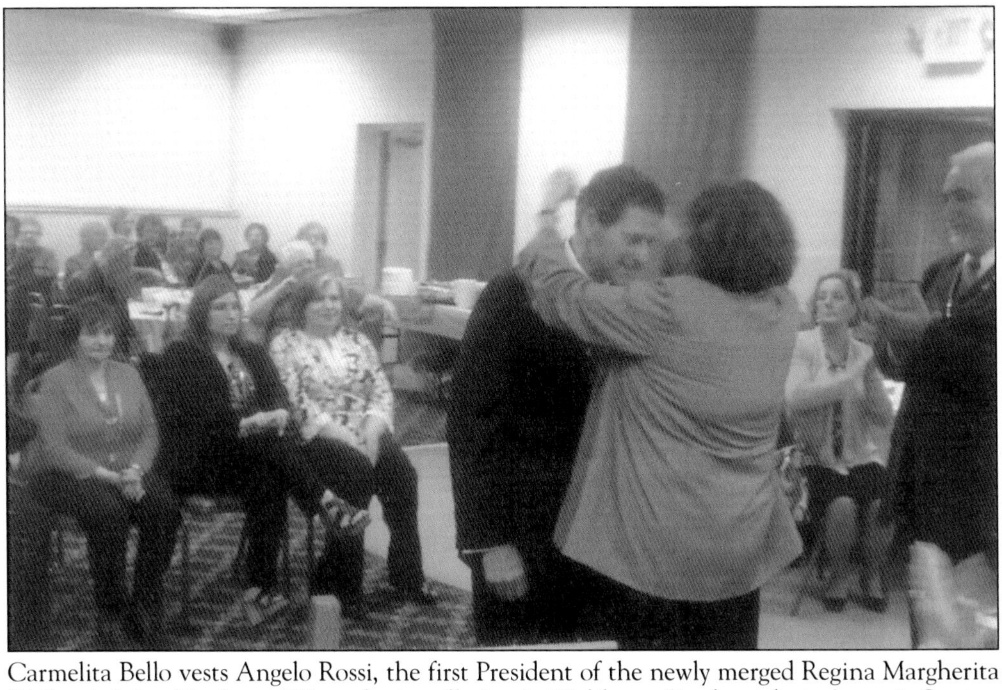

Carmelita Bello vests Angelo Rossi, the first President of the newly merged Regina Margherita Di Savoia Mixed Lodge #1094, at the installation in Waltham. On the right is Antonio Sestito, State First Vice President.

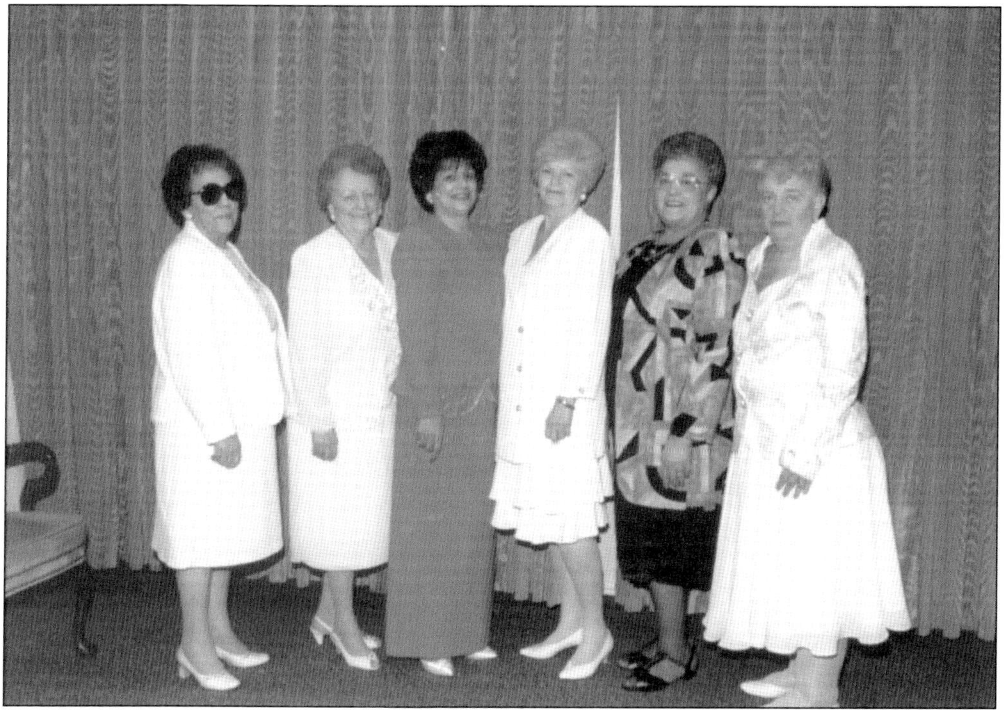

Members of the Braintree Ladies Lodge #1422 in 1990 include Josephine Martino, Midge Zanghi, Marie Graziano, Corinne Fasano, Mary Nickolas, and Phyllis DeGaetano.

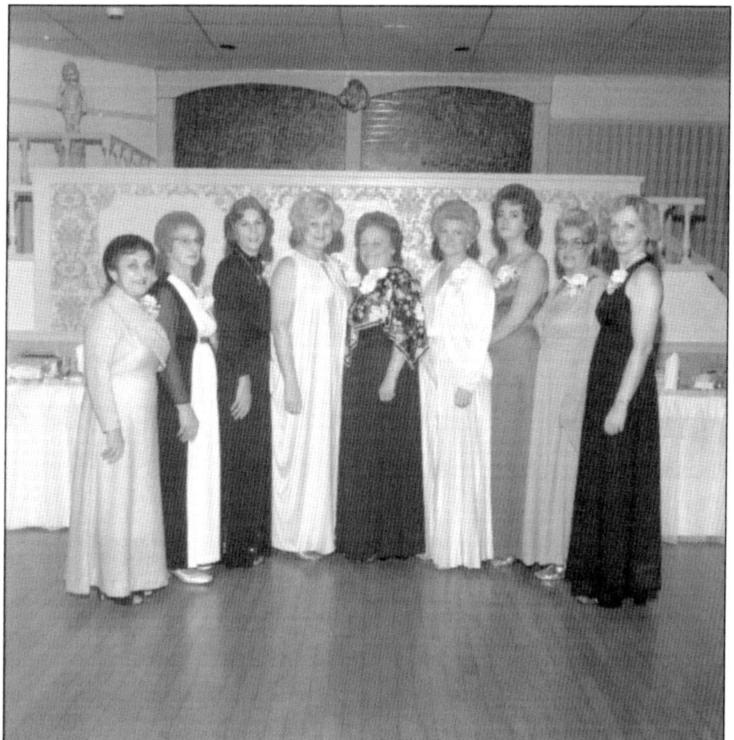

At a formal dinner dance at the Braintree Ladies Lodge #1422 in 1979 are Josephine DiBona, Polly Fuccino, Carol Dunn, Margarette Pettrocelli, Midge Zanghi, Corinne Fasano, Joanne Pistorino, Lenora Spadea, and Joan Fabaizio.

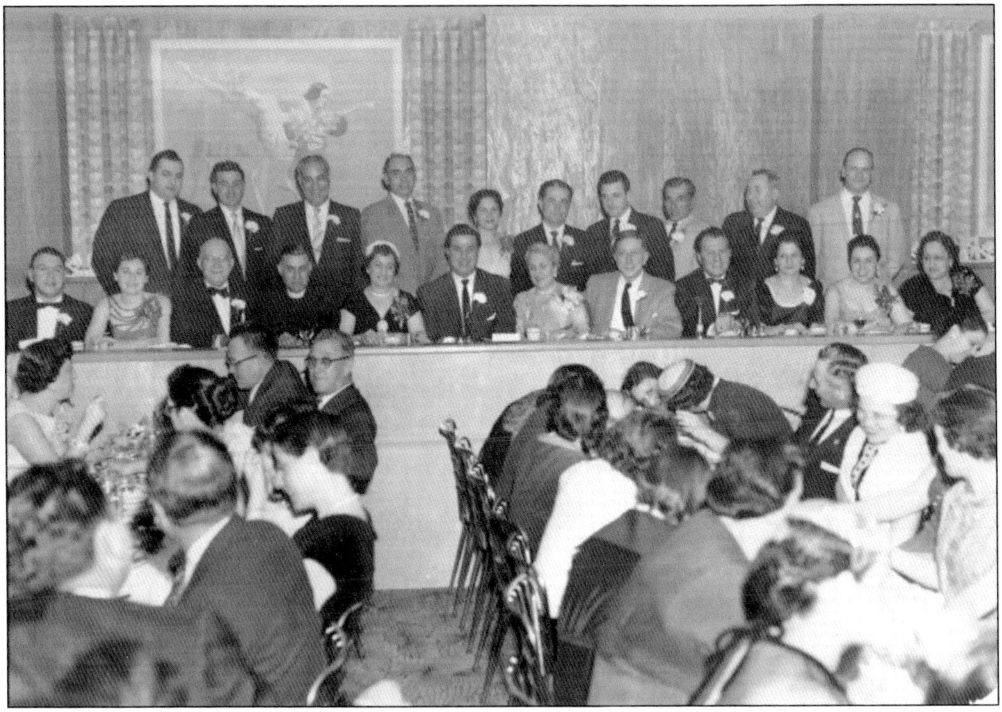

Among those pictured at Worcester Lodge #168 are the Rev. Erminio Mastroianni, Clementina Ursoleo, and Gladys Bello. Standing are John Bello, Ignazio Columbo, Modest Mele, Nicholas DeConza, and Arthur Porcaro. This has long been an active Lodge.

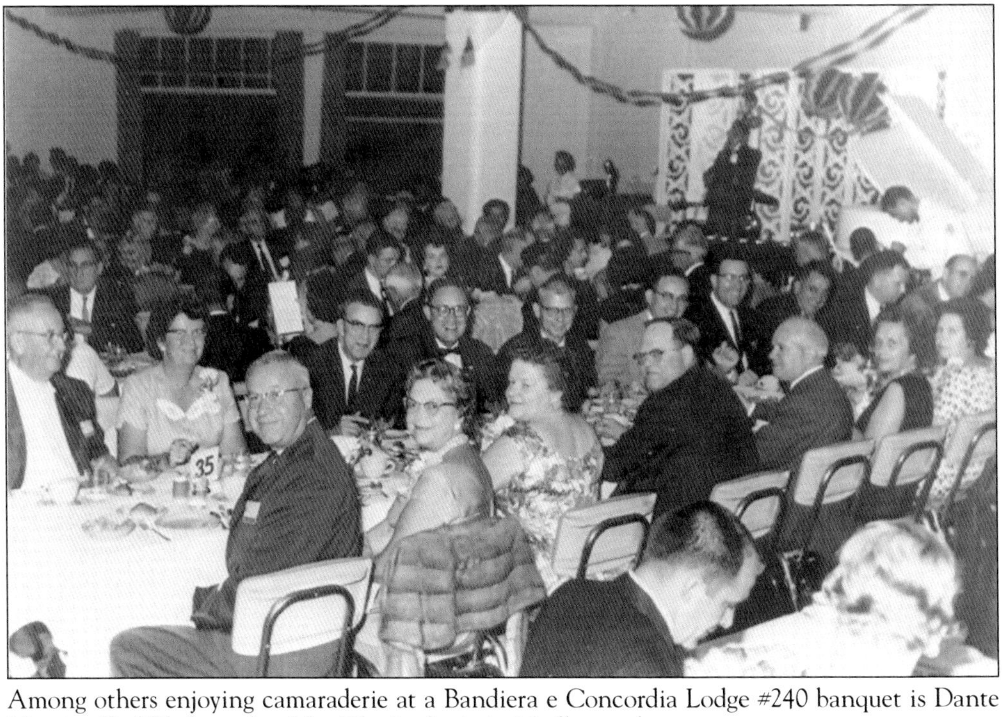

Among others enjoying camaraderie at a Bandiera e Concordia Lodge #240 banquet is Dante Masciarelli, fifth from the right. The Lodge is in Marlborough.

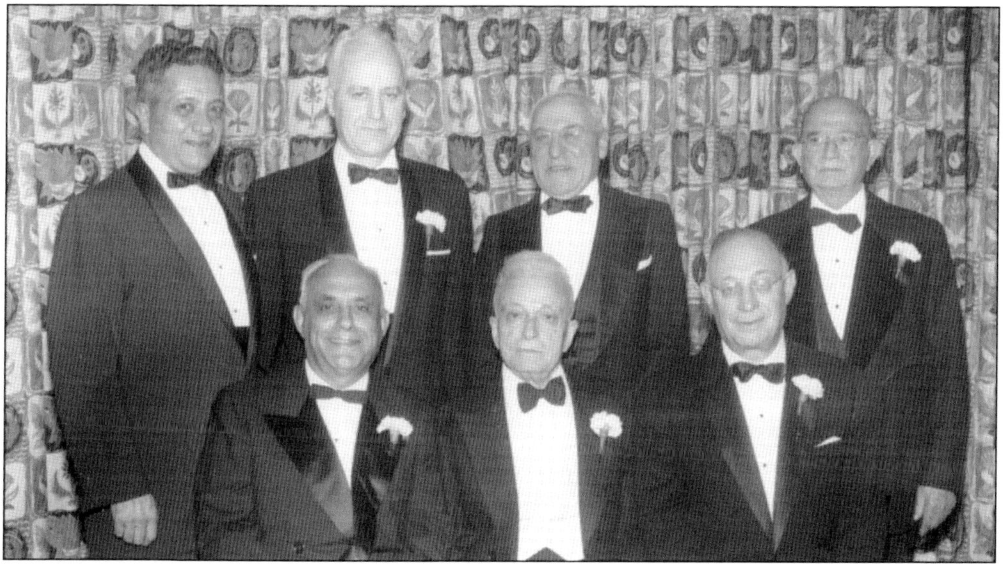

This distinguished group of Venerables (Presidents) of the Grand Lodge of Massachusetts includes, from left to right, (first row) Joseph Gorrasi, President from 1939 to 1946; Saverio R. Romano, founding President from 1914 to 1919; and Felix Forte, President from 1933 to 1937; (second row) John Guarino, President from 1955 to 1959 and again from 1965 to 1969; Anthony Julian, President from 1946 to 1951; Michael A. Fredo, President from 1937 to 1939; and Benjamin Corleto.

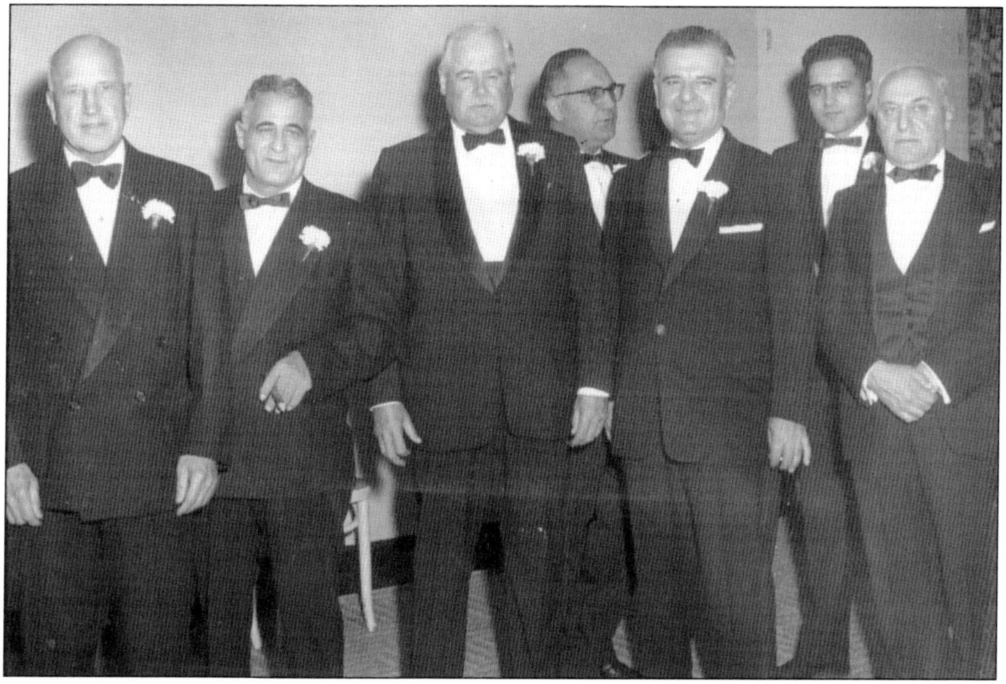

At a reception in honor of the Italian ambassador in 1959 are, from left to right, Carl Ell, president of Northeastern University; Paul D'Agostino, President of the Grand Lodge from 1959 to 1961; Ralph Lowell, noted banker and philanthropist and trustee of the Lowell Institute; Anthony Mosca; Joseph B. Silverio, President of the Grand Lodge from 1951 to 1955; Joseph Furnari; and Michael A. Fredo, President of the Grand Lodge from 1937 to 1939.

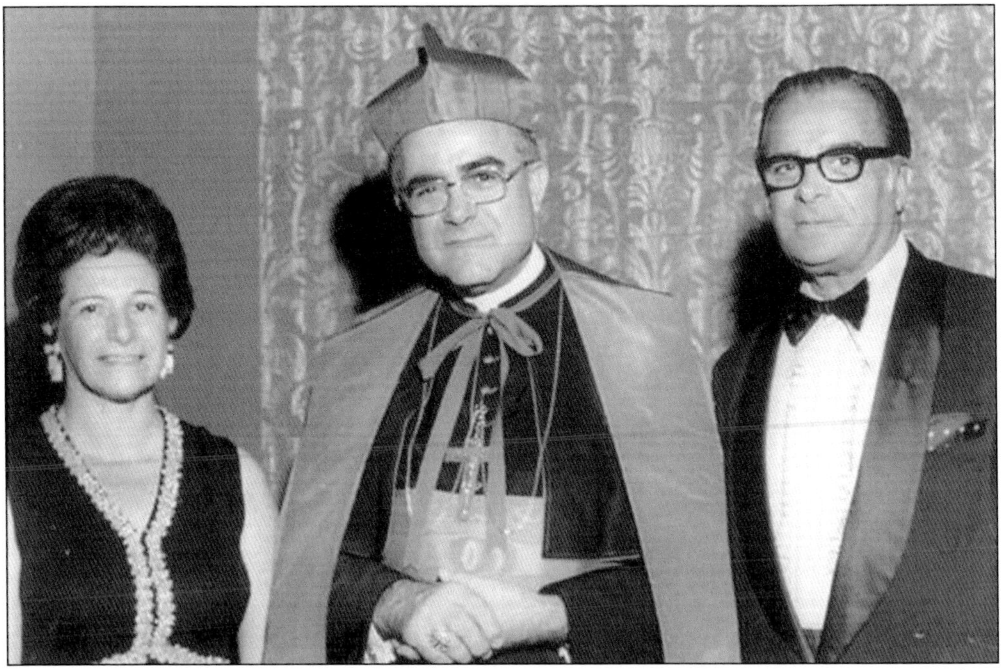

On either side of Cardinal Humberto Medeiros, archbishop of Boston from 1970 to 1973, when he was elevated to cardinal, are Laura Garda Gay and Peter B. Gay, who were among those who honored the cardinal at the Don Orione Home in East Boston in 1974. The Peter B. Gay Lodge #540 in Taunton was named in his honor.

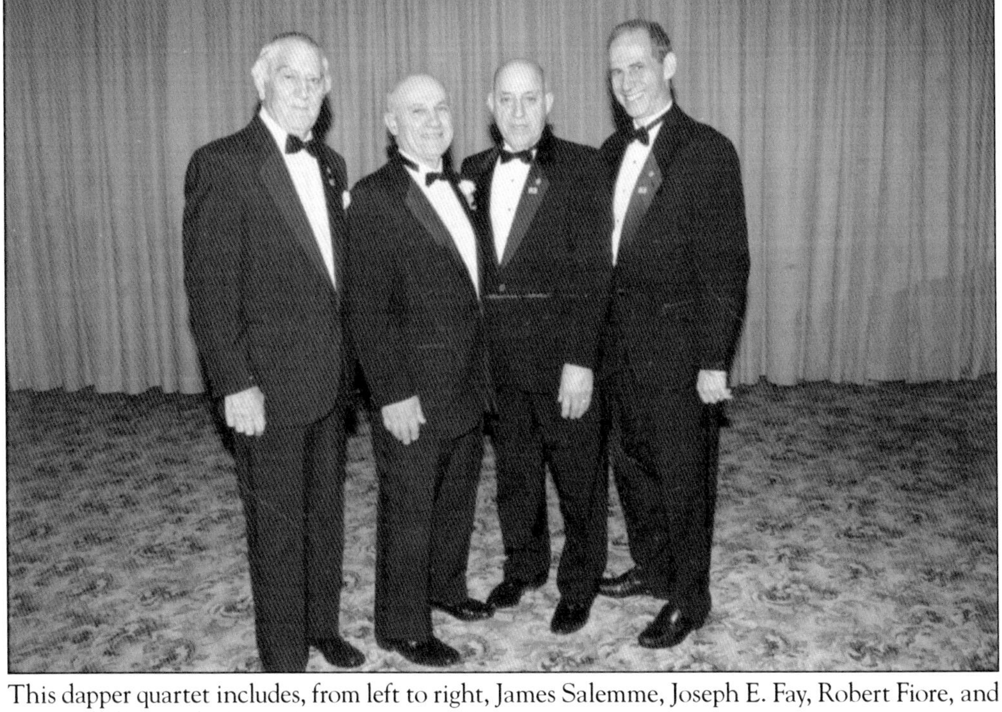

This dapper quartet includes, from left to right, James Salemme, Joseph E. Fay, Robert Fiore, and John Saladino at the State Convention in 1990.

Rev. Gregory Mercurio is the Grand Lodge Chaplain and has been the pastor of Holy Family Church in Lynn since 1999; he is seen here with former State Second Vice President Gloria Ferullo at an event in 1995.

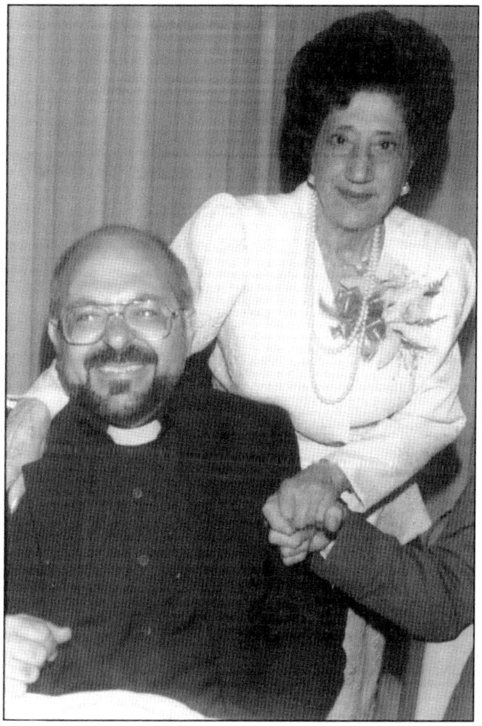

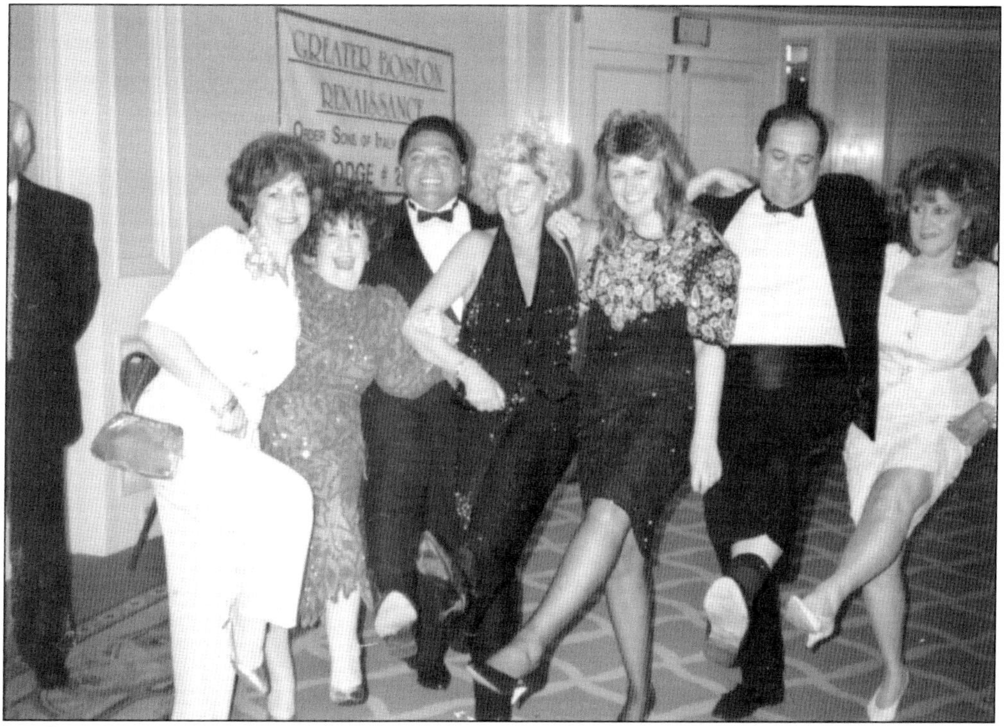

At the Boston University Trustee Ballroom for the Greater Boston Renaissance Lodge #2614 Black Tie Ball are, from left to right, Annette Luongo, Thelma Hawkins, Dr. John Christoforo, Marie D'Eramo, unidentified, Joe DeMaina, and Barbara Summa.

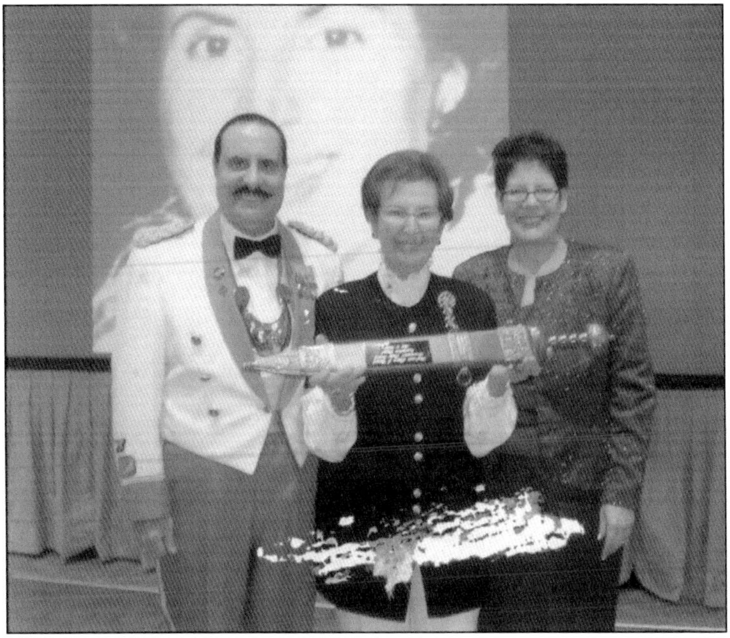

Prof. Nancy Caruso of Northeastern University receives the Legionnaire Sword as the Inspiration Award at the Greater Boston Renaissance Lodge #2614 Annual Black Tie Ball from Col. Dean Saluti and Marjorie Cahn. This award is an actual Roman Legionnaire sword and is presented annually to distinguished recipients.

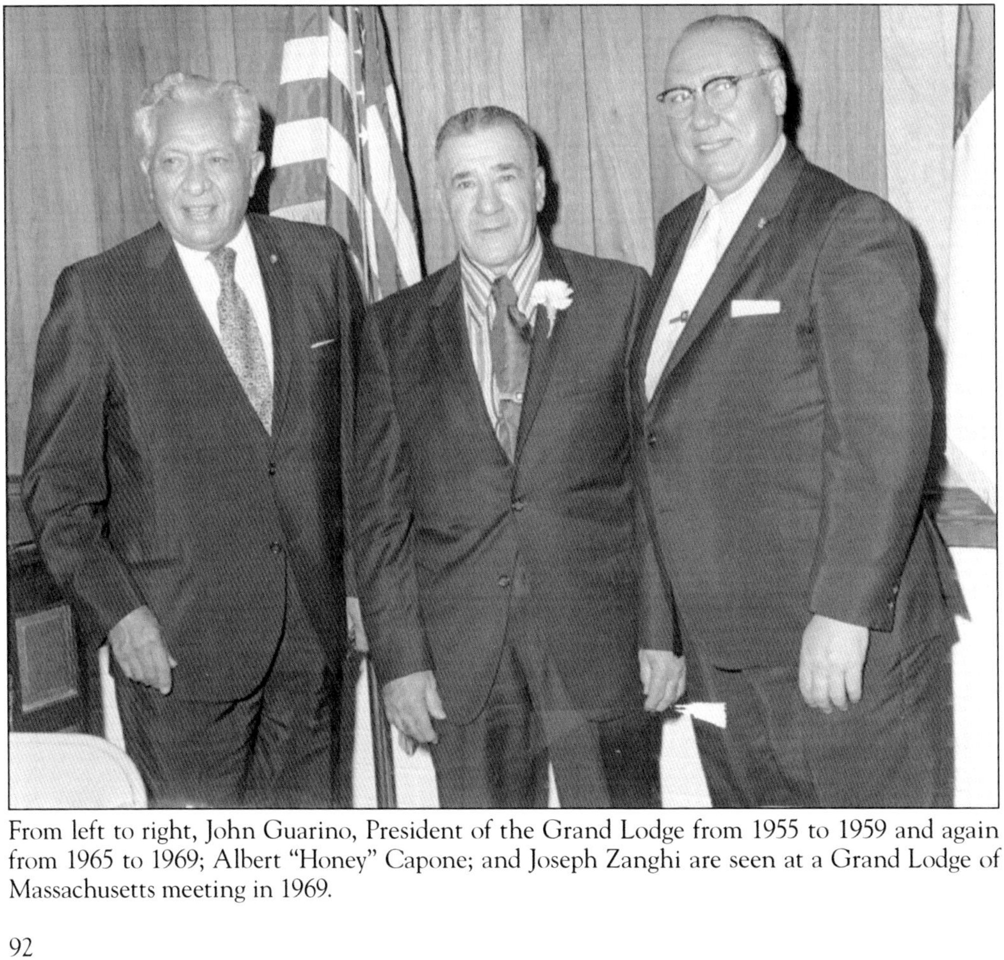

From left to right, John Guarino, President of the Grand Lodge from 1955 to 1959 and again from 1965 to 1969; Albert "Honey" Capone; and Joseph Zanghi are seen at a Grand Lodge of Massachusetts meeting in 1969.

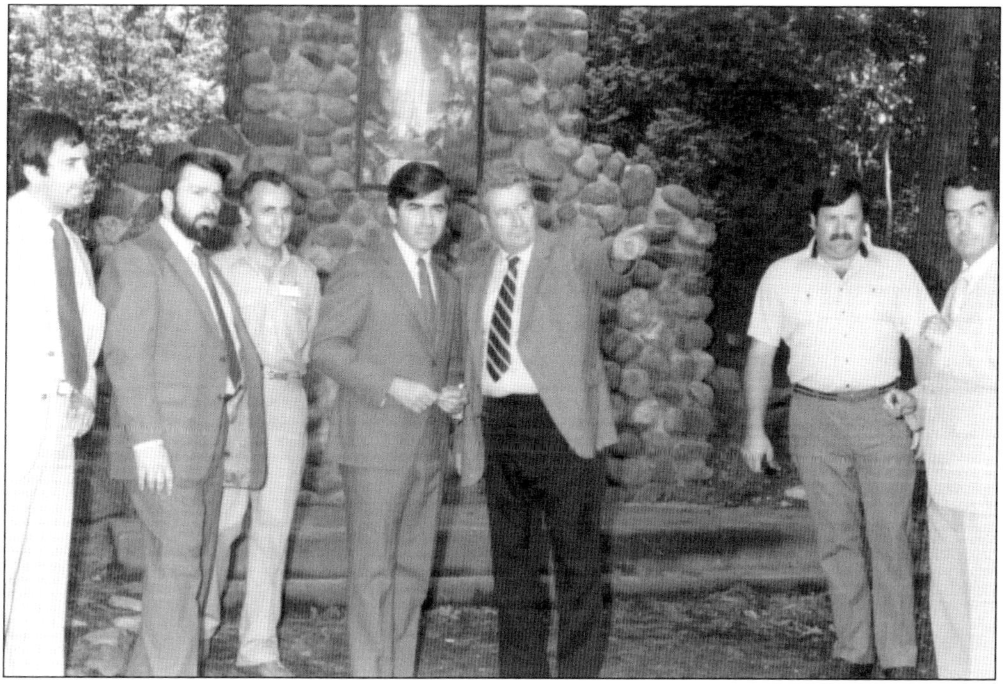

Gov. Michael Dukakis visited Taunton Park in 1983. From left to right are David Gay, President of Peter B. Gay Lodge #540; John Cammarata; unidentified; Governor Dukakis; Robert DeCroce; Robert Cammarata; and Joseph Amaral, former mayor of Taunton.

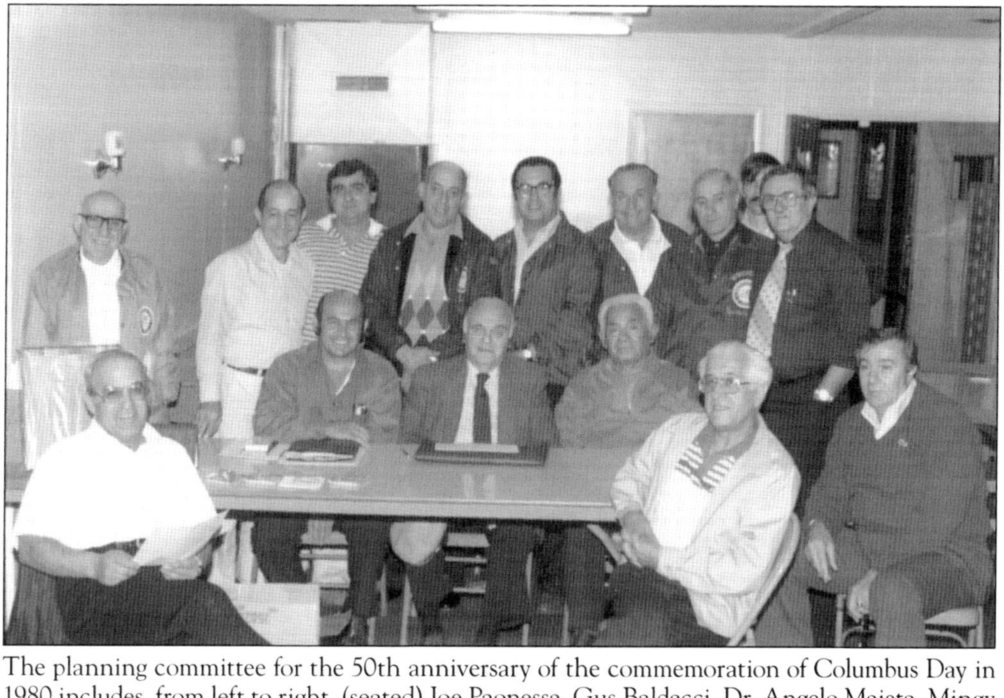

The planning committee for the 50th anniversary of the commemoration of Columbus Day in 1980 includes, from left to right, (seated) Joe Paonessa, Gus Baldacci, Dr. Angelo Maieta, Mingy Frongillo, Joe Cabral, and Frank Dattilo; (standing) Randy Kazazian, Rudy Fiore, Bob Cintolo, Bob Fiore, Tony Staffieri, Jerry Borcini, Bill Fiore, Donald Morris, and Joe Ciarcia.

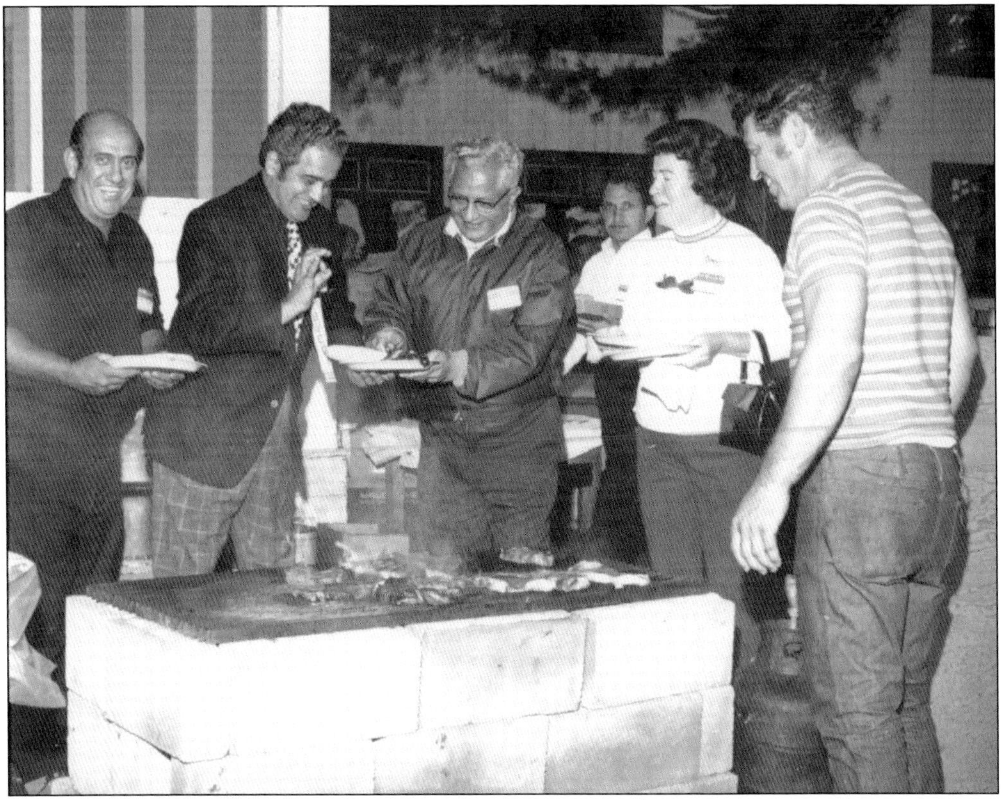

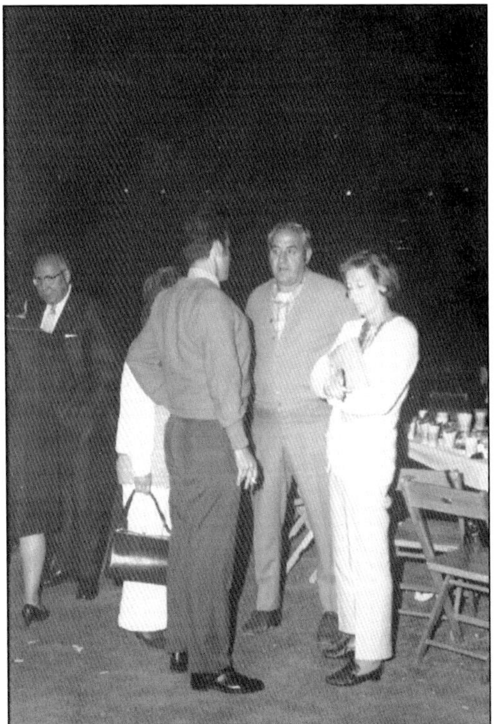

A summer barbecue was one way to entertain lots of members of the Sons of Italy. Standing around a charcoal grill with sizzling steaks are, from left to right, Vinny Massa; Joe Furnari; John Guarino, who served as President of the Grand Lodge from 1955 to 1959 and again from 1965 to 1969; Pat Guarino; and John Spatuzza.

In conversation at a Sons of Italy event are, from left to right, unidentified, Joe Zanghi, unidentified, John Saladino, State President Henry Frissora, and Mary Frissora.

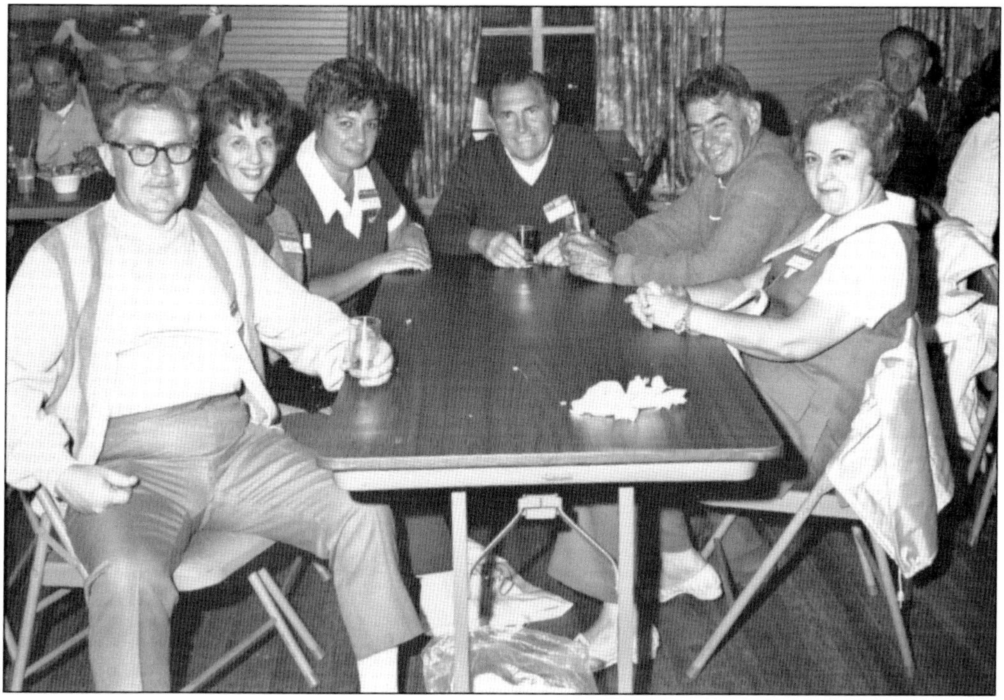

Enjoying one another's company are, from left to right, Jack Cincotti, Josephine Falco, Jennie Polcari, Jerry Polcari, Gene Falco, and Helen Cincotti.

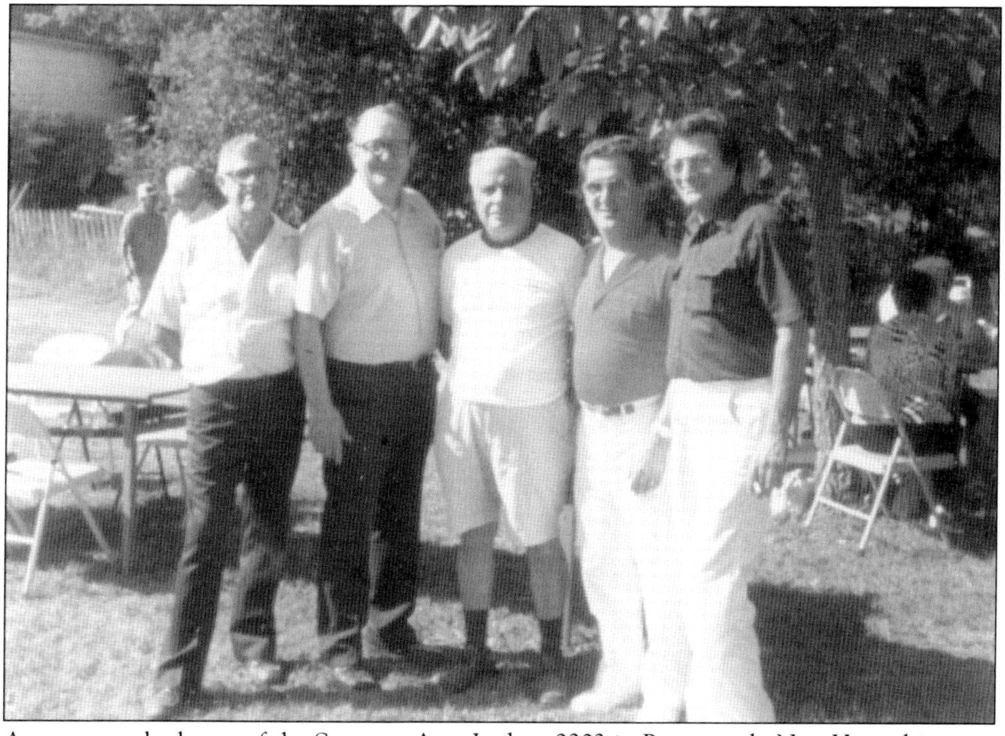

At a summer barbecue of the Seacoast Area Lodge #2303 in Portsmouth, New Hampshire, are, from left to right, Al DiPaolo, Aldo Caira, Carl Anania, Tom DeNofio, and Frank Costanzo.

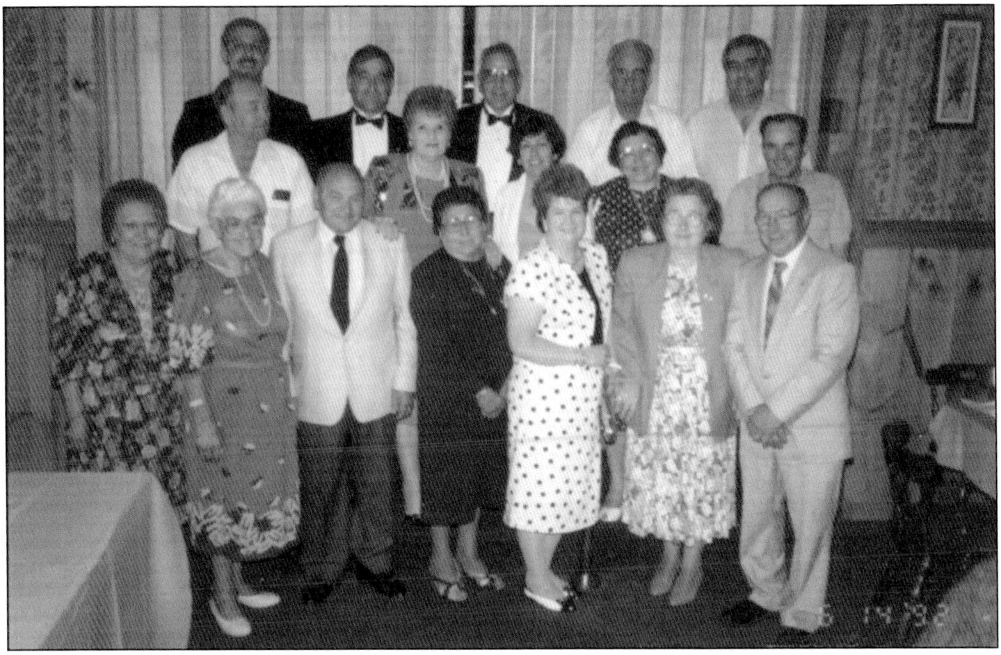

Celebrating their 15th anniversary in 1992 are members of the Granite State Lodge #2380 in Rochester, New Hampshire. From left to right are (first row) Mary Arigo, Rose Russo, Gus DiPrizio, Evelyn DiPrizio, Yvonne Patton, Enid DiPrizio, and John DiPrizio; (second row) William Campbell, Margaret Campbell, Betty Mae Russo, Evelyn Luongo, and Vincent Luongo; (third row) John Krekorian, John Mammone, Salvatore Farina, Nicholas Luongo, and Anthony Lazzaro.

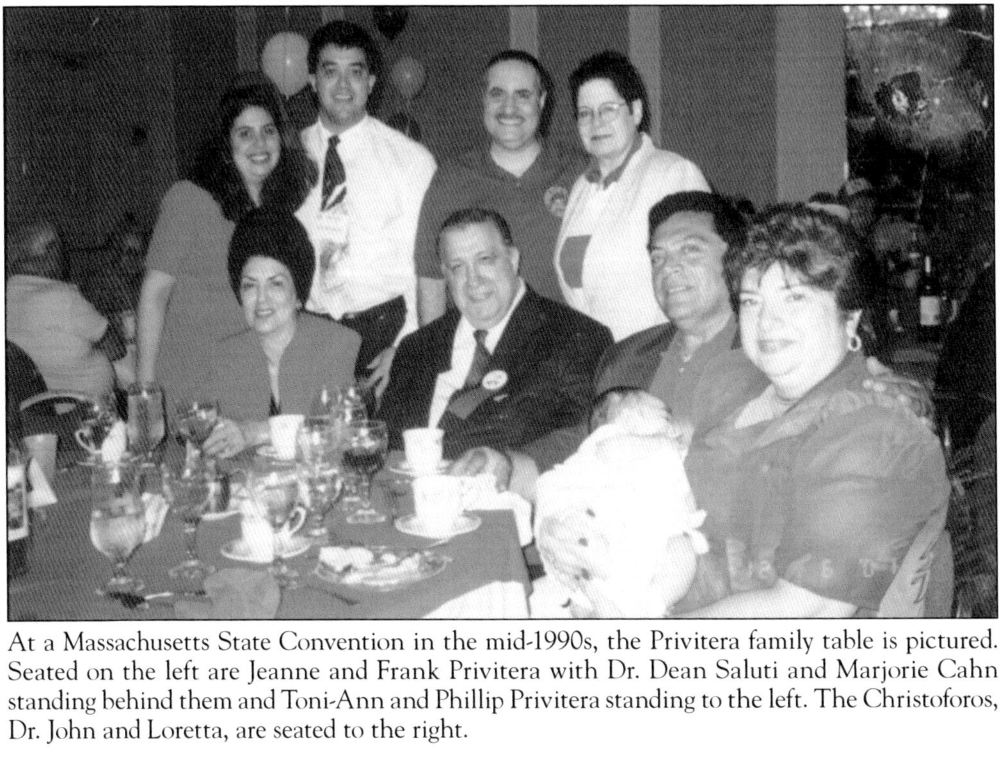

At a Massachusetts State Convention in the mid-1990s, the Privitera family table is pictured. Seated on the left are Jeanne and Frank Privitera with Dr. Dean Saluti and Marjorie Cahn standing behind them and Toni-Ann and Phillip Privitera standing to the left. The Christoforos, Dr. John and Loretta, are seated to the right.

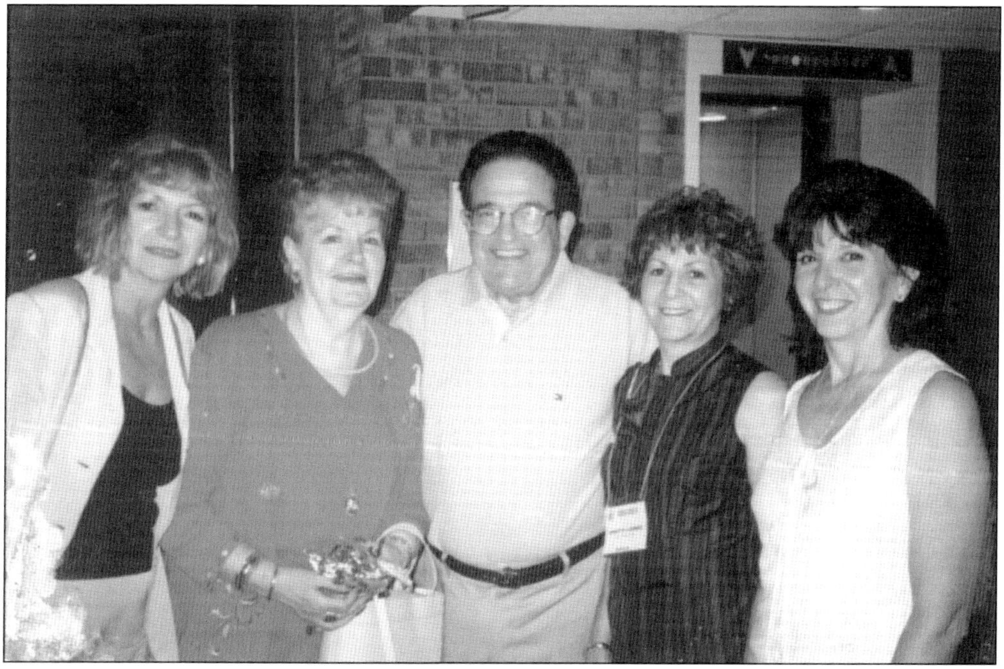

At a Massachusetts State Convention in the Catskills in the mid-1990s are, from left to right, Kathy Cammarata, Natalie and Angelo Furnari, Annette Luongo, and Pam Donnaruma.

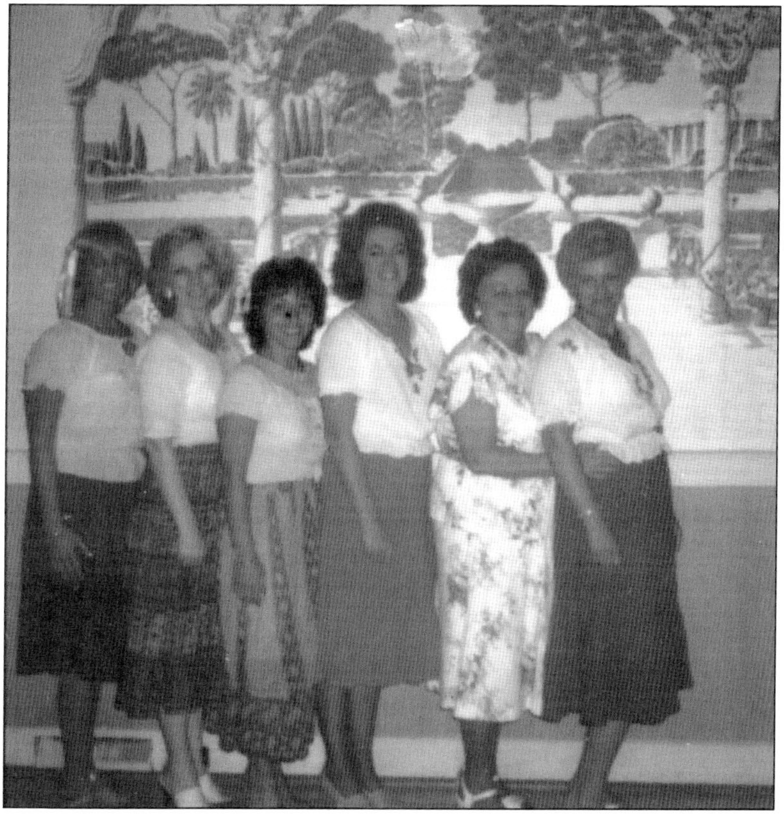

A lineup of members of the Braintree Ladies Lodge #1422 includes, from left to right, Paula Willey, Marta Googins, Joan Fabrizio, Joanne Pistorino, Midge Zanghi, and Corinne Fasano.

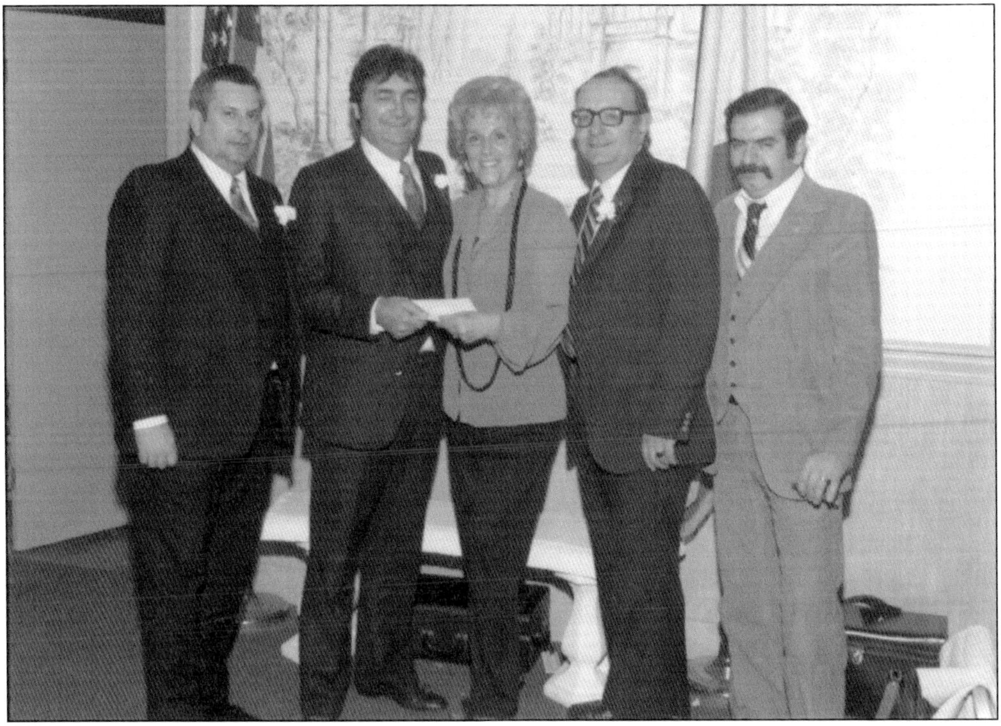

Members of the Massimo D'Azeglio Lodge #760 in Braintree present a check to the Grand Lodge of Massachusetts in 1971. From left to right are John Larmey, unidentified, Irene Granara, Grand Lodge of Massachusetts President Aldo A. Caira, and Bobby Pistarceno.

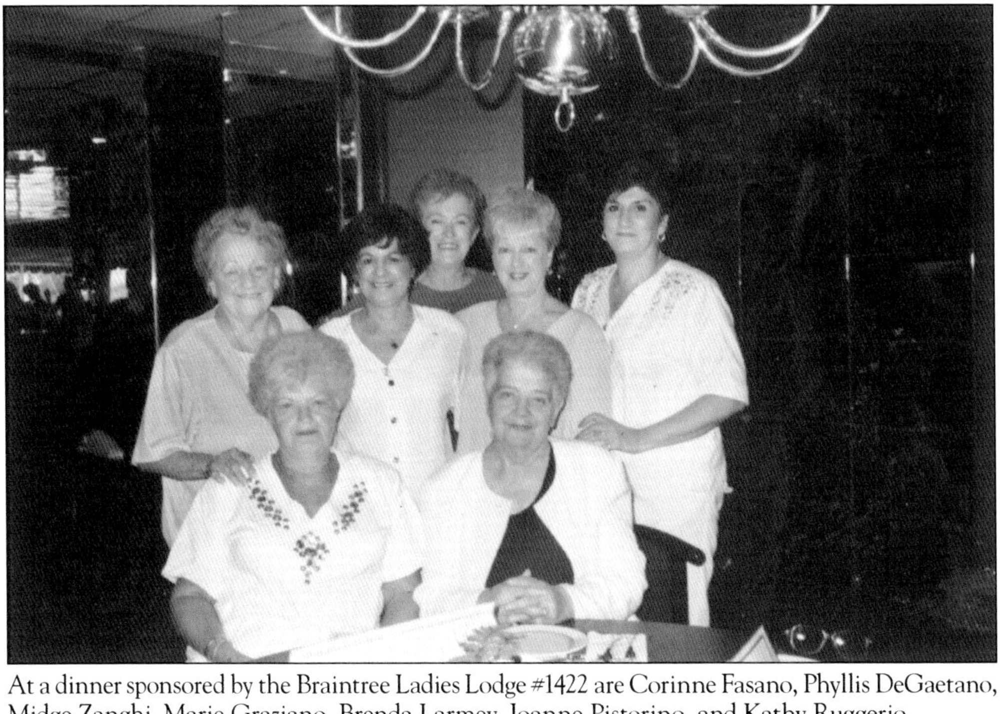

At a dinner sponsored by the Braintree Ladies Lodge #1422 are Corinne Fasano, Phyllis DeGaetano, Midge Zanghi, Marie Graziano, Brenda Larmey, Joanne Pistorino, and Kathy Ruggerio.

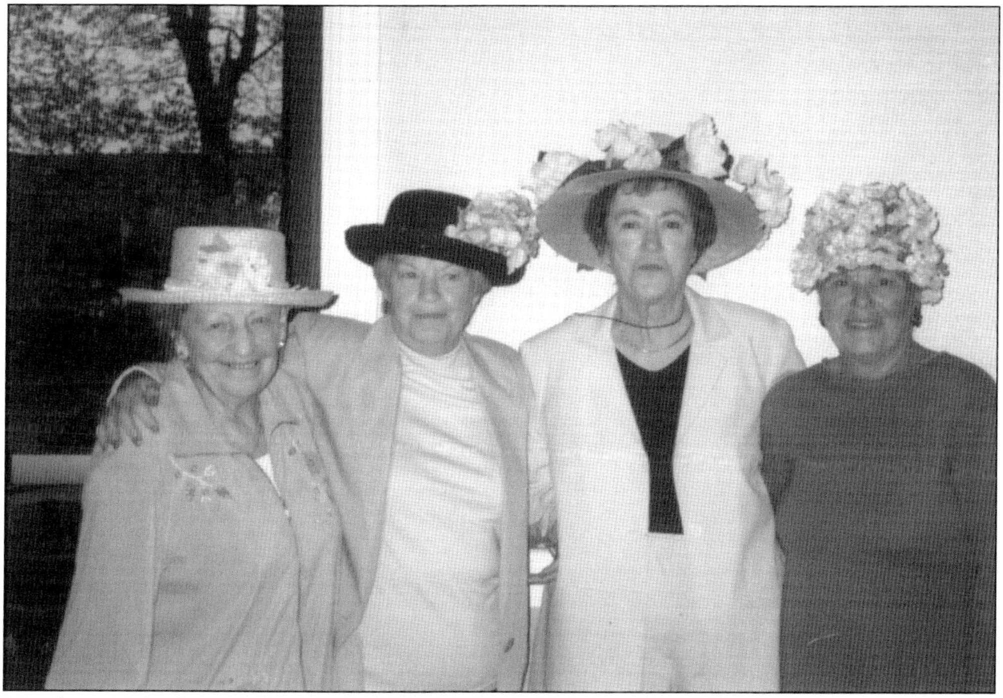

Members of the Braintree Ladies Lodge #1422 sponsored a Hat Party in May 2003 to celebrate spring. From left to right are Midge Zangi, Corinne Fasano, Joanne Pistorino, and Ellie Leo.

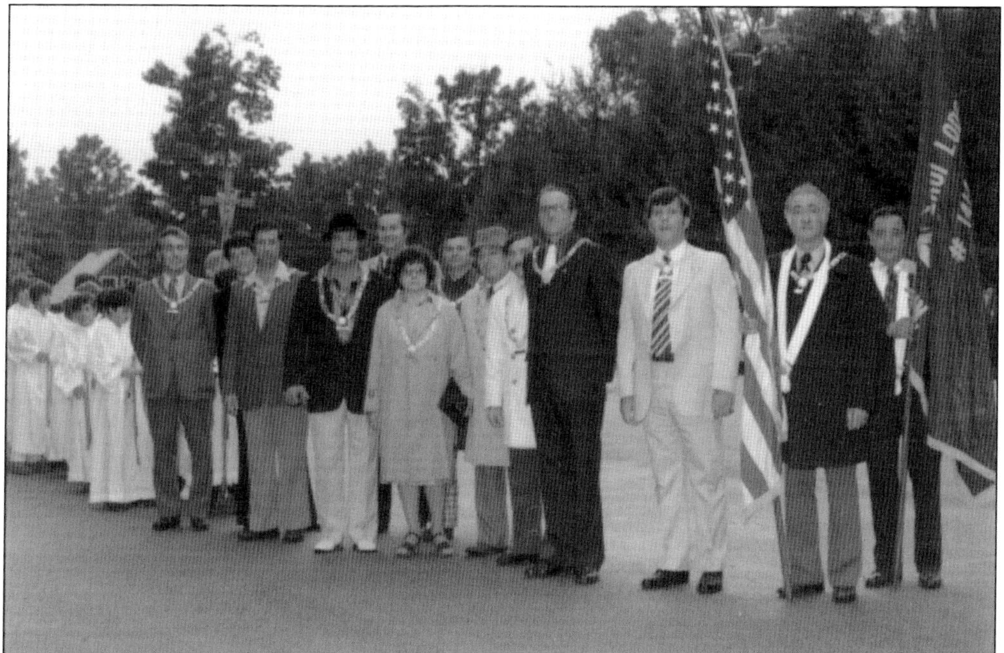

Celebrating the Feast of St. Rocco in 1980 are members of the Quattro Eroi Lodge #1414 in Franklin. From left to right are Laurence Molle, Aldo Tenagloia, Jack Nasuti, Louis Arcaro, Roger Rondeau, Vilma Pascucci, Raymond Mastromatteo, Eugene Pascucci, Ralph Tenaglia, James Ficco, John Vozzella, Steve Dalo, and Lawrence Orlando.

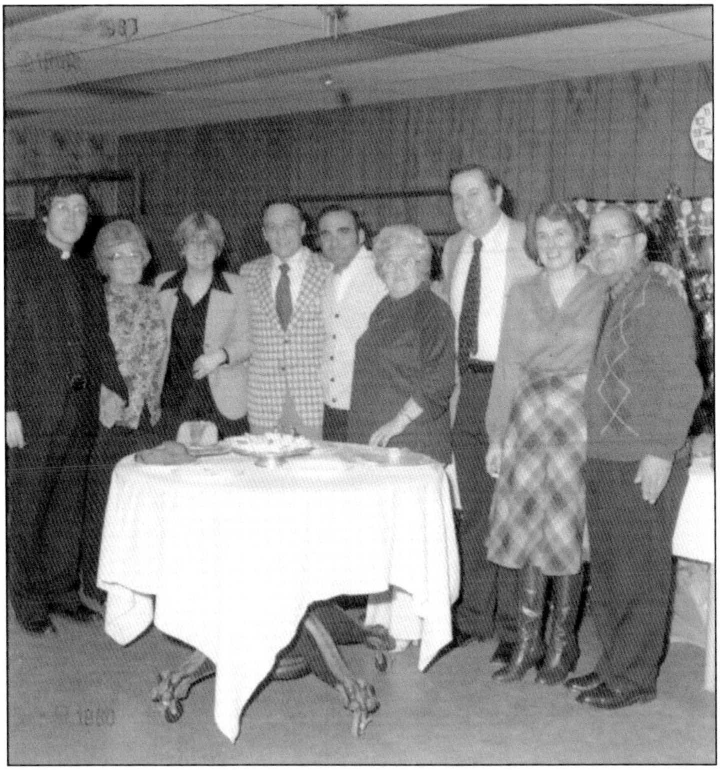

Enjoying a social event in 1980 are members of the Quattro Eroi Lodge #1414 in Franklin. From left to right are Reverend Rocco, Michael Guerino, Sarah Anderson, Donna Oteri, Umberto Tenaglia, Charles Oteri, Carmella Bartolomei, Roger Rondeau, Barbara Rondeau, and Louis Faenza.

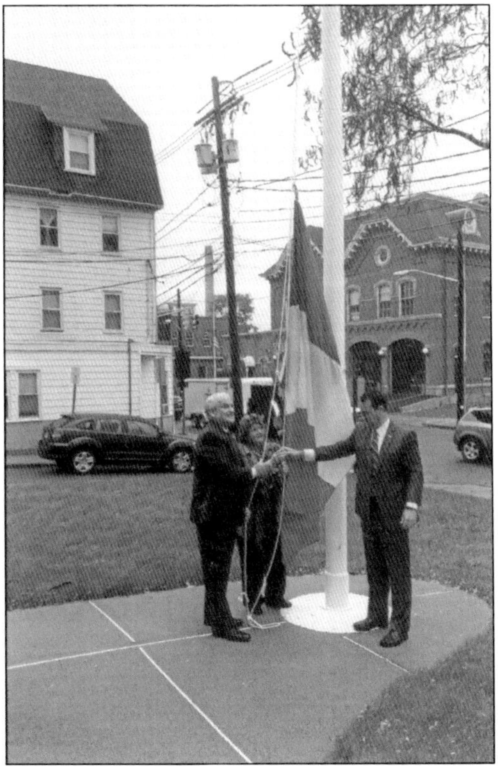

Celebrating Italian Heritage Day in Peabody are Joseph A. Russo, Past President of the Grand Lodge from 1999 to 2003; Angela Fedrico; and Peabody mayor Edward A. Bettencourt Jr. The flag of Italy was hoisted on the flagpole at City Hall by the Peabody Ladies Lodge #1964.

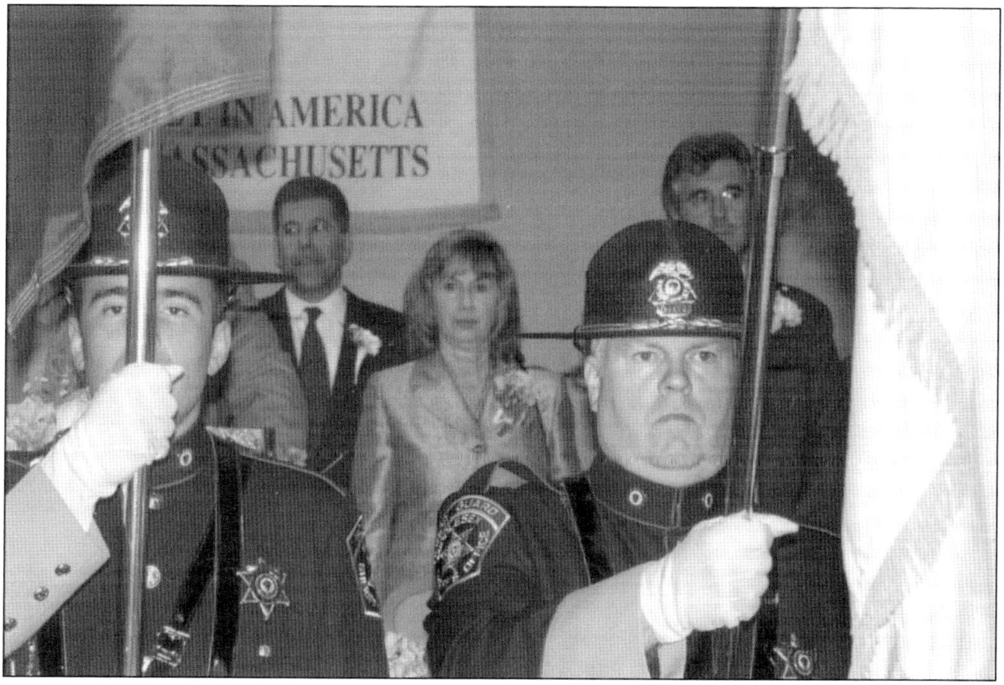

In 2007, then Grand Lodge of Massachusetts President Florence Ferullo Kane is escorted into Law Day at the Marriott in Newton, Massachusetts, with two state guards and the flags of the United States and the Commonwealth of Massachusetts. Law Day was to become part of the Massachusetts Education and Law Awards, a continuation of a long tradition of the Grand Lodge's commitment to social justice, previously known as the Law and Justice Awards.

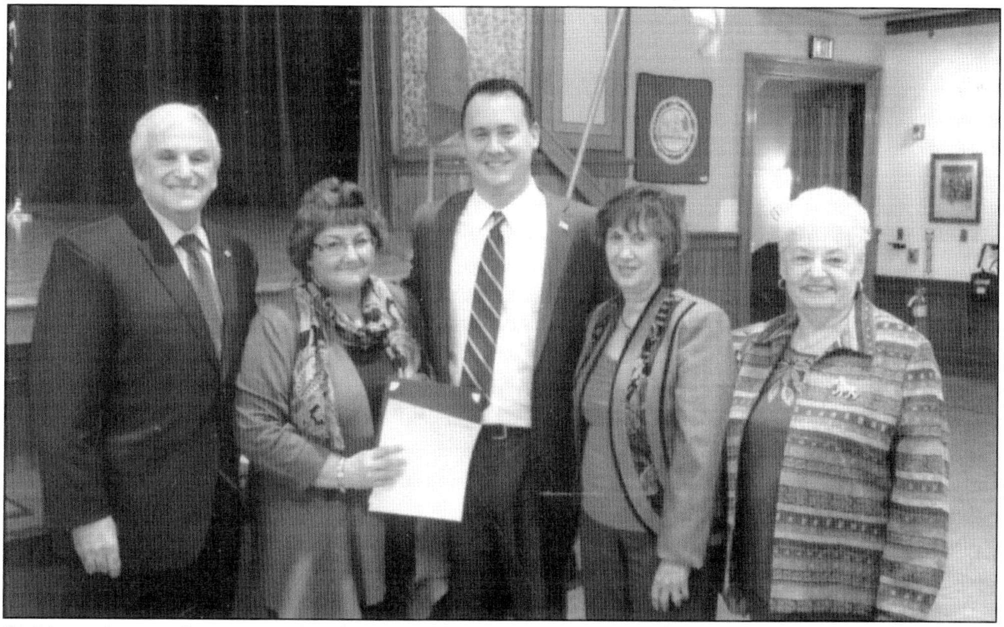

Holding the proclamation of Italian Heritage Day in Peabody are, from left to right, Joseph A. Russo, Angela Federico, Mayor Edward A. Bettencourt Jr. of Peabody, Florence Ferullo Kane, and Marie Jackson.

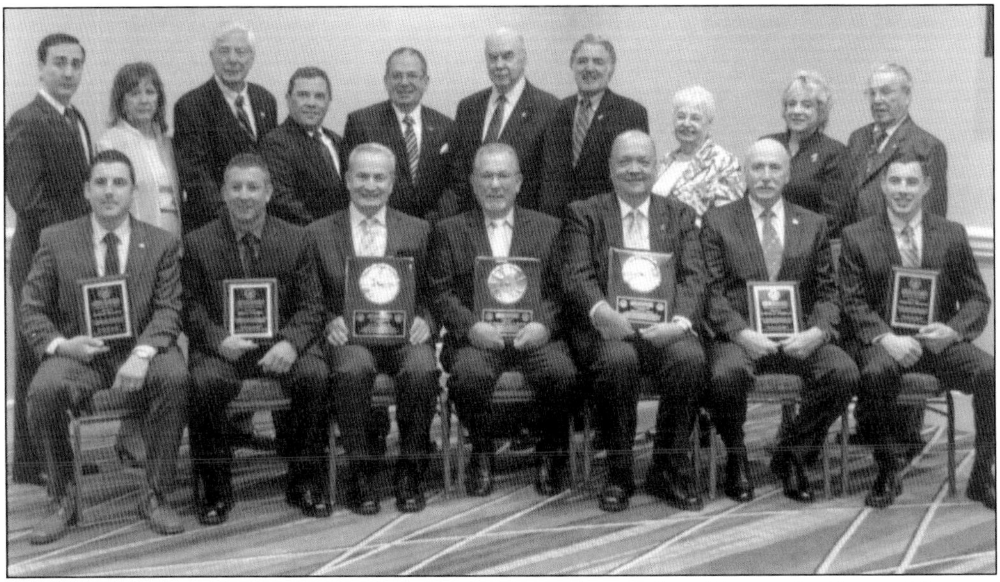

At the first annual Massachusetts Education and Law Awards breakfast at the Boston Marriott Burlington, the Commission for Social Justice awarded plaques to local and state officials for dedicated service to the community. Pictured are (seated) Watertown firefighter Patrick Menton, firefighter James Caruso, Medford police chief Leo A. Sacco Jr., The Honorable Peter C. DiGangi, former Wilmington town manager Michael Caira, Watertown police sergeant Jeffrey J. Pugliese, and patrolman Timothy Menton; (standing) members of the Commission for Social Justice of the Grand Lodge of Massachusetts.

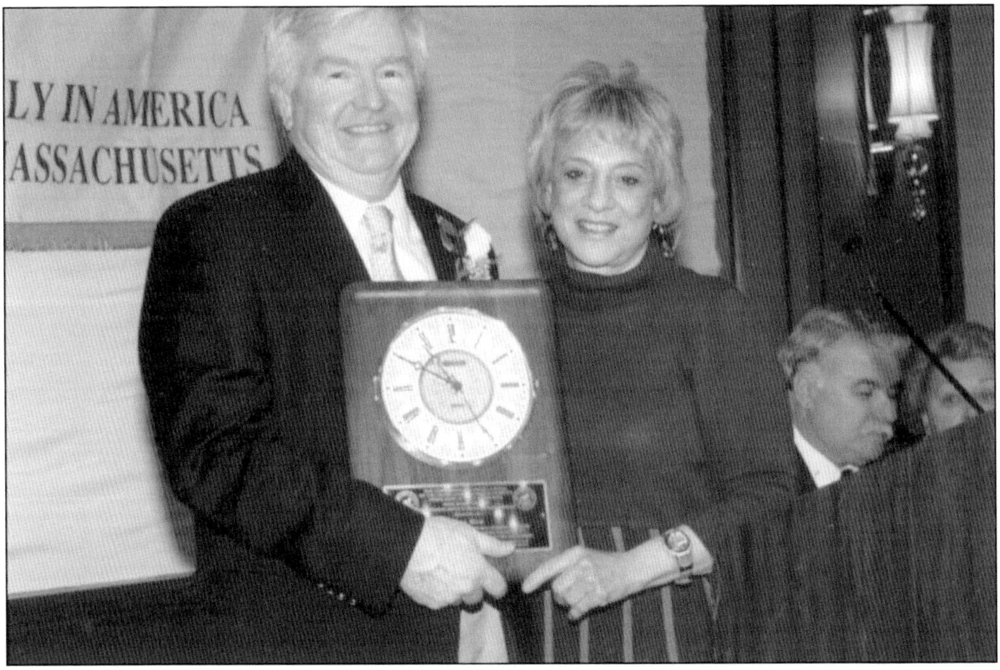

Receiving a Special Recognition Award at the 2011 Law Day breakfast is Dan Rea. Rea is a popular radio host of the program *Nightside with Dan Rea* on WBZ Radio 1030 and a noted journalist. On the right is Marilyn Pettito Devaney, a member of the Governor's Council.

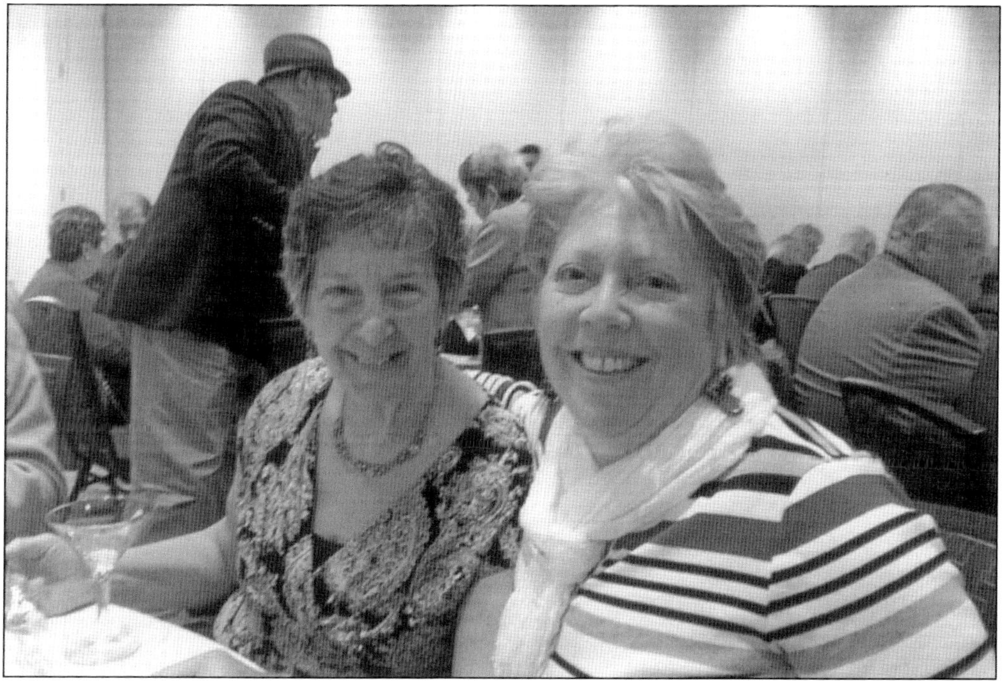

Attending the first annual Massachusetts Education and Law Awards breakfast in 2014 are Donna Killam (right), President of the Victor Emanuel Lodge #1646 in Haverhill, and Lucinda Nolet.

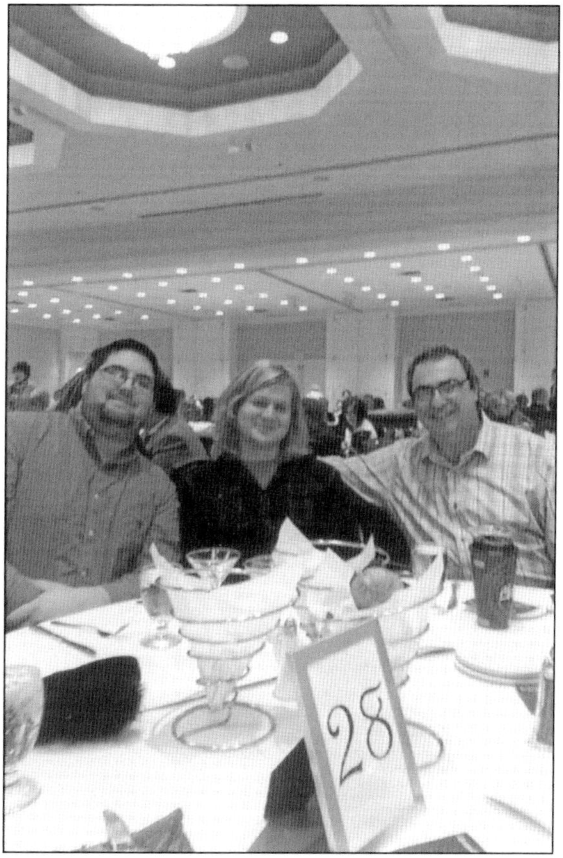

Attending the first annual Massachusetts Education and Law Awards breakfast in 2014 are, from left to right, Anthony LoConte, Nick Thomson, and John Lombari.

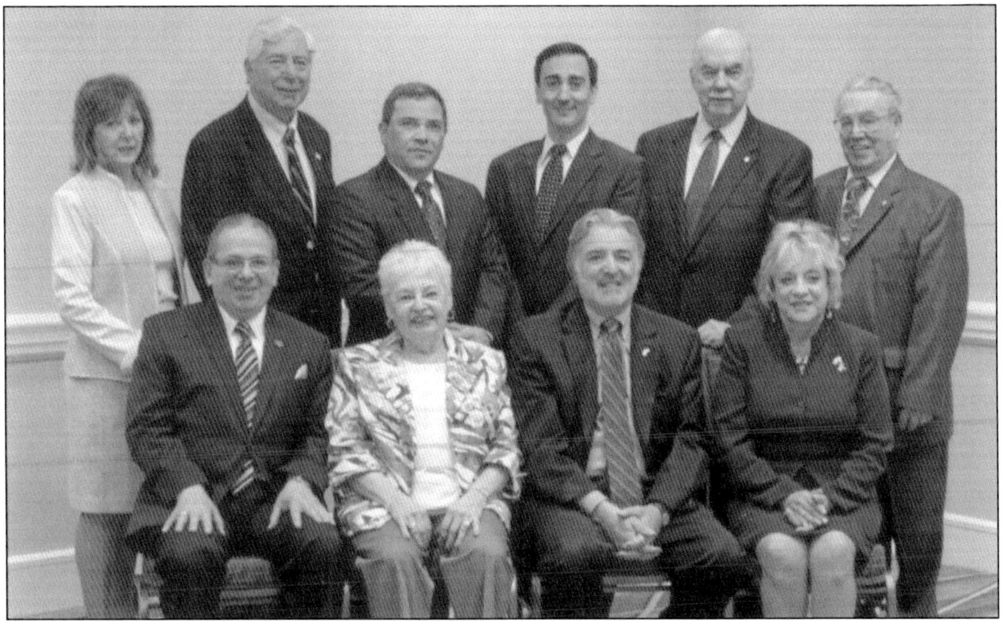

The Commission for Social Justice of the Grand Lodge of Massachusetts members include, from left to right, (seated) Richard Vita, Esq.; Marie Jackson; Chairman Albert DeNapoli, Esq.; and Marilyn Pettito Devaney; (standing) Pamela Donnaruma; Charles H. Perenick; Robert Orsi, Esq.; Carmine Rullo; Vice Chairman Don McGowan; and liaison Stephen Cozzaglio.

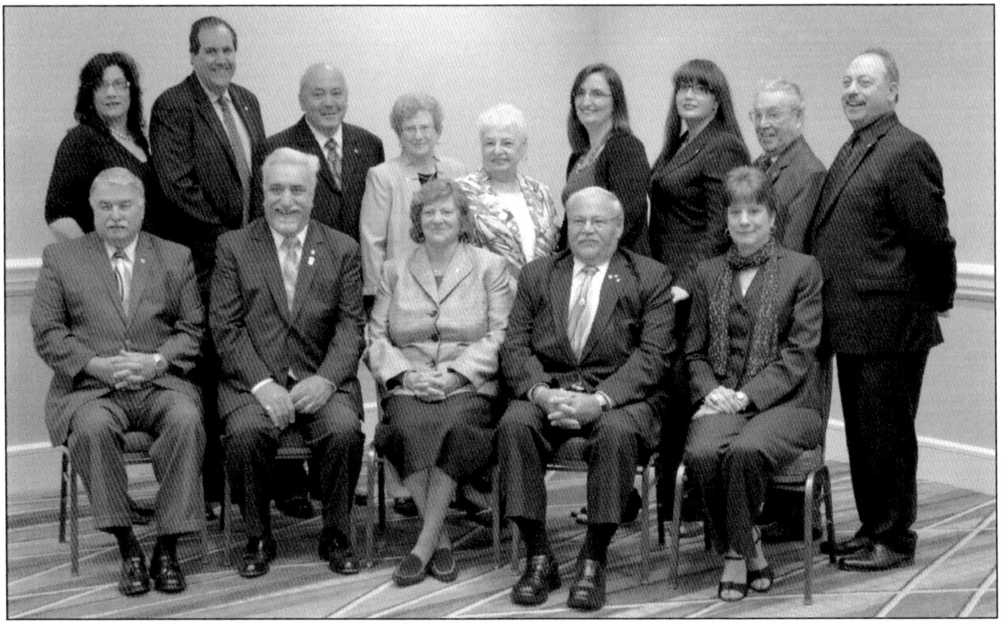

The State Council at the 2014 Massachusetts Education and Law Awards is pictured here. From left to right are (seated) Immediate Past President James DiStefano, State First Vice President Antonio Sestito, State President Carmelita Bello, State Second Vice President Ron Hill, and State Orator Denise Furnari; (standing) State Financial Secretary Margaret Olivieri, State Trustees John Argiro, Charles DeStefano, and Mary Ann Bello, State Recording Secretary Marie Jackson, and State Trustees Marisa Ranalli, Marissa Sestito, Stephen Cozzaglio, and Rodolfo Viscomi.

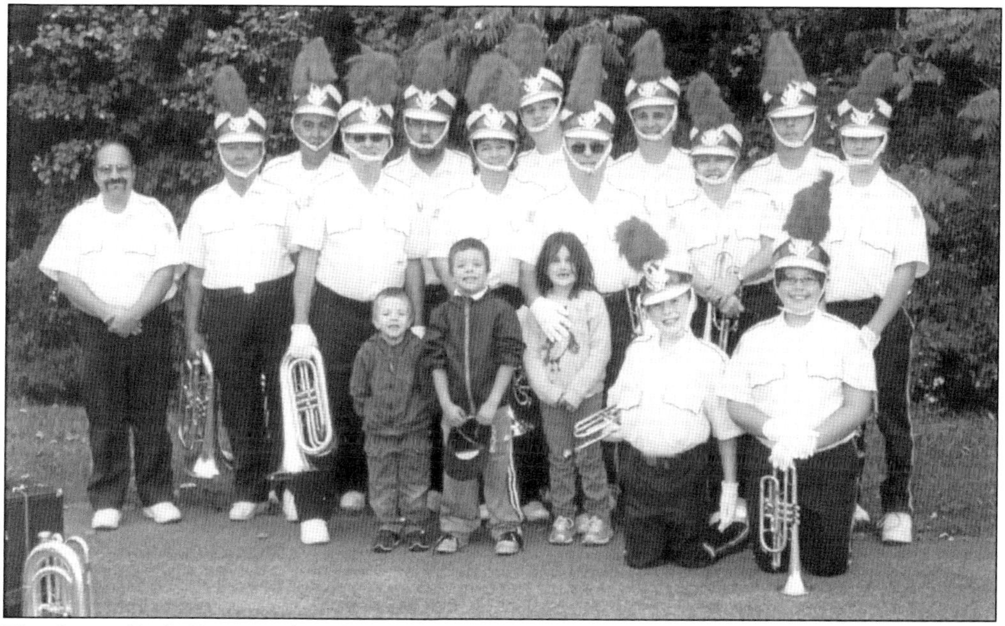

The Sons of Italy Drum and Bugle Corps, which was founded in 1939 and is based in Haverhill, Massachusetts, is a wonderful addition to any parade. Here, the members pose for a photograph in 2014; they are associated with Victor Emanuel Lodge #1646 and are said to be the only remaining Sons of Italy Drum and Bugle Corps in the country.

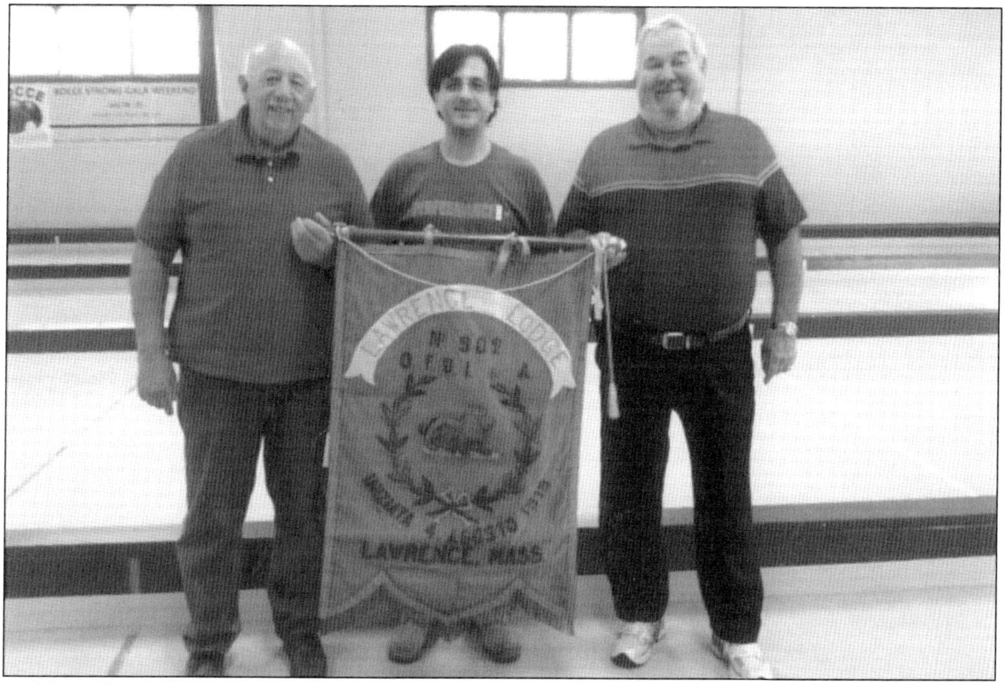

Holding the recently returned Lawrence Lodge #902 banner are, from left to right, Bob Mele, Carmelo Russo, and Mike Cuscia. The banner, dating from 1919, reads "OFDI in A," which were the initials for Ordine Figli d'Italia in America. The banner is now in the possession of the Methuen Lodge #902.

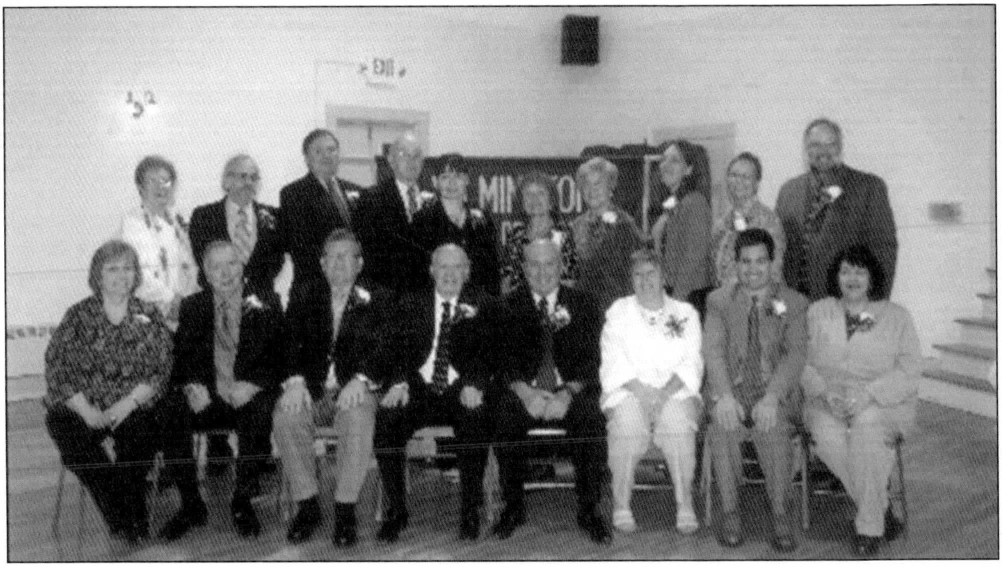

The installation of Angelo Giuseppe Roncalli Lodge #2183 in Wilmington included, from left to right, (seated) Lynne Martell, Jerry Pupa, Robert Dicey, Lou Ricci, Charlie DeStefano, Barbara DeStefano, Chuck Otis, and Betty Sandquist; (standing) Mary Ricci, Lenny Malvone, Joseph Martell, Joseph Maiella, Susan Tocci, Sarah Radomski, Laura Caira, Karen Scalzi, Michele Nortonen, and Kevin Caira.

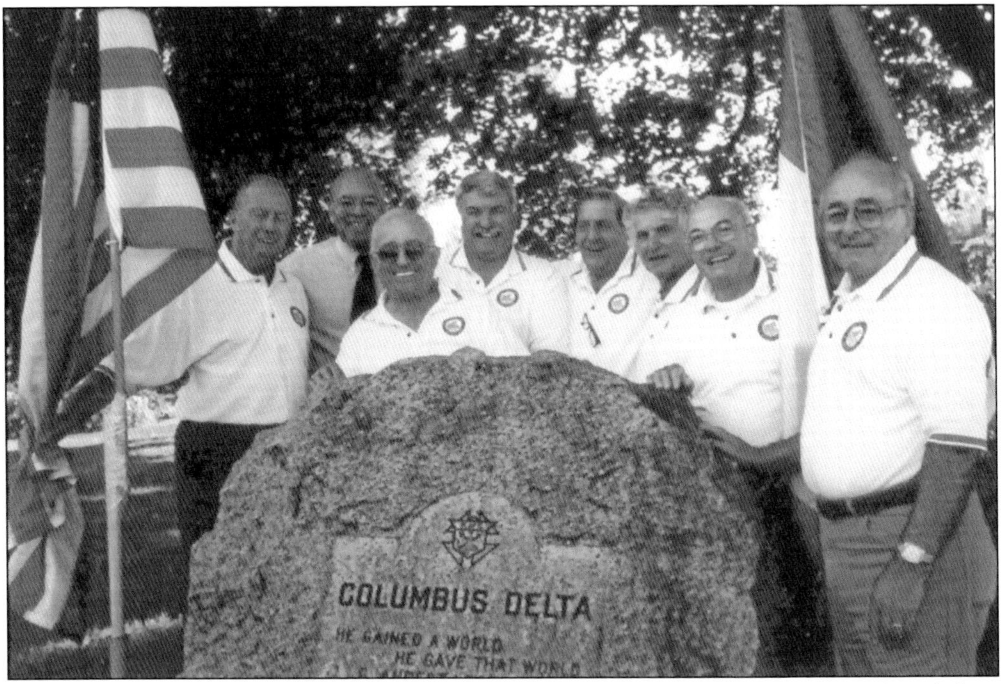

Seen at Columbus Park in Watertown after a Columbus Day parade in 2004 are, from left to right, Fred Pettiglio, Watertown board of selectmen president Clyde Younger; Lodge President Joseph Cimino; State Past President James DiStefano; Lodge Past Presidents Peter Santamaria, Salvatore Pinzone, and Guido DiVecchia, and Lodge Trustee Loreto Leone. This was the Piave Fiume Lodge #1036.

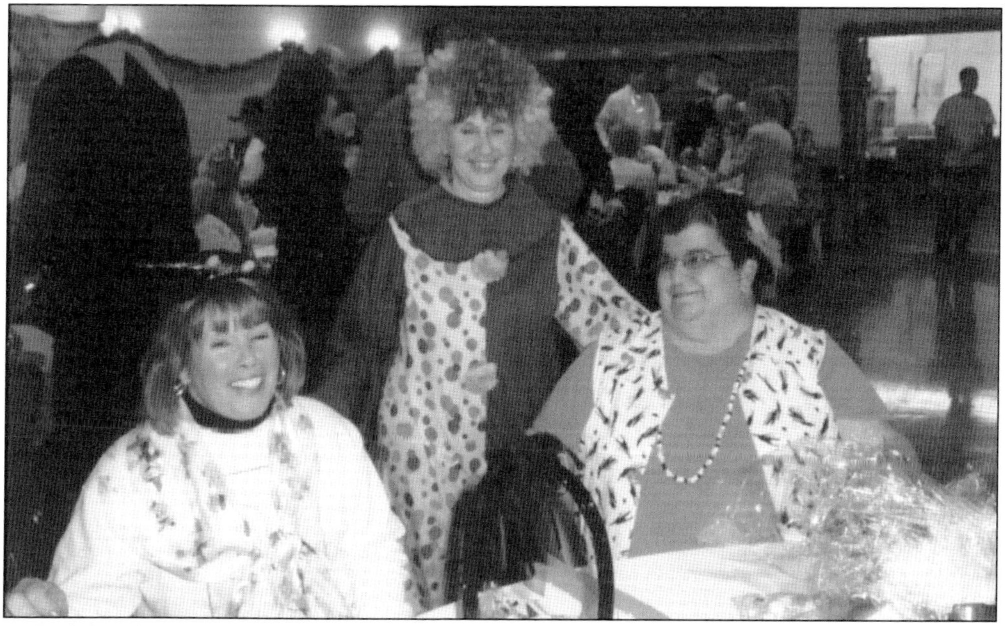

Colorful and fun costumes are often worn to enjoy a Calendar Party, hosted by the Angelo Giuseppe Roncalli Lodge #2183. From left to right are Linda Andreason, Florence Ferullo Kane with a colorful wig and clown outfit, and Anna Sacca.

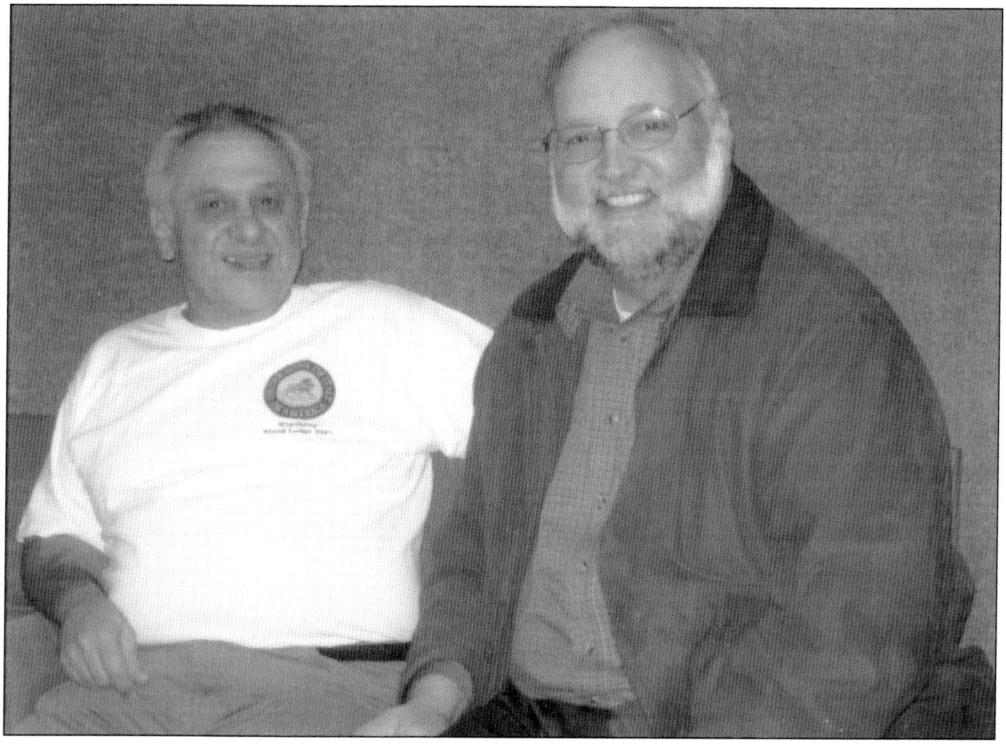

Enjoying one another's company at the Woburn Bowladrome during a bowling tournament in 2011 are Philip R. Boncore (left) and Kevin A. Caira, who served as Presidents of the Grand Lodge in 1993 to 1995 and 2003 to 2007, respectively.

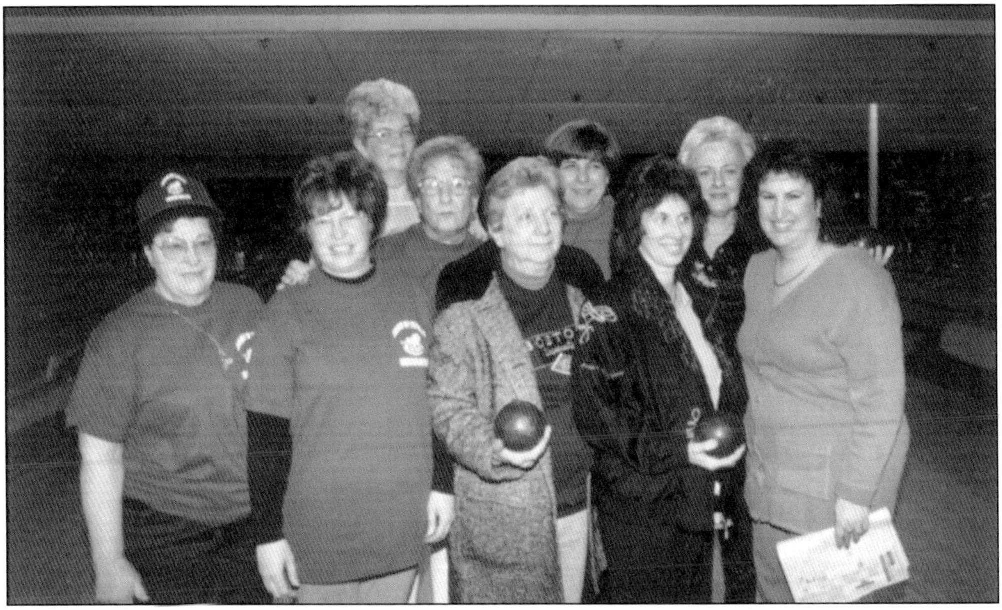

The ladies of the Grand Lodge of Massachusetts and the Wakefield Lodge #1734 are ready to play. In the center holding the balls are Dorothy Berlandi (left) and Florence Ferullo Kane.

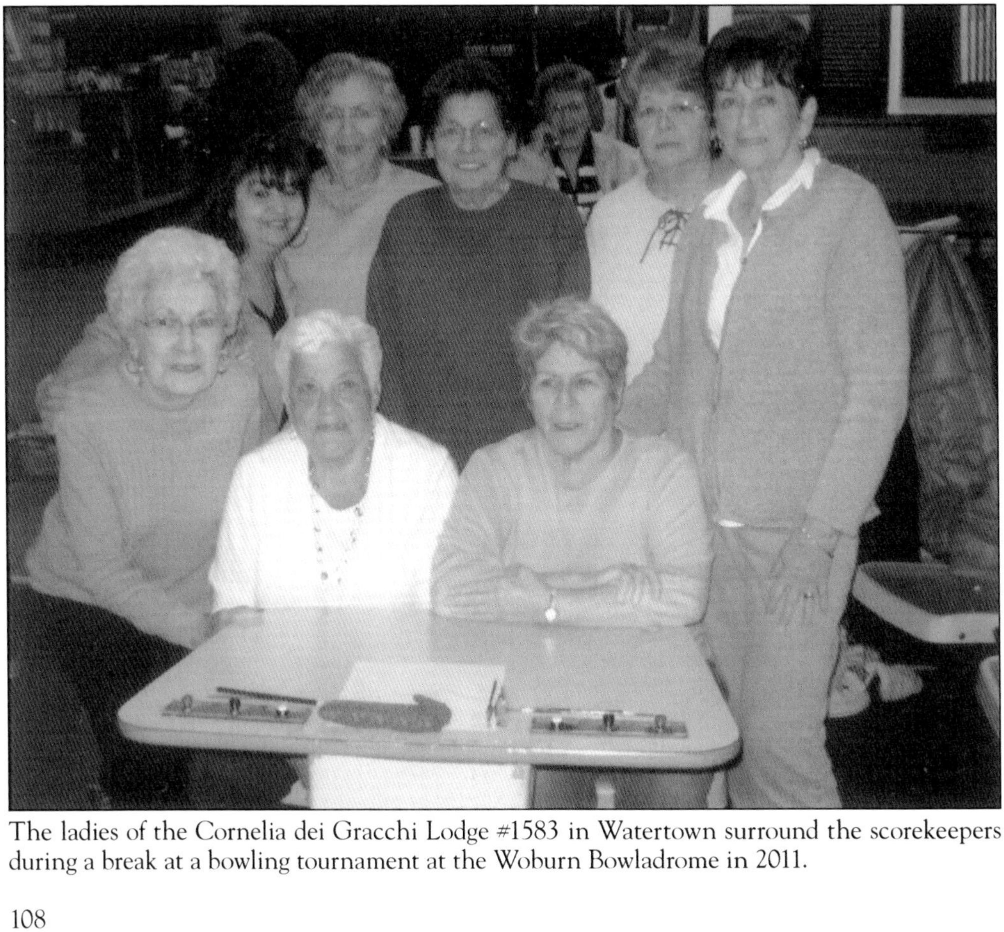

The ladies of the Cornelia dei Gracchi Lodge #1583 in Watertown surround the scorekeepers during a break at a bowling tournament at the Woburn Bowladrome in 2011.

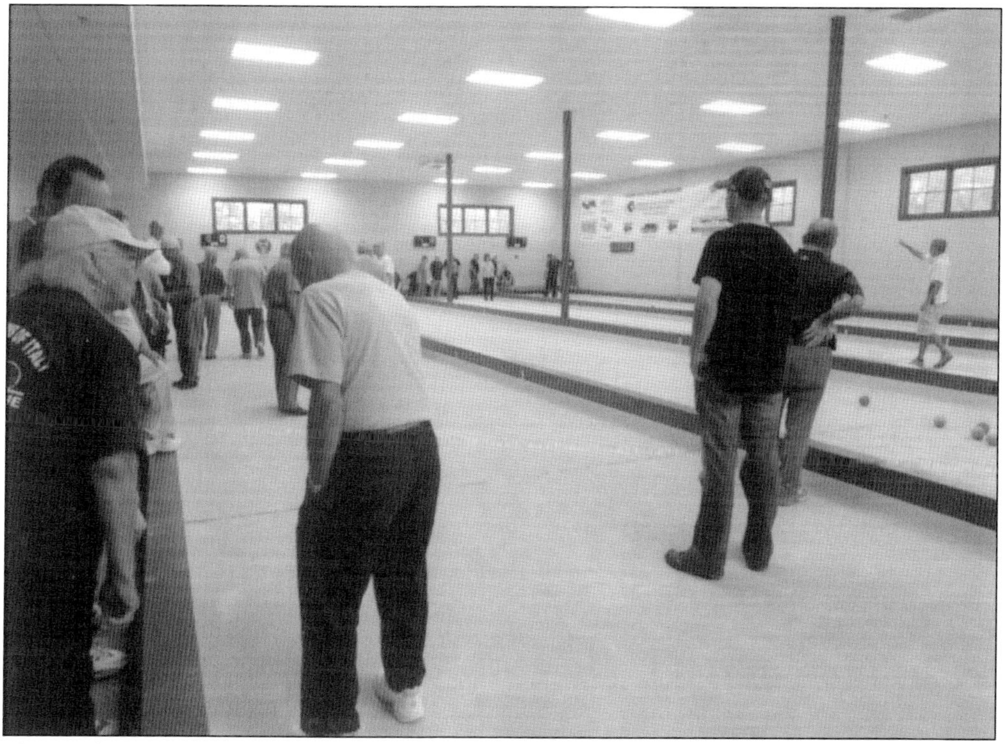

The Methuen Lodge #902 constructed indoor bocce courts in their headquarters, meaning that the game could be played throughout the year, rather than at the mercy of the weather. Here, a group of players enjoys the four courts.

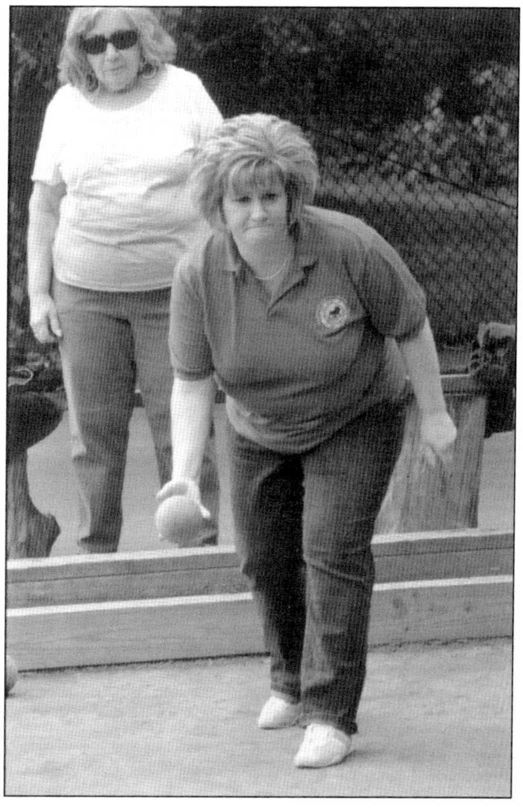

Michelle DiPlacido plays bocce at the Watertown Sons of Italy bocce court in Watertown. There is a decided look of determination as she throws the ball.

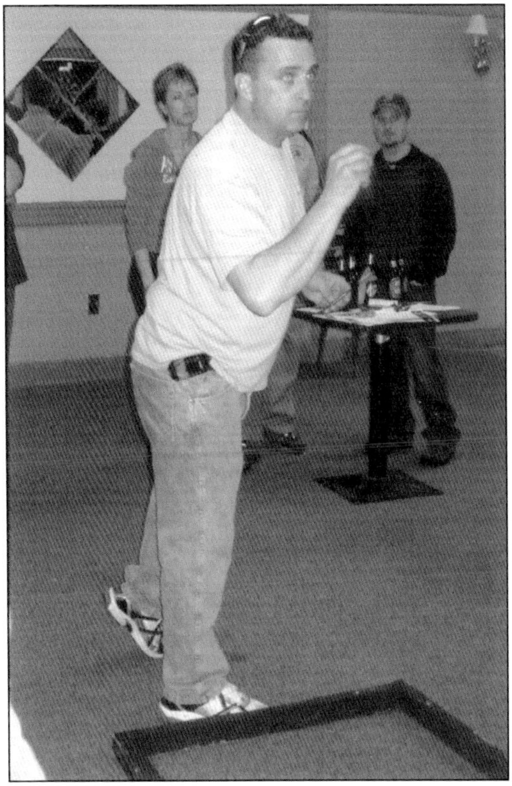

The "Sports Triathlon" included rounds of darts. This player at the Quincy Sons of Italy seems intent on hitting the bull's-eye with his dart.

The Sports Triathlon in 2014 included cribbage at the Quincy Sons of Italy.

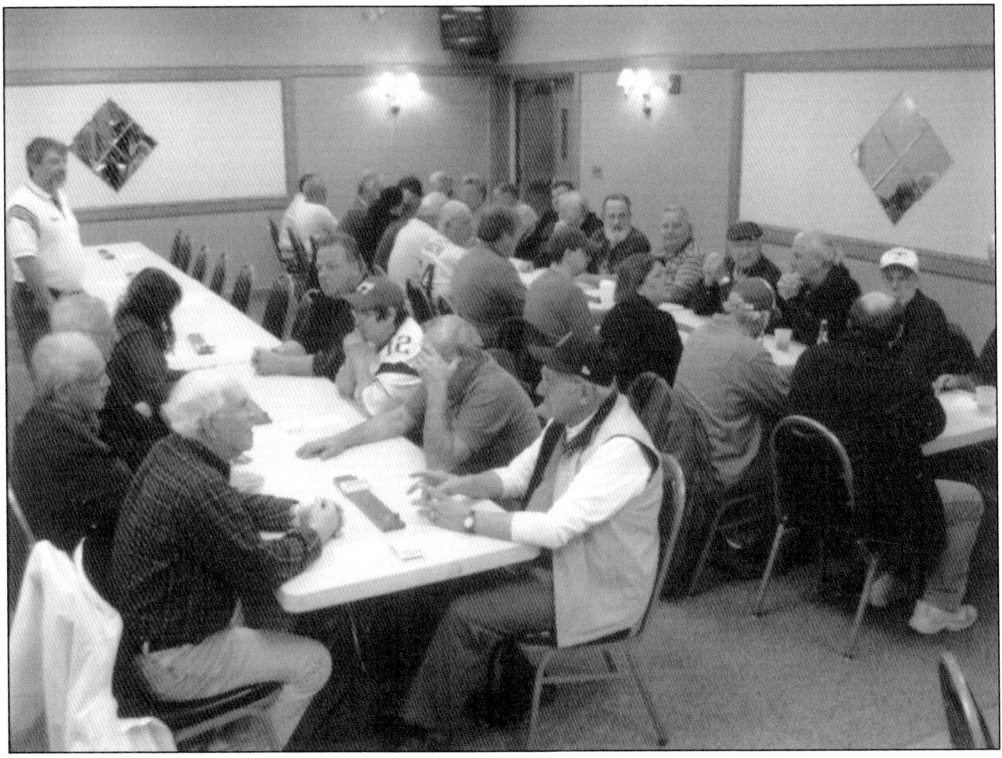

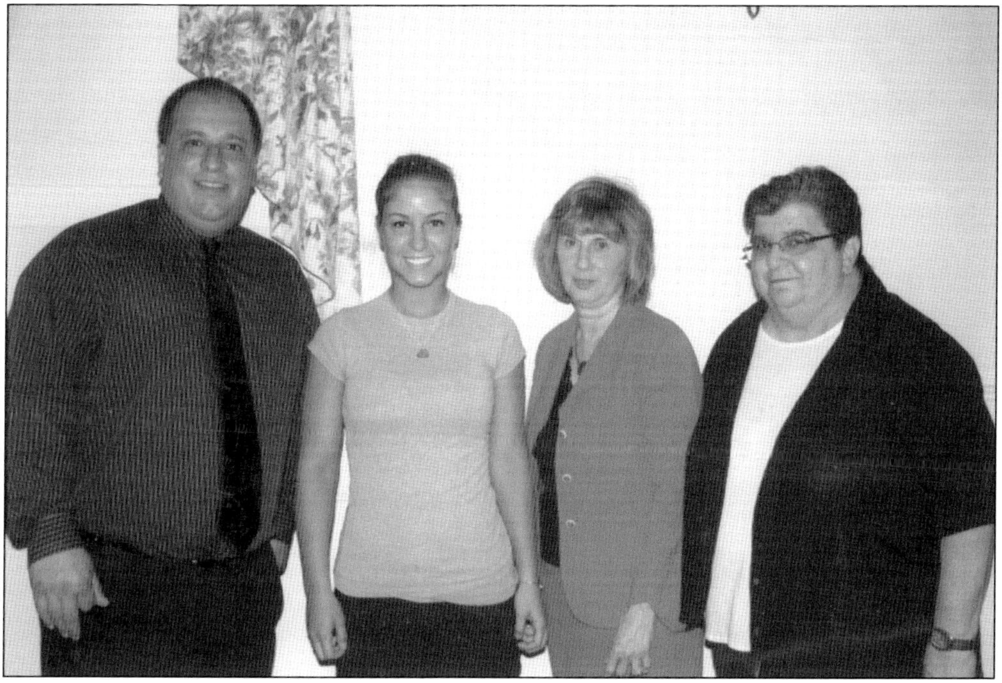

The Sons of Italy awarded a sports scholarship in 2009. From left to right are Steven Cedrone, the Sports Commission Chairman; the scholarship recipient; Florence Ferullo Kane; and Anna Sacca.

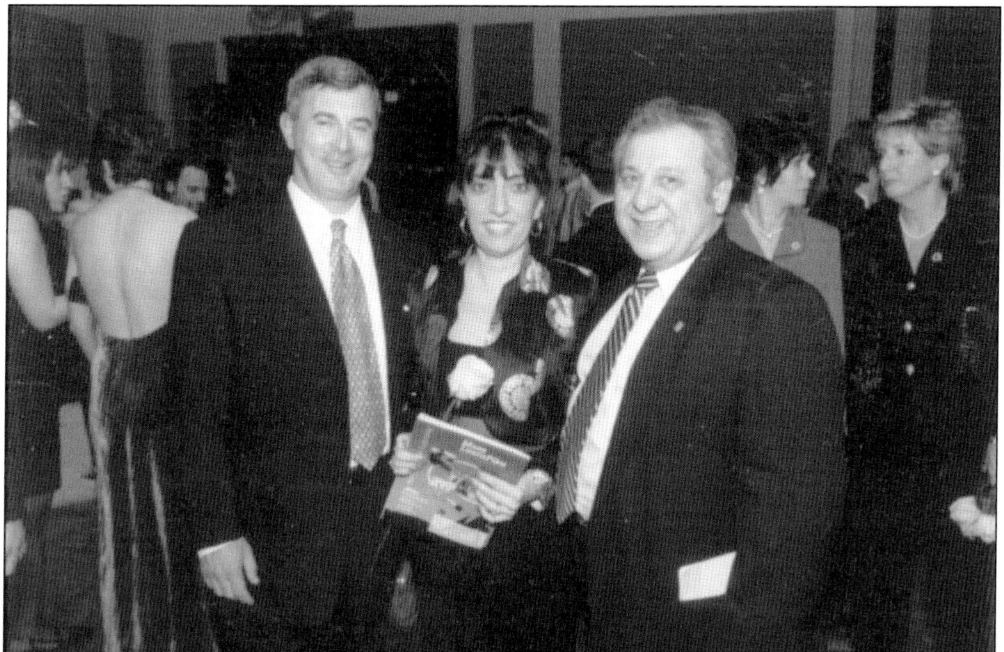

From left to right in 1999 are Gov. Paul A. Celucci, Goldie Boncore, and Philip R. Boncore, who had served as President of the Grand Lodge of Massachusetts from 1993 to 1995.

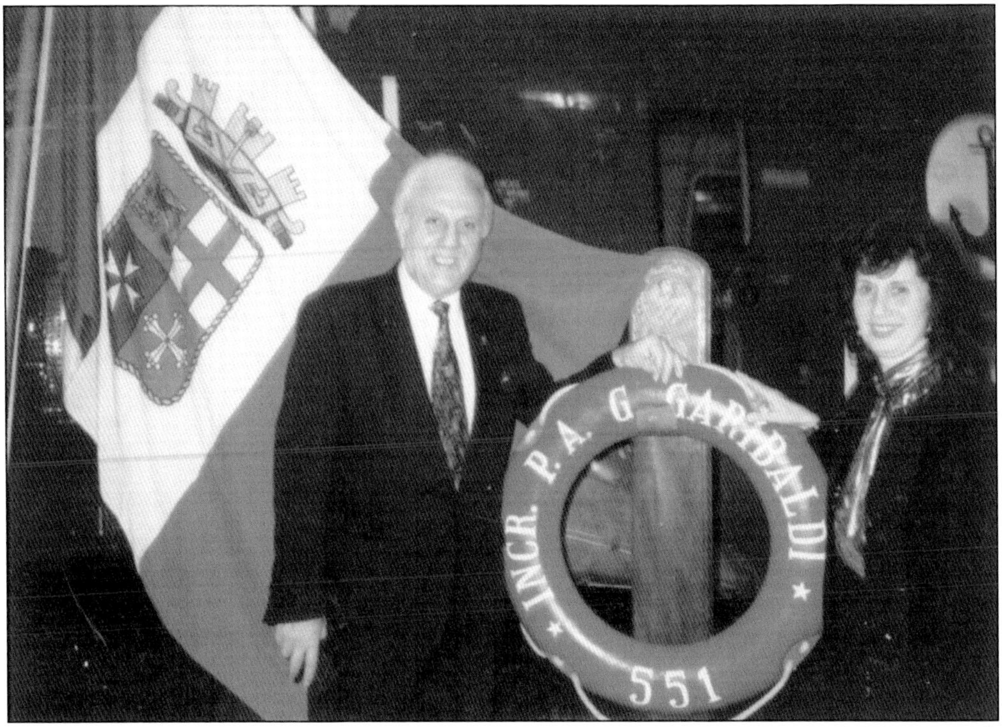

Flanking a life ring from the *Stato Maggiore Della Marina Ufficio D.A.P P.A. Garibaldi* are Joseph S. Giuffrida, who had served as President of the Grand Lodge of Massachusetts from 1995 to 1999, and Florence Ferullo Kane, who served from 2007 to 2009. Note the flag of Italy.

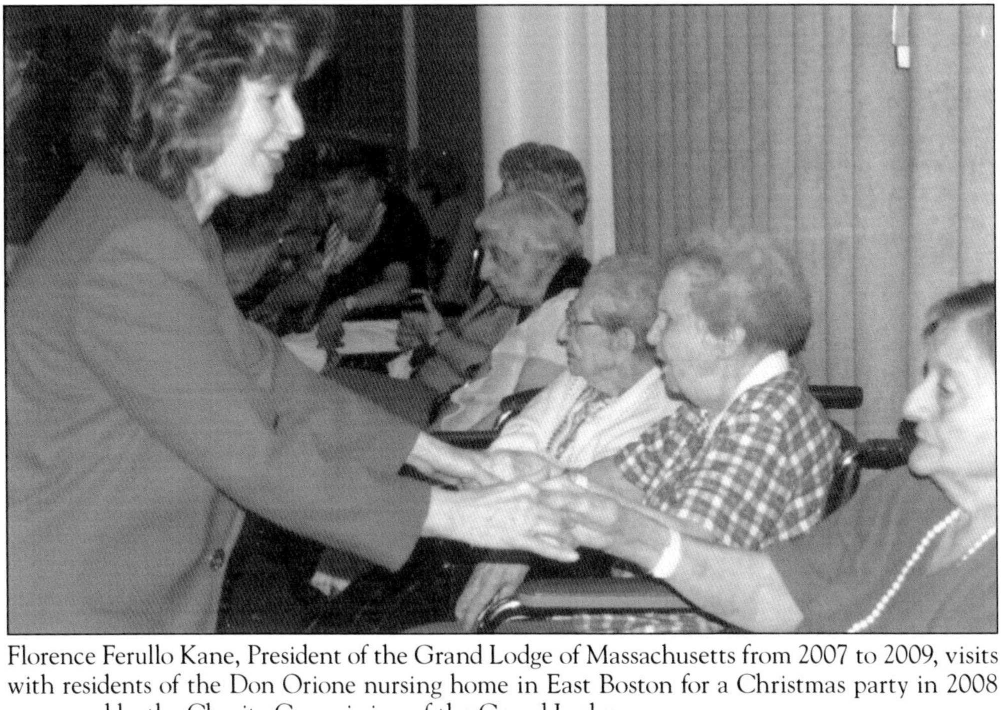

Florence Ferullo Kane, President of the Grand Lodge of Massachusetts from 2007 to 2009, visits with residents of the Don Orione nursing home in East Boston for a Christmas party in 2008 sponsored by the Charity Commission of the Grand Lodge.

Dr. Giuseppe Pastorelli, Consul General of Italy in Boston, on the left, awards a proclamation to James DiStefano bestowing the title of Cavaliere Ordine al Merito della Repubblica Italiana in September 2012. DiStefano served as President of the Grand Lodge of Massachusetts from 2009 to 2013.

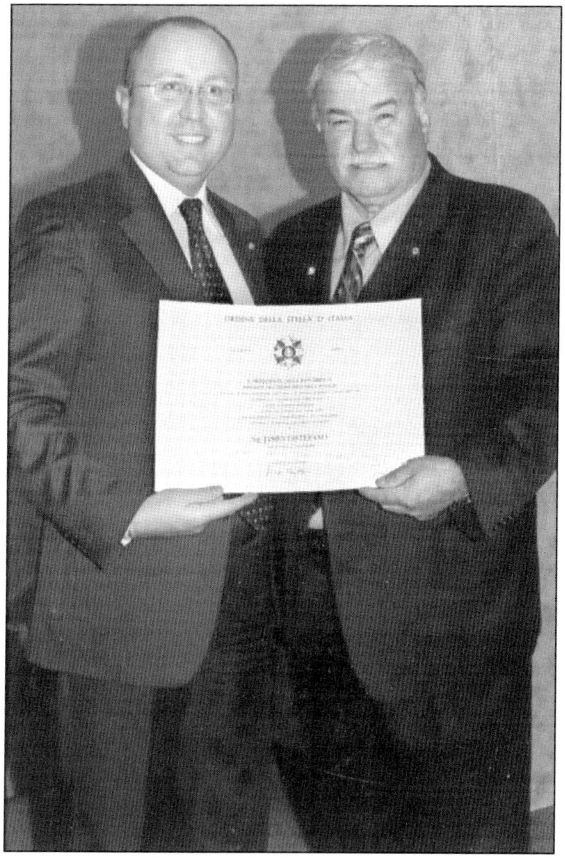

Joe Mantegna, the well-known actor, producer, writer, and director, and Carmelita Bello attended the National Education & Leadership Awards in Washington, D.C., in 2015. Mantegna had served as master of ceremonies numerous times at the event, where outstanding Italian American scholars, business leaders, and humanitarians are honored.

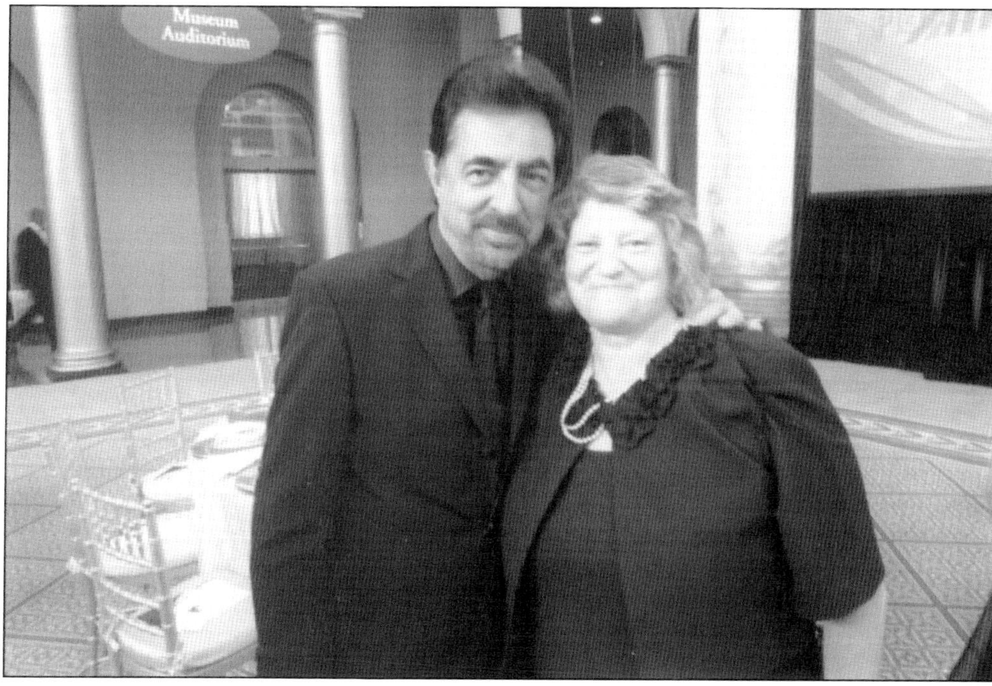

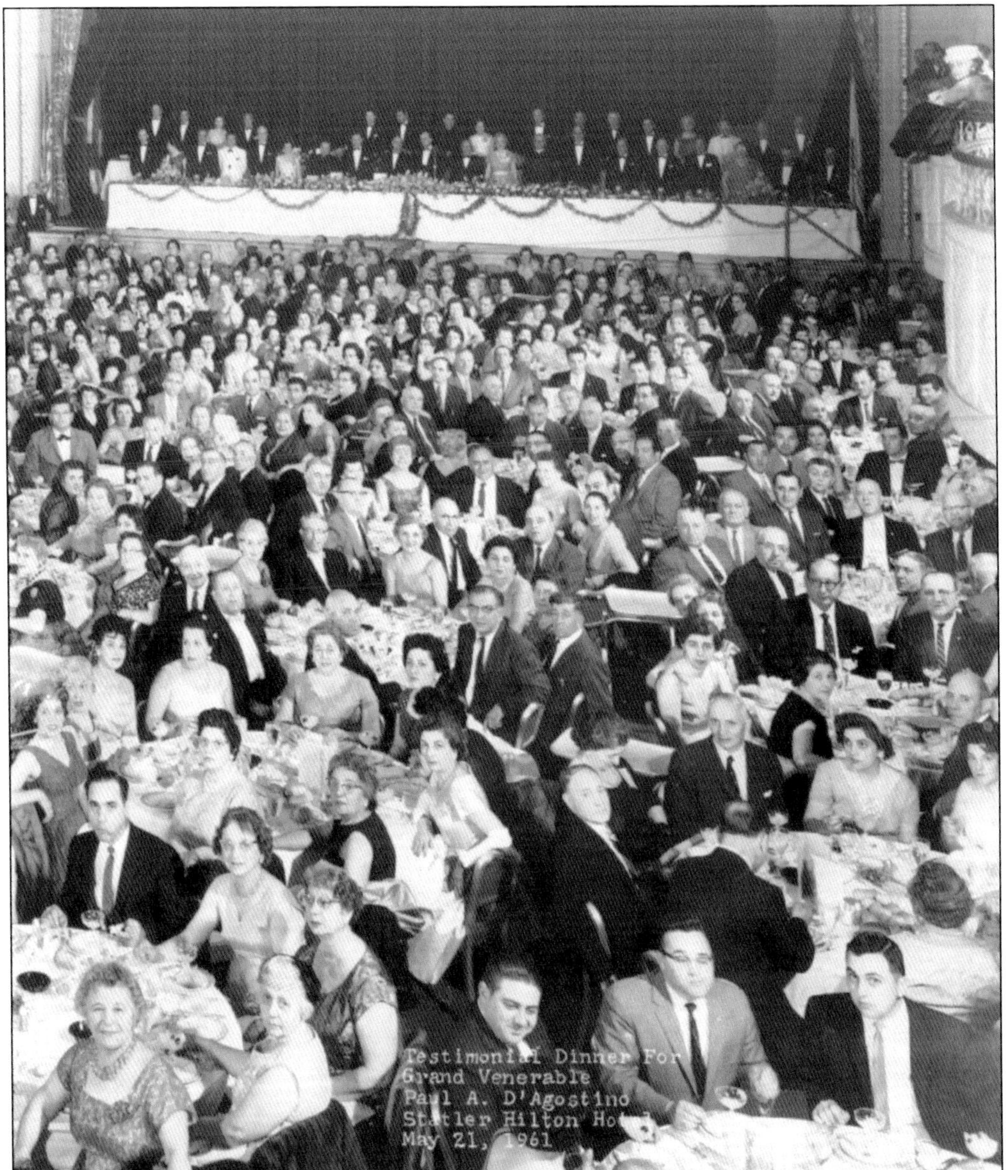

A detail of a very large photograph shows members and friends of the Sons of Italy at a testimonial dinner in honor of Grand Venerable Paul A. D'Agostino, who served as President of the Grand Lodge from 1959 to 1961, on May 21, 1961, at the Statler Hilton Hotel (now the Park Plaza) in Boston, Massachusetts.

Nine

The Centennial Year 2014

L'Anno Centennale 2014

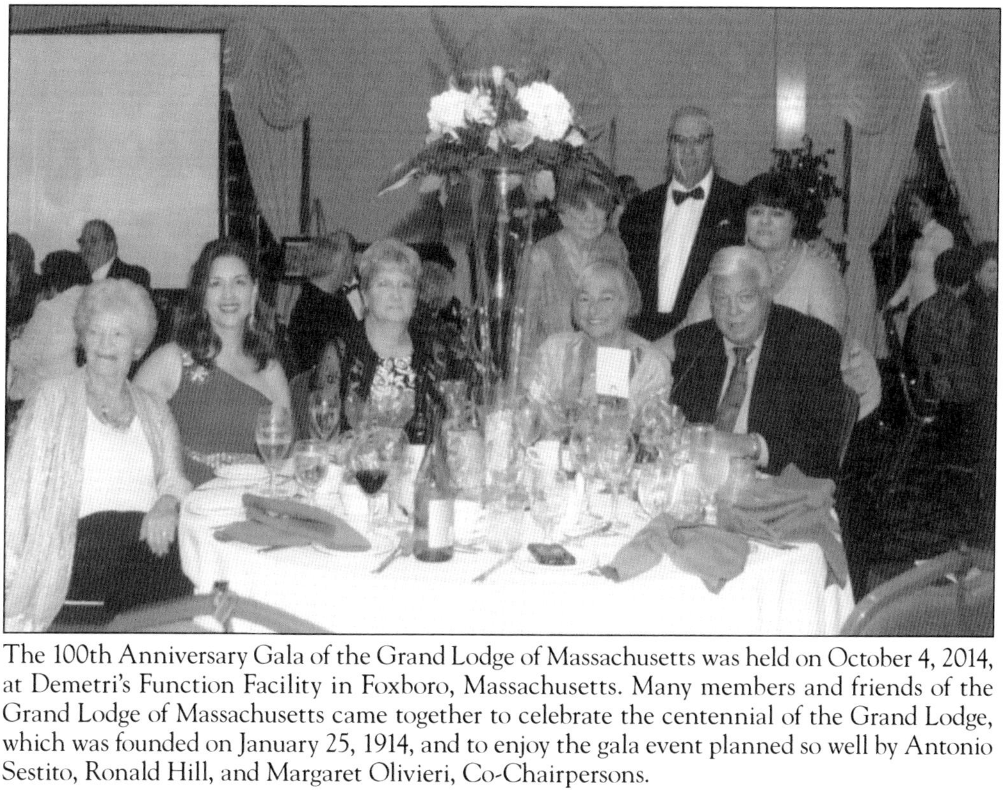

The 100th Anniversary Gala of the Grand Lodge of Massachusetts was held on October 4, 2014, at Demetri's Function Facility in Foxboro, Massachusetts. Many members and friends of the Grand Lodge of Massachusetts came together to celebrate the centennial of the Grand Lodge, which was founded on January 25, 1914, and to enjoy the gala event planned so well by Antonio Sestito, Ronald Hill, and Margaret Olivieri, Co-Chairpersons.

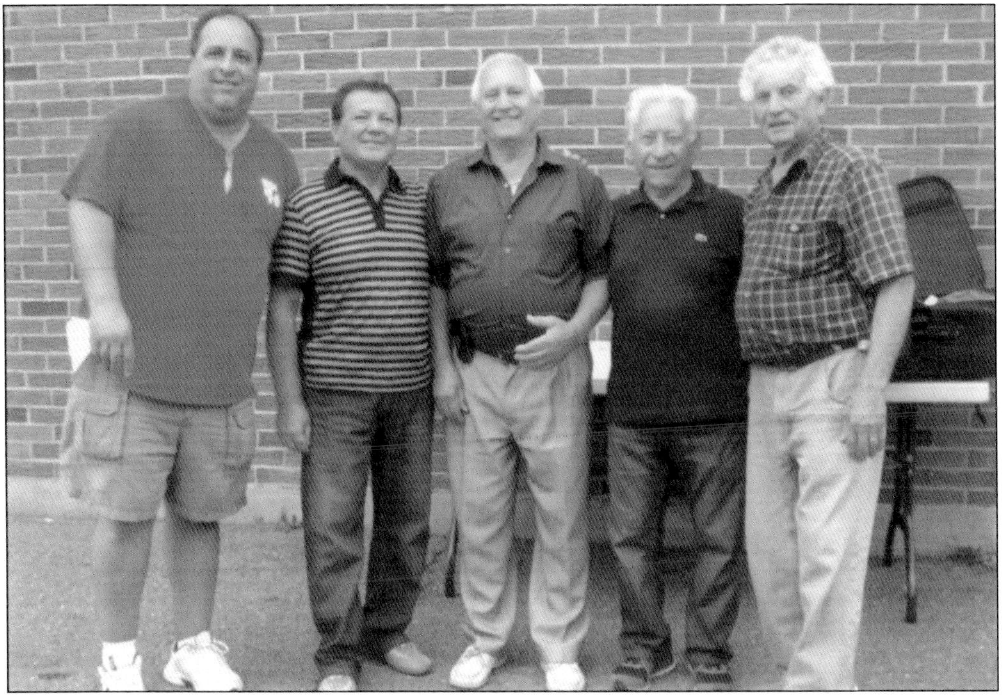

One of the many events held in 2014 was a bocce tournament on September 21 at the Watertown Sons of Italy. The first-place team members in the Men's Division, from the Piave Fiume Lodge #1036, are, from left to right, Sports Commission Chairman Steven Cedrone, Joe Cacia, Vito Varano, Vincenzo Sammartano, and Sal Pinzone.

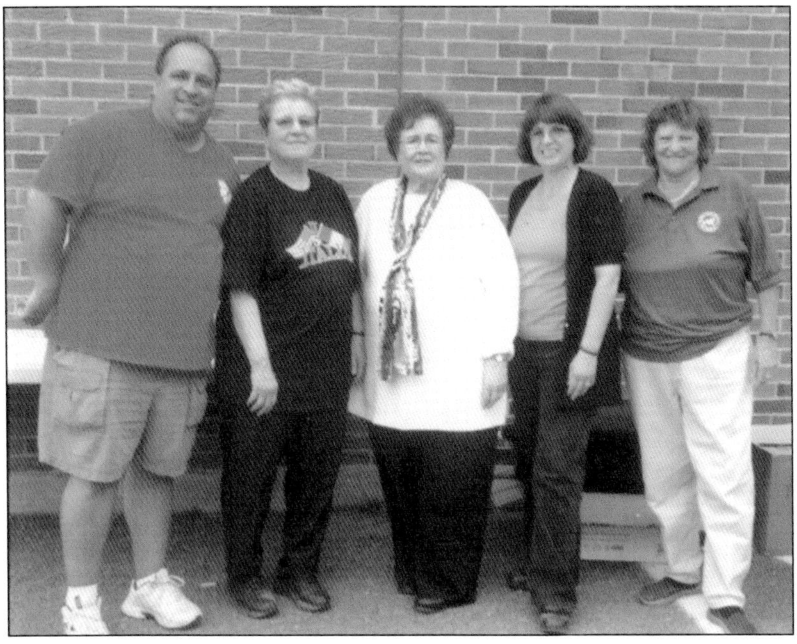

Pictured with Sports Commission Chairman Steven Cedrone (left) are first-place team members in the Women's Division from the Cornelia dei Gracchi Lodge #1583. From left to right are Teresa Iodice, Gerri Cimino, Donna Mazzola, and State President Carmelita Bello.

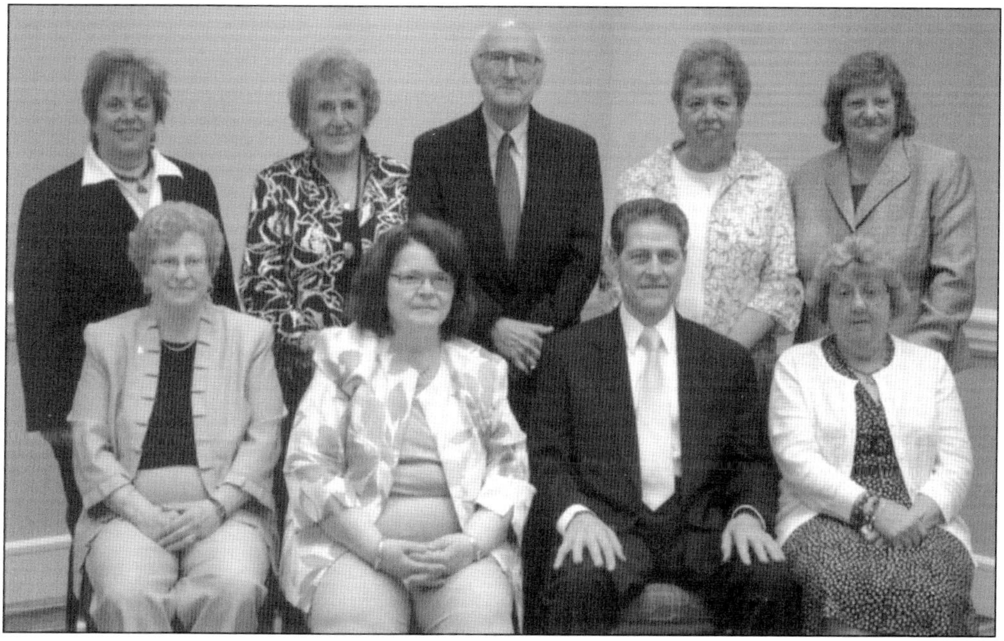

One of the major charitable endeavors of the Grand Lodge is the Scholarship Program, which awards tuition assistance annually to deserving high school students. The 2014 Scholarship Commission members are (first row) Liaison Mary Ann Bello, Chairman Donna Giuliani, Charitable and Educational Trust Chairman Angelo Rossi, and Nancy Gurgone; (second row) Paula Sasso, Mary Cooper, Alex Nardacci, Angela Giovannangelo, and State President Carmelita Bello; they are pictured at the 2014 Massachusetts Education and Law Awards at the Boston Marriott Burlington.

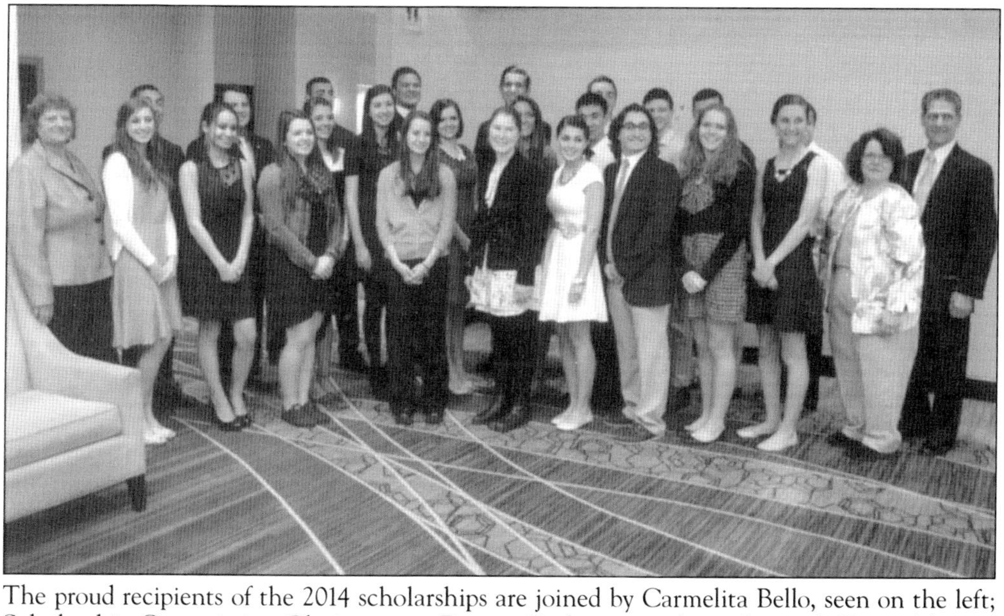

The proud recipients of the 2014 scholarships are joined by Carmelita Bello, seen on the left; Scholarship Commission Chairwoman Donna Giuliani, on the right; and Charitable and Educational Trust Chairman Angelo Rossi, on the far right, for a group photograph at the 2014 Massachusetts Education and Law Awards at the Boston Marriott Burlington.

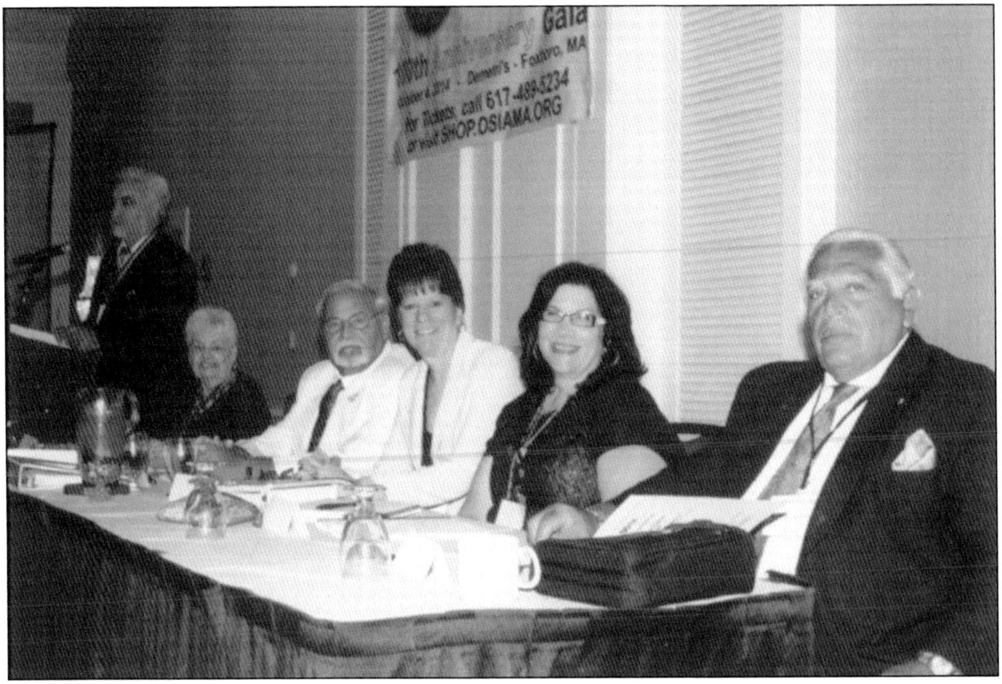

Some of the state officers of the Grand Lodge of Massachusetts at the head table are, from left to right, State First Vice President Antonio Sestito at the podium, State Recording Secretary Marie Jackson, State Second Vice President Ronald Hill, State Orator Denise Furnari, State Financial Secretary Margaret Olivieri, and State Treasurer John Christoforo. They are at the 2014 State Convention at the Boston Marriott Burlington.

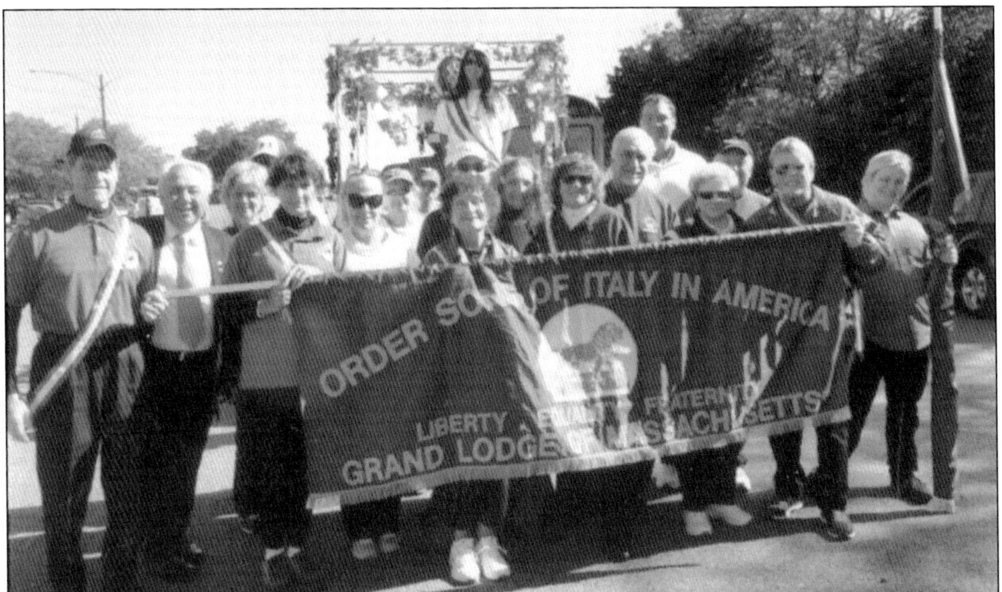

Members and officers from the Grand Lodge of Massachusetts took part in the Columbus Day Parade in East Boston, Massachusetts. In the center with sunglasses is Carmelita Bello, with many state officers, trustees, and members of the Sons of Italy who marched in the parade.

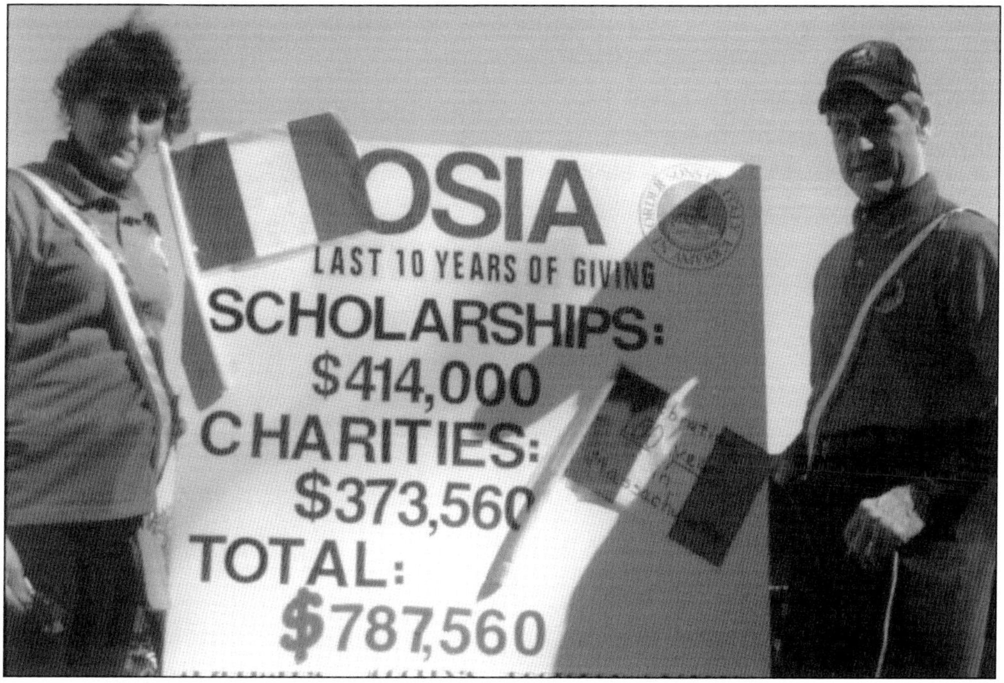

Many people do not realize that the Grand Lodge of Massachusetts is also a charitable organization. Over just the last decade, the Grand Lodge awarded $414,000 in scholarships and made $373,560 in charitable contributions to numerous causes. The Sons of Italy have been doing a lot of giving over the last 10 years! On the left is Carol Rossi, and on the right is Angelo Rossi at the Columbus Day Parade in East Boston, Massachusetts.

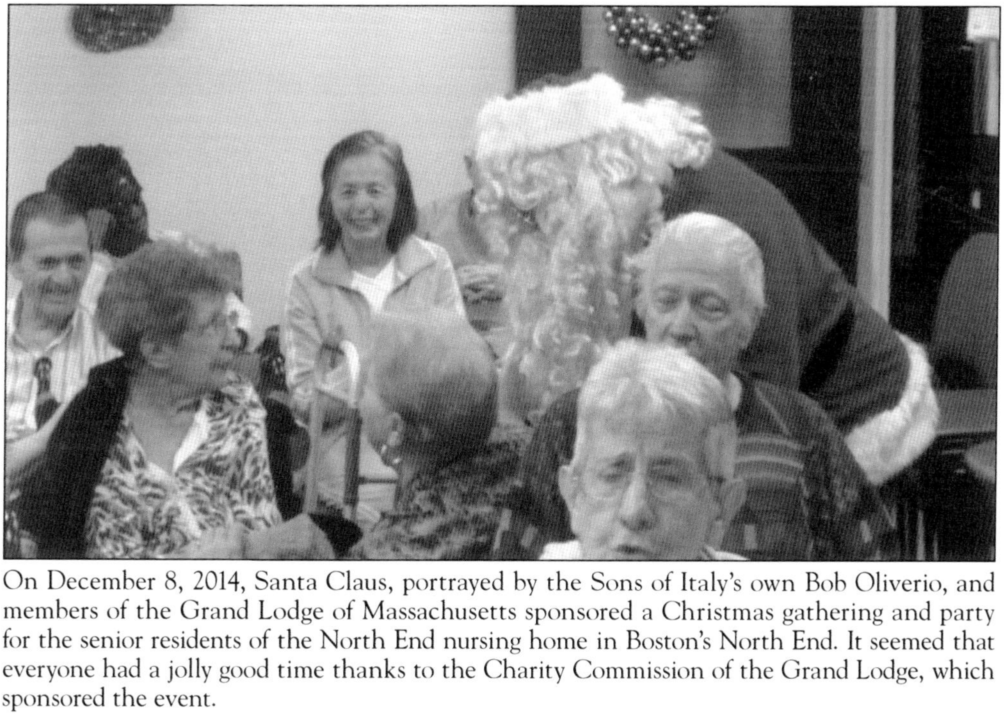

On December 8, 2014, Santa Claus, portrayed by the Sons of Italy's own Bob Oliverio, and members of the Grand Lodge of Massachusetts sponsored a Christmas gathering and party for the senior residents of the North End nursing home in Boston's North End. It seemed that everyone had a jolly good time thanks to the Charity Commission of the Grand Lodge, which sponsored the event.

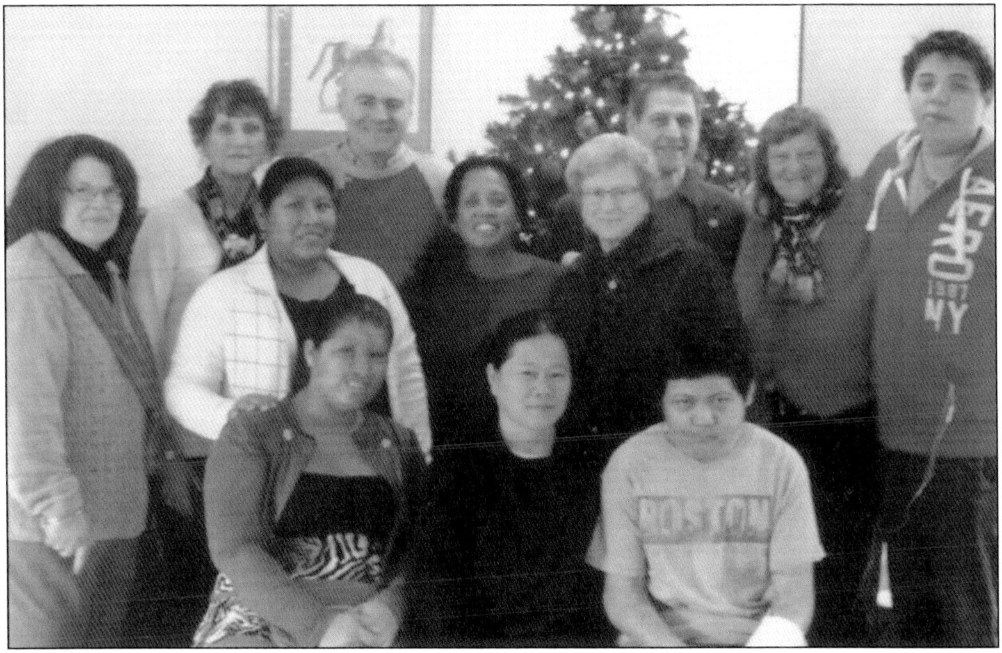

Casa Monte Cassino is a home away from home for patients and their families undergoing extended medical care at Boston area hospitals on Tileston Street in Boston's North End. The Grand Lodge of Massachusetts supports the home as one of its charities. Members of the Grand Lodge are pictured here with people from the Casa Monte Cassino in December 2014.

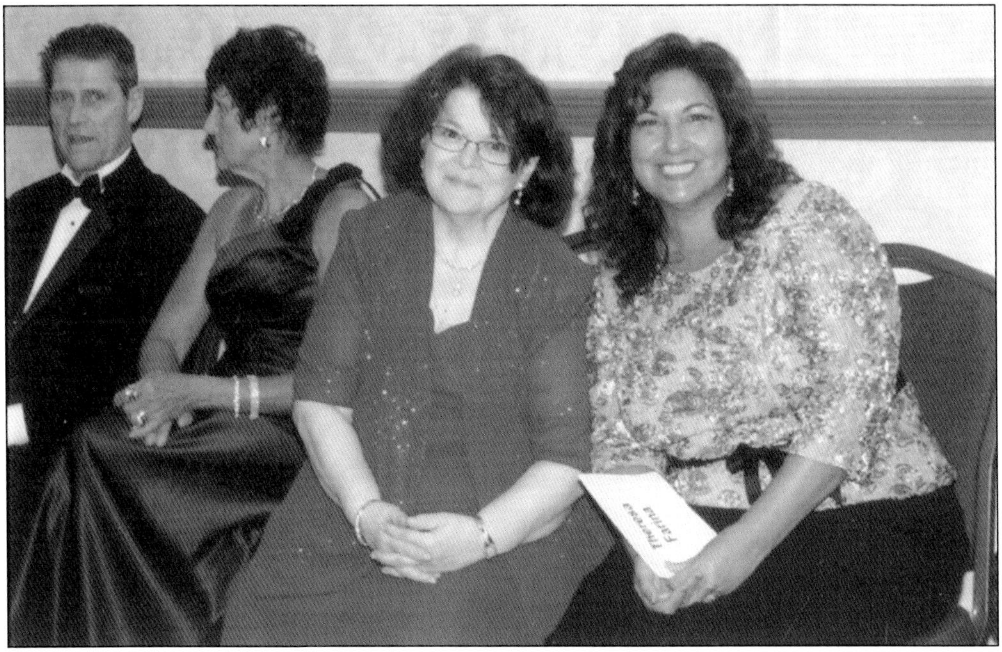

Awaiting their introduction to the members and friends of the Grand Lodge at the 100th Anniversary Gala at Demetri's Function Facility are, from left to right, Angelo Rossi, Carol Rossi, Donna Giuliani and Theresa Busi Farina, the Grand Lodge Historical Commission Chairman, who collected many of the photographs used in this book from local Lodges.

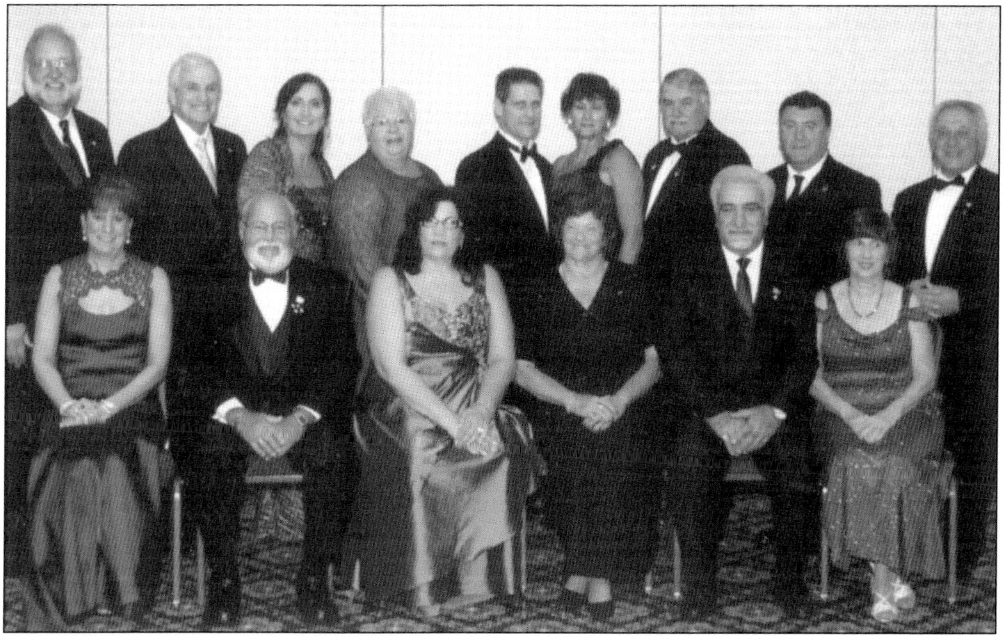

Members of the 100th Anniversary Gala committee of the Grand Lodge of Massachusetts include, from left to right, (seated) Denise Furnari, Ronald Hill, Margaret Olivieri, State President Carmelita Bello, Antonio Sestito, and Florence Ferullo Kane; (standing) Kevin A. Caira, Joseph A. Russo, Marisa Ranalli, Ann Hill, Angelo Rossi, Carol Rossi, James DiStefano, Ross Zagami, and Philip R. Boncore.

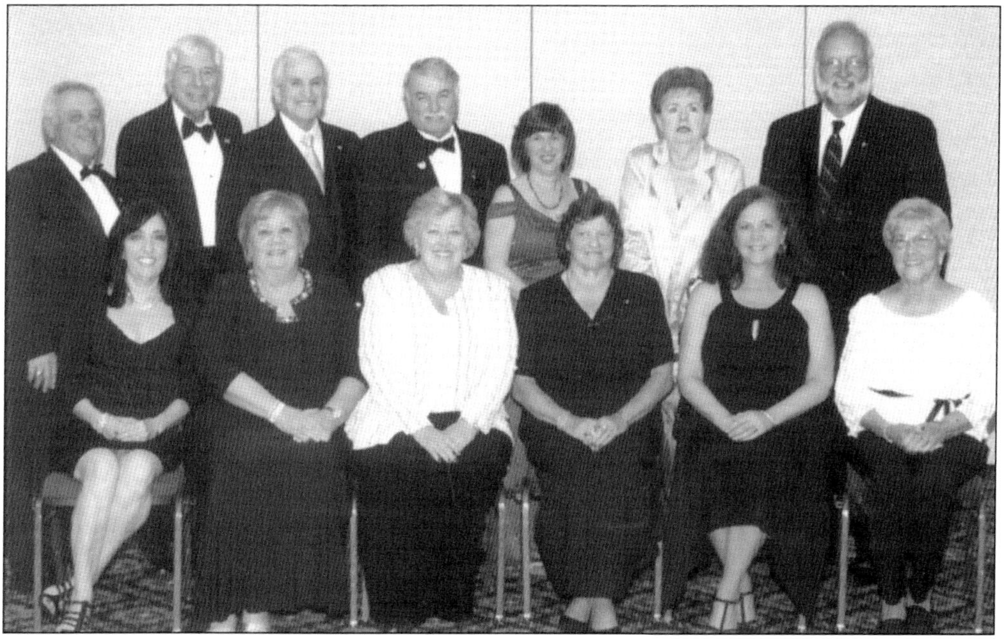

State Past Presidents and First Ladies pictured here are, from left to right (seated) Goldie Boncore, Pauline Russo, Kathy DiStefano, State President Carmelita Bello, Cheryl Lumb Caira, and Laura Caira; (standing) Philip R. Boncore, Charles H. Perenick, Joseph A. Russo, James DiStefano, Florence Ferullo Kane, Natalie Furnari, and Kevin A. Caira.

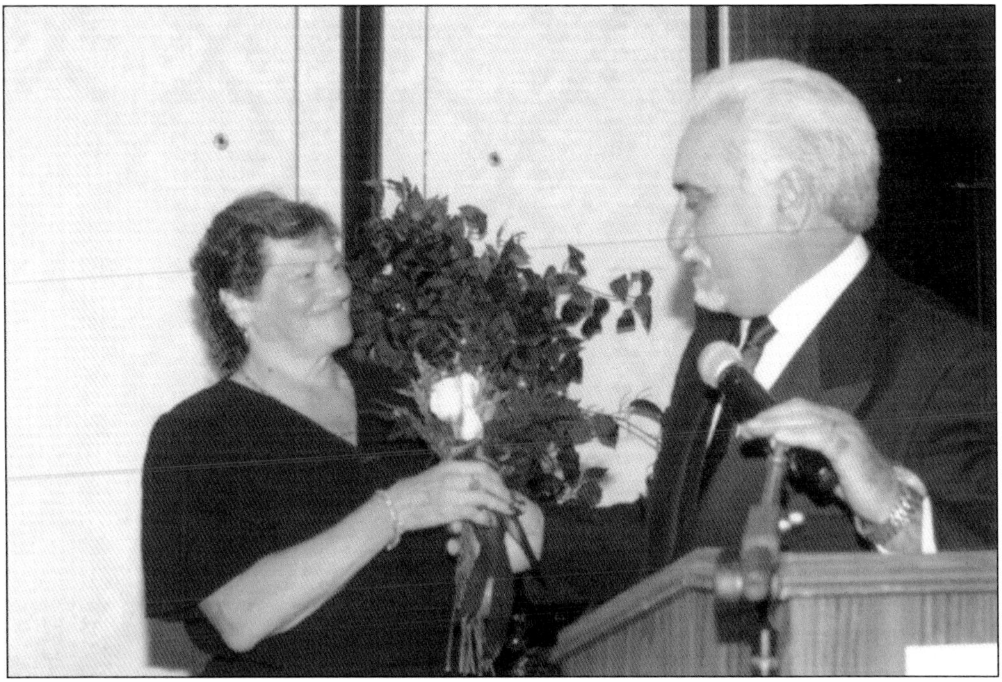

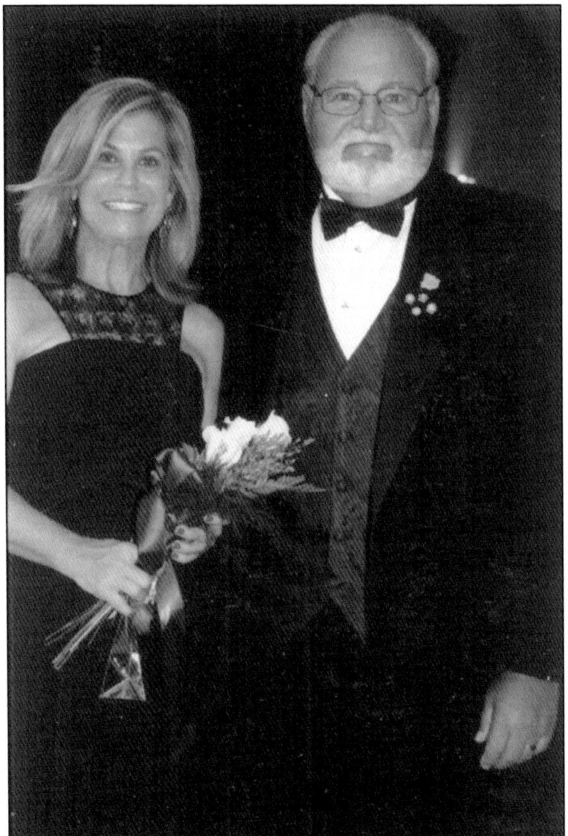

Antonio Sestito presents a lovely floral bouquet to Carmelita Bello at the beginning of the 100th Anniversary Gala at Demetri's Function Facility.

The Toastmaster of the 100th Anniversary Gala was Cheryl Fiandaca, an investigative reporter for WHDH-TV in Boston; she is seen here with State Second Vice President Ronald Hill.

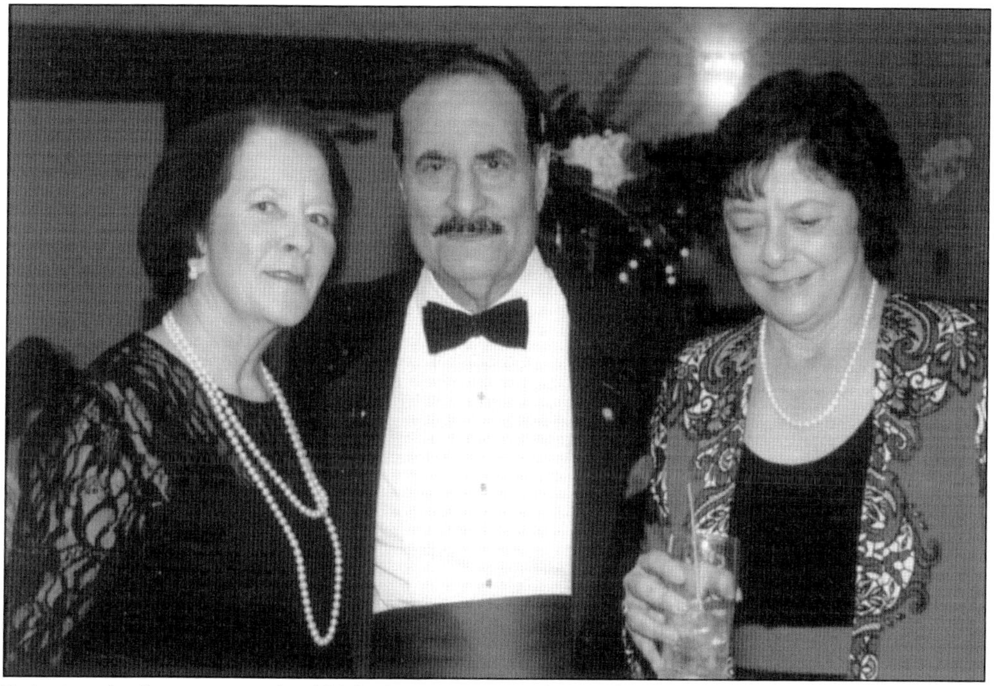

Enjoying the festivities at the 100th Anniversary Gala are, from left to right, Carol McNamara, Dean J. Saluti, and Josephine Matlak.

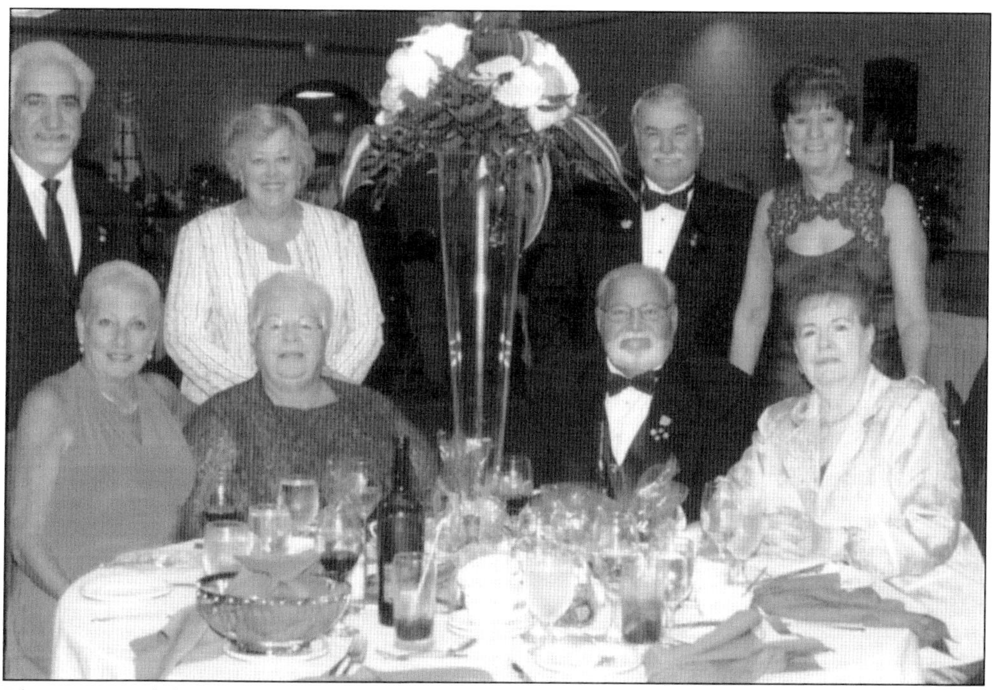

This congenial dinner table includes, from left to right, (seated) Marieanne Sestito, Ann Hill, Ronald Hill, and Natalie Furnari; (standing) Antonio Sestito, Kathy DiStefano, James DiStefano, and Denise Furnari.

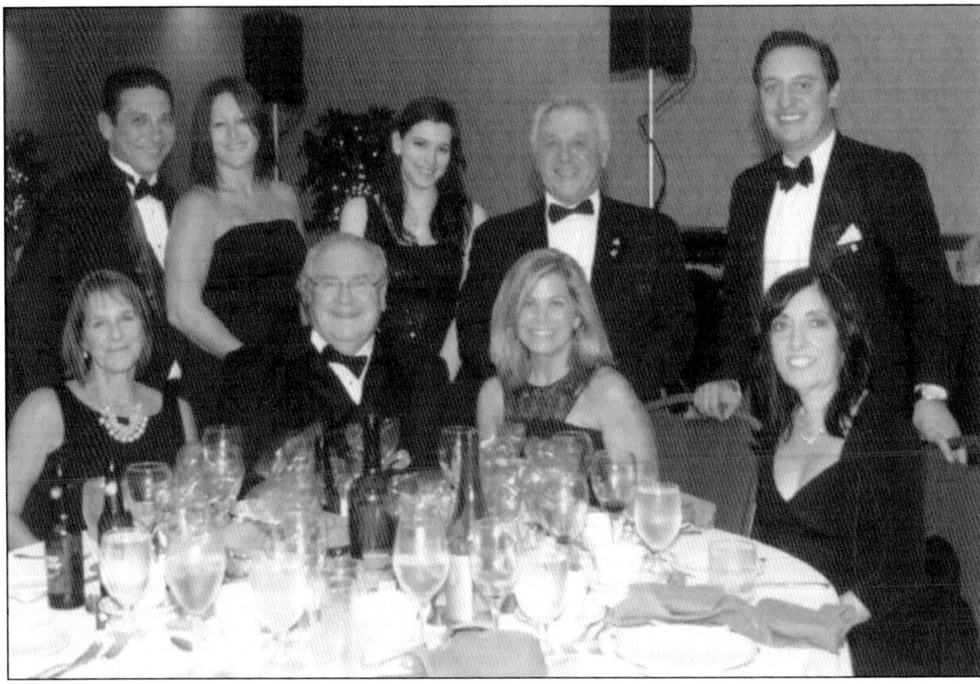

The Boncore table included, from left to right, (seated) Vicky Mucci, Speaker of the Massachusetts House of Representatives Robert A. DeLeo, Cheryl Fiandaca, and Goldie Boncore; (standing) Robert Boncore, Jennifer Boncore, Renata Fiandaca, Philip Boncore, and Joey Boncore.

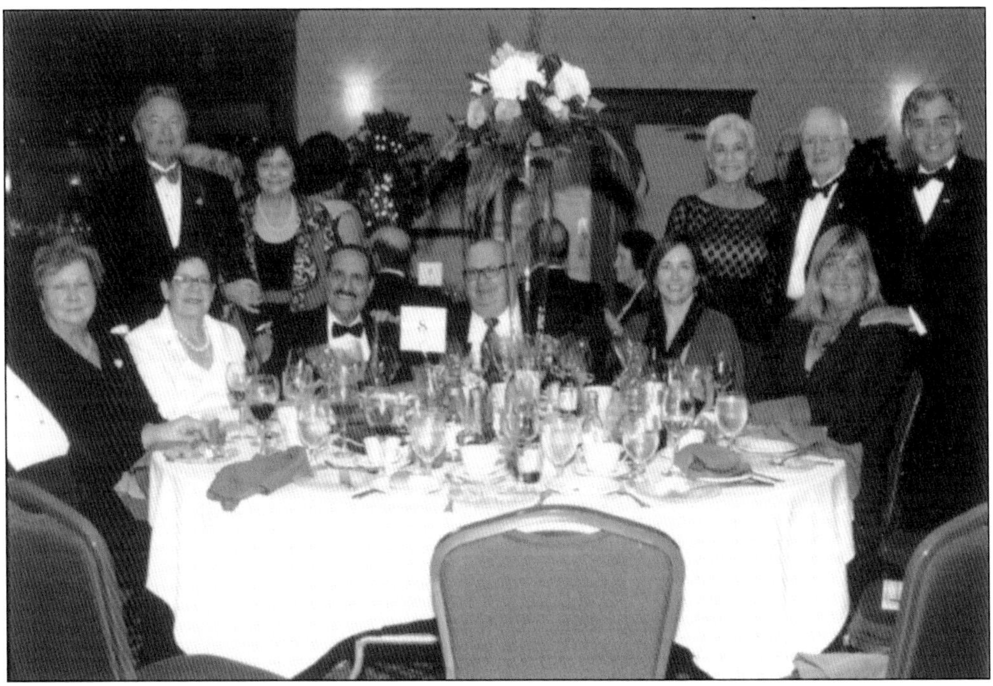

Seated at this dinner table are, from left to right, Eileen DeVito, Marjorie Cahn, Dean Saluti, Les Cavicchi, Kris Cavicchi, and Lori DeNapoli. Standing are, from left to right, Richard Matlak, Josephine Matlak, Nancy Monaghan, Tom Larsen, and Al DeNapoli.

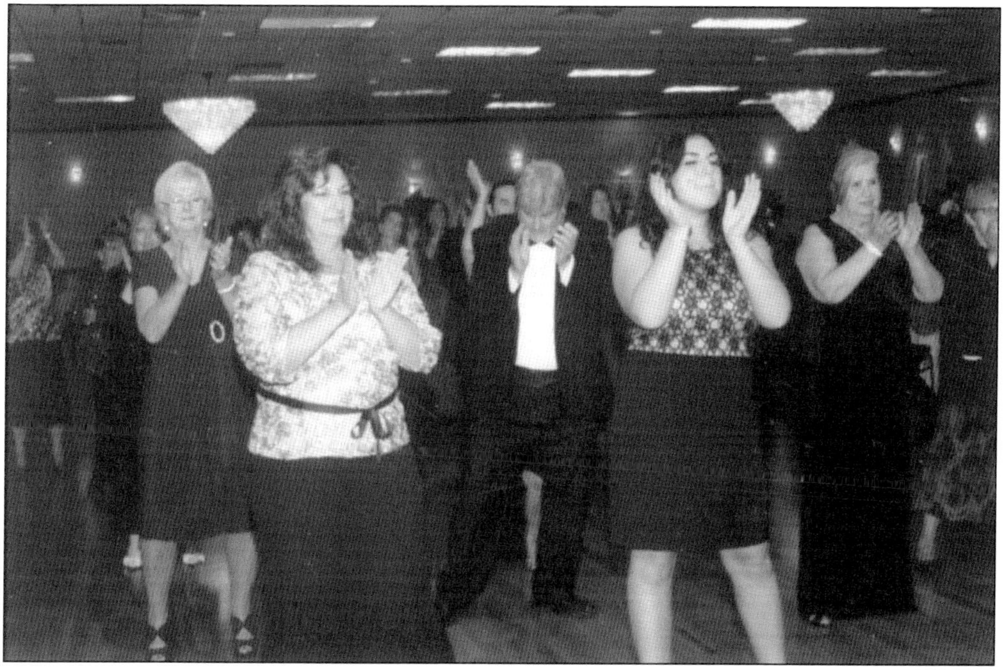

Enjoying the dancing following dinner are Theresa Busi Farina (front left) and her daughter Alessandra Farina (front right), who, with members and friends, danced to the music of *The Italian Connection*.

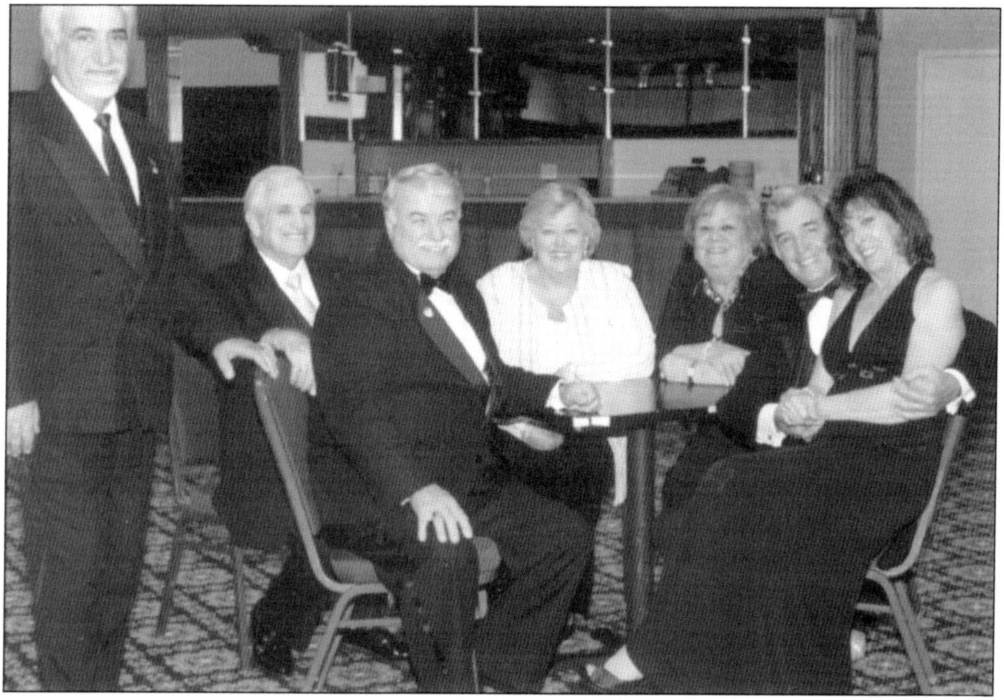

Enjoying one another's company at the end of a wonderful evening at the 100th Anniversary Gala are, from left to right, Antonio Sestito, Joseph A. Russo, James DiStefano, Kathy DiStefano, Pauline Russo, Al DeNapoli, and Pamela Donnaruma.

The Lodges of the Grand Lodge of Massachusetts currently include:

Arlington Men #1349	Arlington, Massachusetts
Billerica #2268	Billerica, Massachusetts
Greater Boston Renaissance #2614	Boston, Massachusetts
Massimo D'Azeglio #760	Braintree, Massachusetts
Braintree Ladies #1422	Braintree, Massachusetts
Christopher Columbus #216	Brockton, Massachusetts
Burlington #2223	Burlington, Massachusetts
Cambridge Italian #506	Cambridge, Massachusetts
St. Catherine of Siena #2215	Canton, Massachusetts
Sempre Avanti #1600	East Boston, Massachusetts
Giuseppe Verdi #278	East Weymouth, Massachusetts
Vittorio Veneto #1035	Fall River, Massachusetts
Cristoforo Colombo Regina Elena #169	Fitchburg, Massachusetts
Quattro Eroi #1414	Franklin, Massachusetts
Victor Emanuel #1646	Haverhill, Massachusetts
South Shore Ladies #1851	Hingham, Massachusetts
South Shore Men #1850	Hingham, Massachusetts
Lawrence Ladies #2026	Lawrence, Massachusetts
G. Marconi #1620	Lee, Massachusetts
Santa Famiglia #2834	Lynn, Massachusetts
Bandiera e Concordia #240	Marlboro, Massachusetts
Medford #1359	Medford, Massachusetts
Santa Maria #1570	Medford, Massachusetts
Melrose #1931	Melrose, Massachusetts
Methuen #902	Methuen, Massachusetts
Milford #1356	Milford, Massachusetts
Francesco DeSanctis #1411	Natick, Massachusetts
Fiore D'Italia #1640	Newton, Massachusetts
Ambrose D. Cedrone #1069	Newton, Massachusetts
Norwood Italian #1235	Norwood, Massachusetts
Peabody Ladies #1964	Peabody, Massachusetts
ITAM #564	Pittsfield, Massachusetts
Seacoast Area #2303	Portsmouth, New Hampshire
Stella Del Nord #1436	Quincy, Massachusetts
Quincy Men #1295	Quincy, Massachusetts
Granite State #2380	Rochester, New Hampshire
Venezia #374	Rockland, Massachusetts
Sgt. Guido Petrilli #1606	Roslindale, Massachusetts
Gorizia #467	Rumford, Maine
Veturia Romana #1200	Salem, Massachusetts
Figli d'Italia #2692	Saugus, Massachusetts
Alessandro Volta #1712	Stoughton, Massachusetts
Minerva #1846	Stoughton, Massachusetts
Peter B. Gay #540	Taunton, Massachusetts
Tewksbury #2872	Tewksbury, Massachusetts
Wakefield #1734	Wakefield, Massachusetts
Walpole-Foxboro Regional #2641	Walpole, Massachusetts
Dante Alighieri #648	Waltham, Massachusetts
Regina Margherita Di Savoia #1094	Waltham, Massachusetts
Cornelia dei Gracchi #1583	Watertown, Massachusetts

Piave Fiume #1036	Watertown, Massachusetts
Angelo Giuseppe Roncalli #2183	Wilmington, Massachusetts
Winchester Men #1580	Winchester, Massachusetts
Winchester Women #1592	Winchester, Massachusetts
Winthrop Mixed #2057	Winthrop Massachusetts
Winthrop Ladies #2071	Winthrop Massachusetts
Woburn Ladies #1584	Woburn, Massachusetts
Joseph Gorrasi #1406	Woburn, Massachusetts
Worcester #168	Worcester, Massachusetts

The Junior Lodges of the Grand Lodge of Massachusetts currently include:

Braintree Junior #2756	Braintree, Massachusetts
Frank P. Consolati #1910	Lee, Massachusetts
Samuel J. Musumeci Junior #2693	Methuen, Massachusetts
Gioventu Junior #2789	Milford, Massachusetts
ITAM Junior #123	Pittsfield, Massachusetts
Wilmington Junior #3729	Wilmington, Massachusetts
Christoforo Columbo Junior #2750	Worcester, Massachusetts

The Loyalty Ode of the Sons of Italy in America

America! America! Home of the brave and of the free.
America! We cherish thee, your faithful Sons of Italy.
You give to all true Liberty, Equality, Fraternity.
America! We'll die for thee, your loyal Sons of Italy.

America! America! Light of the earth and of the sea.
America! Most proud of thee are we, the Sons of Italy.
Through storm and strife with bravery
We will defend our loved country.
America! Fidelity pledge we, the Sons of Italy.

—Dr. Angelo L. Maietta, 1941